英语专业系列教材

BUSINESS ENGLISH:
AN INTERPRETING COURSE

商务英语口译教程

主编 刘春伟
编者 刘晓晖 张华慧 陈向普 魏 立 于红霞

清华大学出版社
北京

内 容 简 介

本书将口译技能渐进式培养与商务专题场景相结合，全面、系统、概要地介绍新文科背景下商务英语口译的技能技巧并覆盖常见口译场景。全书共 12 章，包含商务旅行与接待、电子商务、商务礼仪与文化、对外贸易、物流、经济发展、银行、金融、投资与衍生品、经济危机、气候、能源与环保和人工智能等单元主题。每章由 7 个模块组成，分别是技能概要、译前准备、语料实训、技巧点拨、拓展练习、译海拾贝和译员风采。

本书的听力录音可扫描各章的二维码收听，与同传技能相关的 3 个拓展章节和本书的参考译文可通过扫描前言中的二维码获取。

本书既可以作为英语专业学生的口译教材，又能作为其他口译考试的备考素材，如上海中高级口译、全国翻译硕士专业学位（MTI）和全国翻译专业资格考试（CATTI）等。

版权所有，侵权必究。举报：010-62782989，beiqinquan@tup.tsinghua.edu.cn。

图书在版编目（CIP）数据

商务英语口译教程 / 刘春伟主编；刘晓晖等编者.
北京：清华大学出版社，2025.3. --（英语专业系列教材）. -- ISBN 978-7-302-67747-5
Ⅰ. F7
中国国家版本馆 CIP 数据核字第 2025NH9784 号

责任编辑：倪雅莉
封面设计：李伯骥
责任校对：王荣静
责任印制：刘海龙

出版发行：清华大学出版社
网　　址：https://www.tup.com.cn, https://www.wqxuetang.com
地　　址：北京清华大学学研大厦 A 座　　　邮　编：100084
社 总 机：010-83470000　　　　　　　　　邮　购：010-62786544
投稿与读者服务：010-62776969, c-service@tup.tsinghua.edu.cn
质量反馈：010-62772015, zhiliang@tup.tsinghua.edu.cn

印 装 者：北京鑫海金澳胶印有限公司
经　　销：全国新华书店
开　　本：185mm×260mm　　印　张：18　　字　数：348 千字
版　　次：2025 年 4 月第 1 版　　　　　　印　次：2025 年 4 月第 1 次印刷
定　　价：69.00 元

产品编号：099791-01

前言
PREFACE

中国对外开放新格局的形成、新文科建设和《普通高等学校本科商务英语专业教学指南》的颁布，对商务英语学科建设和教材建设提出了新的时代要求。社会对商务口译能力要求不断提高，CATTI、翻译硕士口译考试、知名公司与国际组织人才招聘的口译考试难度都在不断攀升，本书正是根据这些新的社会发展需求而编写的。

本书以新文科商务英语建设要求为导向，是一部内容全面、主题丰富、层次递进的商务英语口译教材。本书的特征是将口译技能渐进式培养与商务专题场景相结合，全面、系统、概要地介绍新文科背景下商务英语口译的技能技巧并覆盖常见口译场景。通过构建学科交叉融合背景下的商务英语口译场景，归类商务英语话语特征、摸索口译转化策略，结合CATTI/上海中高级口译/MTI等口译考试能力要求，本书实现了从口译基础能力到高阶能力的体系性建构与提升，帮助学生熟悉商务英语背景知识与词汇，培养其跨文化交际意识。

章节布局：

· 模块一为技能概要，全书各章的模块一共同构架起了由浅入深、层层递进、系统完整的口译技能体系框架。

· 模块二与模块三构成一个整体：模块二的译前准备将模块三中的重难点词汇和背景知识进行标注与讲解。在进入模块三的语料实训前，建议学生先对模块二的背景知识和词汇进行深度学习。模块三的英译汉、汉译英练习篇章均与该章节主题高度相关。

· 模块四为技巧点拨，将模块一的口译技能融入具体的音频材料中，帮助学生进一步了解如何应用该章所覆盖的口译策略、技能与技巧。本模块的每个语篇后有单词表，对生词进行了标注和解释。有的语料是完整语篇，有的是将一个完整语篇分成几个例子，每个例子节选了该语料的一部分，以重点练习某一技能。

· 模块五为拓展练习，学生可以进行选择性学习，接触与该章主题相关的更多语篇，加深自己对该章节主题的背景知识、词汇和篇章的理解，巩固学习效果。

· 模块六为艺海拾贝，帮助学生了解口译的实践知识和现场经验。

· 模块七为译员风采，介绍一位知名译员，或者从译员角色走向外交家岗位的著名人士。通过介绍其职业生涯轶事，潜移默化地帮助学生了解译员职业道德标准、学习外交礼节礼仪、把握国际交往准则、洞察译员成长轨迹，为未来职业译员道路奠定基础。

难度分布：

由于每个章节涉及的主题不同，有些主题的语料难度比较大，对于初学者有一定的挑战。为了方便不同基础的学生选择难度相当的语料，每篇语料前面有难度星级标注。学生在起步阶段可以选择难度星级低（一星、二星、三星）的语料来练习，五星级难度的语料适合听力基础好的学生。其中一星和五星难度的语料相对较少。在口译学习的初期，忌讳囫囵吞枣，建议听不懂的反复听，对照文本与音频，直到最后脱稿也可以完全听得懂，再进行下一篇的练习。有的章节整体难度较大，比如第七章，语料是银行业为背景的，技能是数字，两者难度都很大，结合在一起，对学生会造成较大的压力。这种章节就需要学生多次复盘。复盘是口译学习中极为重要的步骤，反复重听、记录单词、查找背景知识是复盘的核心要求。

英汉语料比例：

口译员应该在双语之间灵活转变，具有扎实的双语基本功。但是对于初学者来说，英译汉的难度更大。学生在口译学习的前期会遇到听不懂原文、口语不流畅等突出问题。因此，本书的汉英语料比例的安排是汉语语料略少、英文语料略多，从而帮助学生巩固听力、增强英语语感。这并不意味着学生可以厚此薄彼。

推荐的学习方法：

1. 学习顺序

理解模块一的技巧→熟练掌握模块二的背景与词汇，深度查阅更多背景知识→练习模块三→复盘模块三，听不懂的地方看原文以及译文→通过模块四的技巧点拨巩固口译技能→熟悉模块五的单词→练习模块五→通过模块六和模块七增加口译常识。

2. 复盘

本书每个章节的源语均配有音频、原文和译文。建议学生一开始的时候不要参考原文和译文，听了两三次之后如果还是有没听懂的地方，再去参考原文。口译学习者忌讳贪多吃不烂的学习习惯，精练一篇的作用大于泛练多篇。同时，一篇语料也可以做多种训练，如听辨、源语复述、主旨翻译、无笔记交传、交传、视译、有稿同传和无稿同传。

对于学有余力的学生，本书另外提供法律与法庭、科技与发展、商务谈判与商务会议等3章内容，以供同传进阶训练。本书的参考译文也可通过扫描下面的二维码获取。

最后特别感谢大连外国语大学2022级研究生：陈少华、唐侦凰、施佳静、包雨萱、张路遥、许孟梦、朱倍锋、刘维维、高颖颖、张仕昊、段瑞琳，他们在编写过程中协助完成了部分材料的搜集与整理工作。由于编写时间有限，书中若有不当之处，恳请专家学者及广大读者多多指正。

同传技能
拓展章节

参考译文

编者

2024年12月

目录

第一章 商务旅行与接待 ························ 1

- 模块一 技能概要：听辨逻辑 ························ 1
- 模块二 译前准备 ························ 2
- 模块三 语料实训 ························ 3
- 模块四 技巧点拨：听辨中的逻辑框架 ························ 9
- 模块五 拓展练习 ························ 15
- 模块六 译海拾贝：口译员的基本素养 ························ 19
- 模块七 译员风采：中国外交部翻译的成长历程 ························ 21

第二章 电子商务 ························ 23

- 模块一 技能概要：听辨关键词 ························ 23
- 模块二 译前准备 ························ 24
- 模块三 语料实训 ························ 26
- 模块四 技巧点拨：何谓"关键词"与如何寻找关键词 ························ 30
- 模块五 拓展练习 ························ 41
- 模块六 译海拾贝：译员的职业道德 ························ 44
- 模块七 译员风采："红墙内第一翻译"冀朝铸 ························ 45

第三章 商务礼仪与文化 ························ 48

- 模块一 技能概要：源语复述 ························ 48
- 模块二 译前准备 ························ 50
- 模块三 语料实训 ························ 51
- 模块四 技巧点拨：语篇信息脉络与源语复述 ························ 58
- 模块五 拓展练习 ························ 65
- 模块六 译海拾贝：商务口译中的跨文化因素 ························ 70
- 模块七 译员风采："老虎书生"杨洁篪 ························ 72

第四章　对外贸易 ·· 74

- **模块一**　技能概要：口译记忆 ·································· 74
- **模块二**　译前准备 ·· 75
- **模块三**　语料实训 ·· 76
- **模块四**　技巧点拨：翻译记忆 ·································· 81
- **模块五**　拓展练习 ·· 86
- **模块六**　译海拾贝：达沃斯论坛中的口译错误 ···················· 89
- **模块七**　译员风采：崔天凯从译员到外交官的历程 ················ 91

第五章　物流 ·· 93

- **模块一**　技能概要：笔记的基本要素 ···························· 93
- **模块二**　译前准备 ·· 95
- **模块三**　语料实训 ·· 96
- **模块四**　技巧点拨：如何平衡听辨与笔记记录 ··················· 102
- **模块五**　拓展练习 ··· 112
- **模块六**　译海拾贝：口译员的隐身与现身 ······················· 117
- **模块七**　译员风采：林超伦与他的 KL Communications ··········· 119

第六章　经济发展 ·· 121

- **模块一**　技能概要：笔记符号 ································· 121
- **模块二**　译前准备 ··· 122
- **模块三**　语料实训 ··· 124
- **模块四**　技巧点拨：笔记示范与分析 ··························· 128
- **模块五**　拓展练习 ··· 133
- **模块六**　译海拾贝：口译中听不懂的对策 ······················· 139
- **模块七**　译员风采：四代领导人译员施燕华 ····················· 140

第七章　银行 ... 143

- 模块一　技能概要：数字 ... 143
- 模块二　译前准备 ... 147
- 模块三　语料实训 ... 149
- 模块四　技巧点拨：数字转换与记录 ... 154
- 模块五　拓展练习 ... 159
- 模块六　译海拾贝：译前准备 ... 163
- 模块七　译员风采："银发铁娘子"傅莹 ... 165

第八章　金融 ... 167

- 模块一　技能概要：脱壳翻译 ... 167
- 模块二　译前准备 ... 169
- 模块三　语料实训 ... 170
- 模块四　技巧点拨：脱壳翻译技能 ... 173
- 模块五　拓展练习 ... 179
- 模块六　译海拾贝：口译专业考研规划 ... 184
- 模块七　译员风采：从翻译官到外交官之路 ... 186

第九章　投资与衍生品 ... 188

- 模块一　技能概要：言语重构 ... 188
- 模块二　译前准备 ... 190
- 模块三　语料实训 ... 191
- 模块四　技巧点拨：言语重构技能 ... 197
- 模块五　拓展练习 ... 200
- 模块六　译海拾贝：口译中突发状况与现场应变 ... 204
- 模块七　译员风采：女承父业，闻生闻声 ... 205

第十章　经济危机 207

- **模块一**　技能概要：基础影子训练 207
- **模块二**　译前准备 208
- **模块三**　语料实训 210
- **模块四**　技巧点拨：基础影子技能 214
- **模块五**　拓展练习 224
- **模块六**　译海拾贝：巴黎释义派 228
- **模块七**　译员风采：跨过厚厚的大红门，穿过是非成败 229

第十一章　气候、能源与环保 232

- **模块一**　技能概要：高阶影子训练 232
- **模块二**　译前准备 233
- **模块三**　语料实训 234
- **模块四**　技巧点拨：影子中的延时跟进与干扰任务 239
- **模块五**　拓展练习 245
- **模块六**　译海拾贝：CATTI 与上海中高口证书的介绍 248
- **模块七**　译员风采："武大"郎的翻译之路 250

第十二章　人工智能 252

- **模块一**　技能概要：视译 252
- **模块二**　译前准备 255
- **模块三**　语料实训 256
- **模块四**　技巧点拨：视译技能 262
- **模块五**　拓展练习 270
- **模块六**　译海拾贝：口译失误与外交风波 274
- **模块七**　译员风采：如何成为翻译国家队的一员 276

第一章
商务旅行与接待
Business Travel and Reception

模块一

技能概要：听辨逻辑

听辨作为口译活动的起点和基础，是口译员应当具备最基本的口译能力。听辨要求学生在听懂原文的基础上，对获得的信息进行分析，厘清所听内容的逻辑关系，提取重要信息，最后进行信息整合，为译文的输出作好准备。成功的译员并不是将源语的所有元素都体现在译语中，而是将源语中的关键部分精准转换。如何抓住要点成为口译的关键。在抓要点的过程中，学生要能够透过多样化的语言形式，听辨出话语的核心内容，要从语言层面的理解上升到信息层面的理解。为了达到听辨的最佳效果，学生需要掌握以下两个重要技能——逻辑辨识和关键词抓取：辨识逻辑有助于把握原文的组织框架和脉络；关键词既是架构逻辑框架的提示，也是每个逻辑框架下具体内容的凝练。两者互为条件，有机构成了源语篇章的主旨。我们在第一章的技能概要中首先学习如何听辨逻辑。

逻辑辨识要求学生在听懂源语的基础上，对获得的信息进行分析加工，厘清信息层次及前后逻辑关系，将关键信息按照逻辑进行整合，然后输出翻译。逻辑辨识包括纵向分析和横向分析两个层面。纵向分析是指分清讲话内容的关键信息和辅助信息，找出逻辑层次；横向分析是指明确各信息点之间的逻辑关系，如因果关系、对比对照、举例说明等。听辨过程中，学生可以在脑海中简单勾画讲话内容的逻辑框架，如下例所示：

>> 例一

热络的中外经贸交流，促进了各种商务旅游此起彼伏，也为中国旅游业带来了无数商机。有关资料表明，我国的商务客人的比重逐年加大，在北京等大中城市，商务客人的比重已占当地接待的旅游总人次的50%左右，并且有继

通过纵向分析和横向分析，例一有两个逻辑层次：第一个层次是阐述中国旅游业充满商机的事实；第二个层次是通过数据和调查结果对上述事实进行例证。在第二个层次上，两个例证之间是并列关系。通过逻辑辨识，我们对源语的把握更加透彻，也更有利于记忆和译

续上升的趋势。据有关部门对北京、上海20家星级酒店的调查显示，海外旅游者来华的主要目的依次为商务、投资考察、观光游览。

文输出。在输出过程中，译者需要把握的是总分的行文逻辑：旅游商机＋数据证明（两个数据例子）。

例二

For MICE and corporate travel service providers, it's important to identify which areas of the market are likely to recover first, to optimize product development, and guide sales and marketing. Based on our panelists' experience in China in the past year, association or corporate events look like the key starting point, with incentives following later.

例二给出的英文例句信息较多，但是逻辑层次很清晰。根据纵向分析，我们可以得出源语有两个逻辑层次：第一个逻辑层次为商旅服务行业从业者需要关注和做的事情；第二个逻辑层次是商业预测。通过横向分析，我们可以发现，虽然源语第一句在语法结构上是几个不定式的并列，但是在语义层面上，这几个不定式之间是递进关系。这也体现了听辨的要点：不仅听其音，更要听其意。若只听不辨，则很有可能在逻辑上犯错误，从而影响翻译的质量。相反，只要抓住了主要层次结构，哪怕有少许遗漏，就不会太影响翻译质量。

模块二　译前准备

◎ 1. 背景知识

旅游业在我国第三产业中占有重要地位，作为旅游业的一个重要组成部分，商务旅行在经济全球化的大背景下得到迅速发展。商务旅行和接待翻译要求学生不仅掌握口译技能，还要熟悉商务背景知识和接待礼仪。

本模块涉及的概念主要有商务旅游与接待、《迷失东京》、费尔南多·博特罗、皇家唐桥井。

商务旅游与接待（business travel and reception）：商务旅行是指人们外出处理以盈利为目的的事务而引发的旅游活动，其主要特点为消费水平高、多方位推动经济发展、具有重复性以及较少受季节气候影响等。商务接待是建立在商务旅游基础上的高规格接待服务。

《迷失东京》（*Lost in Translation*）：2003年8月29日上映的一部喜剧爱情片，由索菲亚·科波拉执导，斯嘉丽·约翰逊、比尔·默瑞等人主演。该片讲述了两名身处异国他乡的美国人之间的特殊友情和情感联系。

费尔南多·博特罗（Fernando Botero）：哥伦比亚著名雕塑家、画家，被视为哥伦比亚国家的荣耀和"人民信仰之父"。博特罗的作品带有浓郁的民族色彩，体现了哥伦比亚的文化风格，从传统人物到反映社会的暴力题材，无一不呈现出他个人的才智和绘画的超人智能。

皇家唐桥井（Royal Tunbridge Wells）：英格兰肯特郡西部的大型城镇，距离伦敦市中心东南方约40英里（约64千米）路程，靠近东萨塞克斯郡的边界。

◎ 2. 核心词汇

global business travel market	全球商务旅行市场	public transportation	公共交通
World Trade Organization (WTO)	世界贸易组织	Madrid	马德里
Southeast Asia	东南亚	Rotterdam	鹿特丹
business travel	商务旅行	Porto	波尔图
business reception	商务接待	Amsterdam	阿姆斯特丹
commercial entity	商业实体	Romania	罗马尼亚
emerging market	新兴市场		

模块三　　　　　　　　　　　　　　　　　　　语料实训

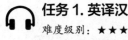

任务1. 英译汉
难度级别：★★★

> 训练要点：本文介绍了商务旅行的定义、目的和商旅市场。全文专业术语较少，对于有一定基础的听者来说难度较小。在听解过程中，学生应在厘清逻辑的基础上尽量听全，并且注意数字信息，平衡听辨主体信息、主要逻辑框架和细节信息之间的关系，抓大放小，切忌眉毛胡子一把抓。

What Is Business Travel?

What is business travel? If you fly somewhere on behalf of your company, you are one of the millions of people involved in business travel each year worldwide. The term "business travel" refers to travelling for work purposes. We call each individual journey a business trip. If you drive across town to visit a client, that is not business travel. Business trips are longer. Although the term business travel suggests that the trip is for profit-making purposes, its meaning also includes non-commercial situations. Government representatives who are flying to a United Nations meeting are involved in business travel. Anybody who is away for work purposes regardless of whether their employer is a commercial entity, is away on business. Put simply, business travel means work-related travel.

Business travel worldwide is a massive market. A WTO study forecast that the global business travel market will reach $2.71 trillion by 2027. The US market, the world's biggest, represents $368 billion's worth of business annually. China's market is expected to surpass the US' during the second half of this decade. Business travel is also growing rapidly in many emerging markets. The coronavirus or COVID-19 has changed the outlook for business travel dramatically. 2020 saw an alarming decline in all types of travel. Business traveler numbers plummeted. Companies and other organizations have been forced to embrace modern telecommunication tools to communicate with clients, suppliers, employees and other stakeholders. Will this new telecommunication trend continue after the pandemic is over?

Traveling is great for learning new things. However, if you have a family, there is definitely a price to pay. Missing family events, especially if you have children, may contribute to relationship difficulties. Many business travelers say they don't like the loneliness. Doctors have found that frequent business travelers have a higher risk of developing mental health problems.

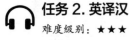

任务 2. 英译汉
难度级别：★★★

> **训练要点：** 本文介绍经济全球化背景下，商务旅行兴起的原因。来自不同行业的受访者分享了他们商旅旅行的经验，帮助我们了解商务旅行的具体情况。在听辨过程中，学生要把握每段话的逻辑，不必过于追求原文每个字词的完整，翻译时也不必过于拘泥于原文的表达，而是用符合中文的语言习惯和语言逻辑将其翻译出来，增加输出语的可理解性。

Business English—Business Travel

Narrator: In a global economy, many companies do business overseas, this means that workers often travel to see their colleagues or clients abroad. There are many reasons why people travel for work.

A: I go abroad to complete projects which are set by my company. Those projects can include setting up certain systems, laptops, docking stations, etc.

B: I need to travel for work because sometimes the projects I do are based somewhere outside London where I live, so I've been travelling to France, to Italy, to Spain, to Romania.

C: I need to travel because we work with big brands and multinationals and they want to understand different people in the different markets and countries, so we travel across the world.

Narrator: An important part of business travel is organizing transportation. When people travel internationally, they often fly, though in some cases taking the train is an option.

A: I travel for work once or twice a month on a regular basis. I tend to fly a short haul and I use two different airlines.

Narrator: Alex makes the most of his travel time and keeps busy during the flight.

Alex: When I fly for business, I tend to get my laptop out and do some work during the flight, and half an hour before my plane lands, I remove my laptop, put it back in my bag and get ready for the landing.

Narrator: On business trips, you may need to stay overnight. It's important to book accommodation that is suitable for your trip, and has everything you need so you can keep working during your stay.

B: The accommodation where I like to stay when I travel for work is hotels, usually, but they need to be very close to the place where I need to go to work. What I expect at my location is Wi-Fi, because I need to work most of the time when I'm back in my room and, of course, parking, because usually I need to hire cars or a vehicle from the airport to the workplace.

Narrator: When travelling for work, you may not know much about the local area and how to get around. Find out about transportation before you go and when you get there, ask for help if you need it or ask for directions.

C: When I have to go from a business meeting to another meeting, I either use public transportation because it's a really good way to mix with the locals or I use a ride sharing app.

I always worry about getting lost but it's part of the adventure. I carry an online map on my phone and if I do get lost, I just ask people and they're really helpful.

Narrator: Even if you've planned ahead, things can still go wrong. Your flight could be delayed or there might be a mistake with your hotel reservation. It's rare, however, to find a problem that cannot be solved.

C: I remember once I was at the airport lounge waiting for my flight and I got really confused with timings and then I get to the gate and it's written in huge red letters: Gates closed. I started panicking and thankfully the staff were really helpful. They helped me through and they rushed me to the plane through a back door. And I made my flight.

Narrator: Like anybody who's done the same thing several times, regular business travelers have advice they can offer to others.

B: My top travel tip when travelling for work is to be very efficient in organization because this gives you time also to enjoy the place where you're going after you've done your business.

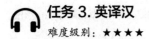

任务3. 英译汉
难度级别：★★★★

> 训练要点：本文分享了商务旅行对个人造成的负面影响，同时也分享如何在这种频繁出差中找到商务旅行的价值，探索商务旅行的乐趣。学生在听辨过程中，要把握演讲者整体的逻辑，对商务旅行先抑后扬的主基调。同时，本文中出现大量地名，学生在听的过程中也要着重注意。在平时学习过程中，也可多积累一些国家和城市名称的表达。

Discover the Joy of Traveling for Business

In March 2020, the COVID-19 pandemic rocked economies worldwide. Millions of people lost their jobs, and many businesses struggled to survive or shut down completely. Governments responded with some of the largest economic relief packages in history—the United States alone spent $2.2 trillion on a first round of relief. So where did all this money come from?

I'm so glad to finally be here in Royal Tunbridge Wells. The name of your town has been in my diary for the last four months. During these four months, I have been in Paris,

Rotterdam, Mexico, Porto, Shanghai, a couple of times in London, three times in Amsterdam. In the next four, I plan to be Madrid, London, Shanghai again, Mexico, Peru, Florida, New York, and a couple of times in Amsterdam as well. For those of you who love travelling, you might be thinking: Wow! How nice! It must be fantastic to travel so much! But what if I tell you that all these trips are purely for business, in other words, there are no sunny pictures of Cancun; there are no nice pictures of the Inca trail to Machu Picchu. On the contrary, there are long waiting hours in airports, lack of sleep, some food surprises, many phone calls home reminding my three kids that they still have a loving and caring father. And it can be worse, someday you can find your own wife asking you why did you always choose a job that makes you travel so much, and this is scary.

So where is the joy or how I discovered the joy of traveling for business? What did I do when I travel for business? I bring with me the curious boy that is still in me. That boy makes me play with history, with geography, with politics, wrap up together with imagination and create my own stories, stories that for instance make me cross London's Victoria Station looking for secret agents around. I joke about this weirdest room I've ever been in Amsterdam, what you see there the tube is a shower in the middle of the room. I can tell you that I couldn't sleep, just thinking that any alien would just come down from the shower. I love conferences, I learned so much from them. This one in Paris, my colleague John Paulson had such a good speech on the Brexit referendum and he was accurate by the way, so, in Paris, I learned from you British people. When I'm alone, I take long walks at night through the city. For instance, in London, I really love and feel magnetized by Saint Paul's cathedral. In Latin America, I discover the materialism of Latin America through the sculptures and paintings of Botero. Thanks to my friend Angel who lives in Colombia for the last five years. In Tokyo, for instance, after six days of meetings, I realize and understand the deep sense of the movie *Lost in Translation*, listening to a fine banjo from a jazz band vajaspan while drinking the "Lost in Translation" cocktail on the Hyatt Tokyo hotel. Singapore, Singapore may be the place where I've dedicated more efforts to understand the tricks of his success. I recall this such an interesting meeting with this client, an Indonesian-Chinese origin, from Chinese origins, so after the meeting, I just told him: look, I've been always interested in understanding the role that the Chinese people have played in the Southeast Asia because I had read some things before, so he was so delighted that after one hour I had just got the best lesson I could get about this subject. I also train in time, I control in time as well. Let's move to Romania.

Let's move to Timisoara. After the whole day of meetings, I just passed by this such beautiful cathedral, Orthodox cathedral; I listened to these people singing inside. I got in and I've seen, for the first time in my life, the liturgy and the ceremony of orthodox liturgy, so I just stood there in silence and my mind just travelling time. I could imagine how impressive, how powerful this liturgy had to be for uneducated people in previous ages.

So which are the main factors of these stories and many others that I could explain to you? From my perspective, the first one is people, second one: introspection and the third one: language. People, a true willingness to understand and connect with people. Apart from setting my business meetings, what I do when I travel to a city for some days? I look in my LinkedIn account and search for people that I could get in touch with. Not people straightly from my own industry, just a broad search and I organize sort of blind dates, so a dinner, a lunch, meeting, whatever, and I try to understand what this person is doing in this, in that country, in that city; how is life there; how is the profession there; how is business. And when you get this connection, when you feel this connection, you know that something has changed in the other and in you.

 任务 4. 汉译英
难度级别：★★★

> **训练要点**：本文介绍了商务接待中迎接部分的礼仪，文章逻辑清晰，表达清楚，语速适中。学生在听辨过程中，要把握其总分式的结构，同时重点把握要点的主旨信息（通常在首句）。汉语因为语言特点，在表达过程中会出现词语或意群重复现象，在听辨过程中，应适当舍弃，整合出最关键信息。

接待工作礼仪——迎接礼仪

迎来送往是社会交往接待活动中最基本的形式和重要环节，是表达主人情谊，体现礼貌素养的重要方面，尤其是迎接，是给客人良好第一印象的最重要工作。给对方留下好的第一印象，就为下一步深入接触打下了基础，迎接客人要有周密的部署。应注意以下事项：

一、对前来访问、洽谈业务、参加会议的外国或外地客人，应首先了解对方到达的车次、航班，安排与客人身份、职务相当的人员前去迎接。若由于某种原因，相应身份的人员不能前往，前去迎接的人员应向客人做出礼貌的解释。

二、到车站、机场去迎接客人，应提前到达。恭候客人的到来，绝不能迟到，让客人久等，客人看到有人来迎接，内心必定感到非常高兴。如果迎接来迟，必定会给客人心里留下阴影，事后无论怎样解释，都无法消除这种失职和不守信用的印象。

三、接到客人后，应首先问候，一路辛苦了，欢迎您来到某某城市等，然后向对方做自我介绍。如果有名片可送予对方。

四、迎接客人，应提前为客人准备好交通工具。不要等到客人到来才匆匆忙忙准备交通工具，那样会因让客人久等而误事。

五、应提前为客人准备好住宿，帮客人办理好一切手续，并将客人领进房间。

模块四　　　　　　　　　　　　　技巧点拨：听辨中的逻辑框架

 任务1. 英译汉
难度级别：★★★

训练要点：本段音频中挑出两个实例来分析如何培养听辨能力。音频较长，听第一遍的时候，将全篇音频听完，尝试提炼全文主旨框架。第二遍复盘时，体会两处例子如何进行具体的框架提炼。

>> 例一

The **GBTA** expects corporate travel to rebound sharply this year and return to its pre-pandemic peak by 2024. That is a relief to full service airlines which **counted on** business travelers for 30% of revenues and a higher proportion of profits and big global hotel chains which earned 2/3 to their sales from executive guests for corporate road warriors.

词汇

GBTA
全球商务旅行协会

count on
依赖

译文

　　全球商务旅行协会（GBTA）预计商务旅行将在今年大幅度反弹，并且于2024年回到疫情前的峰值。这对于全服务航空公司来说真是一种宽慰，这些航空公司依靠商务旅客获得30%的收入和更高比例的利润，而大型全球连锁酒店的销售额有三分之二来自商务旅行的高管客人。

逻辑听辨

预计商务旅行将大幅回暖，2024 年恢复峰值。航空公司和酒店都开心了，因为前者 30% 以上的利润来自商务旅客，而后者则从商务旅客那里获得了三分之二的销售额。

策略分析

本段落先是提出了预测数据，再叙述了该预测的影响和各方对此的态度，最后说明了这一现象的原因。学生在进行听辨训练的时候，要把握文章整体的脉络，学会抓住核心词汇，进而形成逻辑框架。听辨忌讳眉毛胡子一起抓，讲究的是抓大放小、抓主放次。从关键词的层面来分析，英文中，名词、形容词和动词一般承载的信息较多，学生在听辨时，必须重点把握实词的意思。本文第一句话中，corporate travel、rebound、return 几个关键词点明了本段落的中心话题，即商旅回暖，之后的句子都是基于此话题展开的。而第二句话中的 relief，点明了各方的态度，奠定了行文的基调。学生在听译时，要善于把握关键词中传达的中心信息点，从而把握大致的逻辑脉络。从逻辑辨识的角度来看，本句的纵向分析难点主要在于第二句中 which 所引导的定语从句，是对前文 relief 态度的进一步解释，与前文是因果关系。横向分析，听译版本没有被冗长的修饰语所迷惑，厘清了逻辑脉络，将从句中的两个中心"全服务航空公司"和"大型全球连锁酒店"提前，直接表明态度，还使用了代词"前者""后者"，使译文更加简洁明了。

听辨要点

1. 注意把握关键词所承载的信息点，学会抓句子的主干，不要被过长的修饰语所迷惑。
2. 注意句子的逻辑关系，如第二句的定语从句，学生应该敏锐地察觉出因果关系。
3. 适当运用代词，使译文更加简洁。

》 例二

Over the longer term, the news for the **itinerant** executive isn't all bad. The introduction of touchless technology and online check-in for flights and hotels should speed up travel a little (at least one's pandemic paperwork such as passenger-locator forms and vaccine certificates no longer needs verifying). With many planes sitting idly on the tarmac as a result of COVID-related cancellations, some airlines used the opportunity to spruce them up.

◇ 词汇

itinerant
巡回的，流动的

译文

　　从长远来看，对流动高管而言这并不全是坏消息。非接触式技术以及航班和酒店在线登记的引入应该会稍微加快旅行的速度（至少个人疫情相关的文件，如乘客定位表和疫苗证明，不再需要验证）。由于与疫情相关的航班取消，许多飞机闲置在停机坪上，一些航空公司利用此机会对它们进行了美化。

逻辑听辨

　　长远来看，疫情对于商务旅客也不全是负面影响。非接触式技术以及在线值机能略微加快旅行速度（乘客定位表和疫苗证明等不再需要验证）。由于疫情飞机闲置，一些航空公司借此机会来打理它们。

策略分析

　　听辨的精髓在于抓住最重要的信息，而不是折射所有信息。本段承接上文疫情给商旅带来的不便，引出下文疫情的促进作用。学生要学会找中心句，抓关键词，进而在听辨过程中对接下来的信息作出大致的推断和预判，如本段的第一句为中心句。首先，"News isn't all bad"，抓住这几个关键词便可以作出一定的预测，下面要开始讲利好方面的信息了。这样，若是后一句话中的动词 speed up 没有听出来，也可以通过这一句判断出是一个表示积极态度的动词。另外，第一句话中的 itinerant executive，其实就是代指前文的"商务旅客"。与中文不同，英文不喜欢重复，经常一个概念换各种说法，看似不相同，其实指的是同一事物。若是学生不熟悉 itinerant 一词，也要通过听辨能力，把握逻辑，联系上下文，分析出该词的含义。第二句中出现了抽象名词 introduction，中文喜动，而英文喜静，遇到这样的抽象名词，不可只局限于翻译为名词，要学会化静为动，识别出其动词内涵。第三句中有许多介词结构，如 with 和 as result of，学生在听辨的时候一定要分清主次，分析出它们之间的逻辑关系，另外该句中的 cancellation 与 planes sitting idly 语义重复，所以可以省略。

听辨要点

1. 抓住段落的中心句和关键词，特别是表明段落观点态度的句子，把握好全文的基调，从而对下文的内容进行推断预测。
2. 熟悉英语喜欢变换说法的特点，抓住行文的逻辑，把握各个词的同义替换，如本段落中的 itinerant executive。
3. 学会"得意忘形"，特别是遇上英文中的抽象名词。
4. 为了使译文更加简洁，学生可适当删减语义重复的部分。

任务 2. 汉译英
难度级别：★★★

> 训练要点：本段音频中挑出三个实例来分析如何培养听辨能力。音频较长，听第一遍的时候，将全篇音频听完，尝试提炼全文主旨框架。第二遍复盘时，体会三处例子如何进行具体的框架提炼。

》例一

这次疫情带来很多购买行为的变化，比如以前做一个旅游计划，可能需要提前一个月或者至少半个月，而现在出现了很多说走就走的旅行。跨省游和长时间的度假也在慢慢地缩减。而省内游、周边游、露营等体验类、探索类的项目，满足了有生活理想和探索欲望年轻人的需求。

译文

The pandemic has brought many changes in purchasing behavior. For example, in the past, it might be necessary to make a travel plan one month or at least half a month in advance, but now there are many trips without plan. Inter-provincial trips and long vacations are also slowly being curtailed. Experience and exploration projects such as provincial tours, short-distance tours and camping meet the needs of young people who have ideal life and desire to explore.

逻辑听辨

This pandemic has changed purchasing behavior. In the past, planning ahead is needed; but now you travel without planning. For another, interprovincial and long-distance trips are slowly shrinking, while nearby-traveling is increasing.

策略分析

本段落语句比较散，但其实表达的意思是很明确的，主要阐述了两种事物的对比变化：过去的旅游计划和现在的旅游计划，跨省长途类旅游和短期体验类旅游。学生在听辨的时候要学会抓关键词，选取最重要、最核心的信息进行提取，如本文中"以前做一个旅游计划，可能需要提前一个月或者至少半个月，现在出现了很多说走就走的旅行"，就是以前计划耗时多，现在旅游计划耗时少。

听辨要点

1. 把握逻辑框架，对获得的信息进行分析加工，厘清信息层次及前后逻辑关系，再将关键信息按照逻辑进行整合输出，如本文主要讲了两个对比。
2. 根据意群切分句子，使译文更加流畅。

▶▶ 例二

我们现在考虑从什么方向去发展旗下一些旧改项目、**存量项目**，其实更多是想把空间更扩大化。不仅把自己的圈子扩大，也要破圈、交圈。不光酒店要破圈，商业也要破圈。不同的圈和圈之间交汇，产生新的内容圈。我觉得在未来，尤其在疫情之后的市场会更有前途和发展。

○ 词汇

存量项目
outstanding project

译文

Now we are considering how to develop some of our old projects and outstanding projects. In fact, we want to expand the space. Not only to expand their own circle, but also to break the circle. It's not just hotels that have to break the old circle, businesses, too. Different circles intersect with each other, creating new circles of content. I think in the future, especially after the pandemic, the market will have greater prospect and development.

逻辑听辨

Now we are considering how to develop some unfinished projects and trying to expand our space. We should not only expand our space for development, but also break down boundaries. Then the market will be more promising.

策略分析

本段落主要叙述了商旅行业现在所做的努力以及未来的期望与发展。首先要把握段落的纵向逻辑，即"扩圈"和"打破"，如此才有好的未来，即两个"因"，带来一个"果"。听辨中不要被细节信息缠绕，各种"圈"都是干扰项，不过都是打破旧俗的例子。本段的难点在于"圈"的翻译，学生一定要进行听辨，抓住关键词，把握逻辑，分析不同"圈"在不同位置所表达的含义，才不会把自己绕进去。

听辨要点

1. 学生在进行听辨的时候，要注意通过听取关键词把握行文的逻辑，如本段是按时间顺序论述的。

2. 语义重复可以把握关键信息点，适当省略，如本文的"市场会更有前途和发展"译为"the market will be more promising"。

❯❯ 例三：

我认为数字化分为三个维度，第一是管理维度。保利商旅有丰富的产业背景，但如何快速<u>顺应</u>市场、<u>顺应</u>管理、<u>顺应需求</u>，提高我们的工作效率，还有赖于我们的数字化管理。第二个维度是数字化分析。数字化分析往往为数字化市场做积极的准备。如果你登录某一个酒店预订平台，你关注的酒店房价都低于1 000元，那么同类型预订平台就会推荐很多近似价位的酒店给你，这是一个算法。最后，国际平台很早之前没有数字营销，他们会员就是经营他们的**私域流量**。我们应该学习，也要把它以适合中国国情的方式发展起来。比如SaaS，通过自己设计的SaaS，将公域流量转化成私域流量之后，更好地了解客户，达到及时、多点的触达。

词汇

顺应
adapt to

私域流量
private traffic

译文

I think digitization is divided into three dimensions; the first is the management dimension. Poly Commercial Travel has a rich industrial background, but how to quickly adapt to the market, adapt to management, adapt to demand, and improve our work efficiency depends on our digital management. The second dimension is digital analysis. Digital analysis tends to be proactive in preparing for digital markets. If you log in to a hotel reservation platform, the average price of the hotel you pay attention to is below 1,000 yuan, then the same type of reservation platform will recommend a lot of similar-price hotels to you, which is an algorithm. Finally, international platforms did not have digital marketing a long time ago, and their members simply managed their private traffic. We should learn from it and develop it in a way that suits China's national conditions. For example, SaaS, through their own design of SaaS, the public domain traffic can transfer into the private domain traffic, and we can better understand customers and achieve timely and multi-point reach.

逻辑听辨

Digitization has three dimensions. Firstly, the management dimension. Secondly, the digital analysis which makes positive preparations for the digital market. Finally, the international platforms didn't have digital marketing anymore either. We should develop it in a way suitable for China's national conditions.

策略分析

本段落的关键信息已经标出。本段落纵向逻辑比较清晰，主要为商旅行业数字化发展的三个建议，即管理维度、数字化分析和数字营销，难点在于横向逻辑的分析。如第一大点中的"保利商旅有丰富的产业背景，但如何快速顺应市场、顺应管理、顺应需求，提高我们的工作效率，还有赖于我们的数字化管理"一句，要求学生将让步意思翻出来。本段的最后一句"将公域流量转化成私域流量之后，更好地了解客户，达到及时、多点的触达"不可直接处理为并列关系，而需要将后半部分处理为目的或结果状语。在听辨练习的时候，无法记住细节不要紧，但是三个纵向大点需要被完整折射。

听辨要点

1. 把握好横向逻辑，明确各信息点之间的逻辑关系。
2. 遇到不会的词可以根据上下文推断大概的意思，采取直译或省译。

模块五　　拓展练习

任务1：
句子逻辑层次练习

请参照模块一的听辨技巧找出下列句子的逻辑框架。

1. Economic pressures are going to impact corporate travel in the years to come, and the general rule is that the less hard-hit an industry or company is financially, then the sooner their employees will start traveling again. Sectors such as pharmaceuticals, manufacturing, and construction have thus been identified as those to watch, and McKinsey notes that China and South Korea were both hosting large-scale events for the automotive and construction industries as early as April 2020.

2. Business travel is also getting closer to nature. The Incentive Research Foundation's June 2020 report on COVID-19 and disruption cited several examples of remote, outdoors-

focused destinations hosting incentive travelers and business meetings in the US, with a strong recommendation for service providers to develop outdoor offerings. This move outdoors can be seen around the world.

3. 商务旅行市场同样有买方身份互换，主客体换位的变化。旅游业中的食、住、行等行业，往往此时以买方身份通过市场建立经济联系，从市场上取得人、财、物和技术等各种资源。同时又作为卖者身份向市场出卖有形或无形商品。而在许多情况下，是处于商务旅行市场客体地位。旅游业这个商务旅行的首席客体始终同"大商贸"联系互动，拉动市场，为市场注入活力。

4. 商务旅行市场是经贸、商贸、技贸和文贸参与旅游活动的过程。一项大的商务活动往往涉及上至中央、下至各省市，甚至县区政府行政系统。因此，加强宏观指导尤为重要，应切实做到组织有序、协调行动、目标一致。

> **任务 2：**
> **商务旅行与接待口译练习**

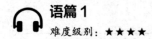

语篇 1
难度级别：★★★★

Business Travel on the Road Again
— Companies are spending more on sending their staff out to win deals

For well over a century people have predicted that technology will make business travel obsolete. In 1889 Jules Verne imagined that the phono, telephoto or the transmission of images by means of sensitive mirrors connected by wires would replace overseas meetings. In the 21st century, **far-flung** communication is no longer science fiction.

Yet far from **stowing** their suitcases, putting away their passports and signing into **Skype**, the corporate world's road warriors are clocking up more miles than ever. According to a report by the Global Business Travel Association, or GBTA, firms around the world will spend a record 1.25 trillion dollars this year on sending employees on work trips. This largely reflects growing

词汇

far-flung
遥远的

stow
塞，塞进去

Skype
远程视频会议软件

business confidence in the **downturn** following the global financial crisis suspending foreign **jaunts** was a quick way to cut costs. Now firms are looking to grow by sending staff out to hunt for deals. A recent survey by **Morgan Stanley**, a bank, found that 63% of American firms increase their travel budgets for 2015. A similar proportion said that they would increase spending again next year. Another survey by business travel news suggests that management consultants and makers of expensive hardware remain the biggest spenders on travel among American companies. And businesses and other organizations in China will collectively soon be spending more than their American counterparts, the GBTA reckons.

Organizations still place great store by face-to-face meetings. Kathryn Bell of the **Boston Consulting Group** says, although clients do not always demand personal contacts with its consultants, when they are working on operational improvements to a customer's plant, for example, there is no alternative to being on the ground. Isabel Bader Baznew, the dean of Desotel, a Canadian business school, says a big part of her job is **scouring** the world for potential benefactors. "When you are asking someone for money, it is better to do it in person", she observes. Some firms also use foreign jaunts as a reward for high-performing staff. That might be less demand for expensive jet setting, if promises of seamless tele-conferencing but not proved so hollow. Anyone, who has endured a **jerky muffled** video call, might wonder, if like one's **phono**-telephoto was being transmitted through distant mirrors. "Sony is a leader in virtual presence technology", says Chris Bowden, a former executive at that company, now at Carlson WAGonlit, a travel management firm. Yet if it's potential customers and competitors were gathering at a conference on the other side of the world, it would not send a **hologram** to attend. Even as they increase their budgets, corporate travel managers continue to seek ways to **pinch pennies** on each individual trip. A survey by

词汇

downturn
下降；衰退

jaunt
远足；短途旅游

Morgan Stanley
摩根士丹利（投资银行和财富管理公司，总部位于纽约）

Boston Consulting Group
波士顿咨询集团

scour
搜索；擦洗

jerky
不平稳的；抽筋的

muffled
听不清的；沉闷的

phono
声音的

hologram
全息图；全息摄影

pinch pennies
严格节约，紧缩开支

the Association of Corporate Travel Executives, or ACTE, found that over the past two years, firms have become **stingier** about letting staff upgrade their flights or hotel rooms and stricter about demanding that all trips go through their centralized booking systems.

Yet one obvious way of cutting costs is going largely unexplored, making use of the sharing economy. According to the ACTE, over half of firms have ruled out alternative suppliers of accommodation, such as Airbnb, mainly citing their duty of care to employees. Carol Neil, a travel manager at Norma, says the bank **vets** all the suppliers of travel services before letting staff use them, and so far it has not approved any sharing economy firms because of doubts about safety. Indeed, hotel rooms are built to a standard design with safety in mind, whereas Airbnb host's homes may contain unexpected hazards.

What of the road worries themselves? As their employers expect them to do more **schlepping** around the world with fewer **perks**, life on the road has become tougher. Stricter airport security, business traveler's biggest **gripe** eat up time and patience. And as more airlines offer in-flight Wi-Fi, the chance of enjoying a few hours of **downtime** is **evaporating**. Yet despite this, most executives say they enjoy life on the road. According to the GBTA, around half was happy with the amount of traveling they do and over a third said they would like to do more. This may be because the daily **grind** back at base has got a lot tougher too. An executive from a big professional services firm who flies around 20 times a year says that modern office life has got so unpleasant, trying to run a business from an open-plan desk, higher levels of expectation and having to inspire the hell out of people merely to stop them from being tempted away, that he looks forward to foreign trips simply to take a break from it all.

词汇

stingy
吝啬的，小气的

vet
审查，仔细检查

schlepping
费力地携带或搬运沉重的物品
perk
津贴，补助
gripe
抱怨；肠胃绞痛
downtime
停工；停机
evaporating
蒸发；消散
grind
苦差事，磨碎

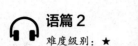

语篇 2
难度级别：★

Prepare for a Business Trip

　　I'm going to a conference this weekend back in my home state of Minnesota. I am going there to address a convention full of librarians, believe it or not. For me, the worst part of going on the road for business is not the traveling, it's all the preparation you have to do. I created a whole checklist of things that I have to do when I travel. First, I confirm that my flight will be on time departing from LAX. Next, I call to double-check on my reservation for the hotel and the **renter**-car. After that, I pull out my suitcase and start packing. I'm a light packer, so I bring only the pants, shirts, socks, and underwear I'm going to need, nothing more. I throw in my **toiletries** bag with the usual stuff: shaver, shaving cream, toothbrush, toothpaste, and **floss**, and then I'm just about done. Finally, I go through my briefcase to make sure I have the things I'll need for the conference: my badge, my laptop, my overhead transparencies, a notepad, and some pens. Now I'm ready. Off I go to my old home.

○ 词汇

renter
承租人

toiletry
洗漱用品

floss
牙线

模块六

**译海拾贝：
口译员的基本素养**

　　在翻译（translation）的概念框架内，口译与其他翻译活动最明显的区别在于它的即时性：从根本上说，口译是为想要跨越语言和文化障碍进行交际的人们提供即时即地的便利。英语中的"译员"一词来自拉丁语 interpres（意思是详述者，解释晦涩难懂之事的人）。口译分类标准多样，但是业内普遍接受的是将口译工作分为联络口译和会议口译（包括交替传译和同声传译）。从工作难度角度来看，联络口译相对简单，交替传译难度加大，而同声传译则难度最大，但三种口译形式对译员的能力也有一些共性要求，其专业素养主要包括以下方面：

对翻译事业的热爱

这是一名译员应该具备的最基本素养。如果对一个行业没有热爱之心，又怎么会在行业中钻研深造，会花费时间和精力去练习交传、同传，学习相关理论和文化知识呢？所以，在谈论口译员的基本素养时，对翻译事业的热爱是最首要的。

扎实的双语能力和口头表达能力

口译员在翻译的过程中需要充分理解源语，然后用流畅的目标语将其表达出来，所以平时双语的语言积累至关重要。除了要有扎实的双语能力外，译员还要有较强的口头表达能力，联络口译和交传译员要具备一定的演讲能力；而同传译员为了能紧跟发言者，其讲话速度和思维加工转换速度要比一般人稍快。同时，译员要做到逻辑清晰、吐字清晰、语音语调流畅利落。反观在一些重要的口译场合，译员的迟疑、过多的填充词（language filler）、重复、不流畅，都会直接影响会议的交流效果，甚至引起外交风波。

坚定的政治立场和敏感度

译员的输出语表达，需要字斟句酌，从而维护国家尊严与利益。这既需要扎实的语言功底，也需要爱国热忱和政治敏感度。例如，1972年1月尼克松派国家安全事务副助理黑格来华，将尼克松"访华公报草案"送交周恩来总理。周总理仔细阅读公报草案，其中有这样的表达："美国政府关心中国人民的生存能力（viability）"。为弄清viability的准确含义，总理请外交部翻译室专家认真查明该词含义，该词尤指"胎儿或婴儿的生存能力"。周总理问黑格："你们为什么非要在公报中使用viability这样的字眼？"黑格振振有词地解释说："我们完全是为贵国着想。你看苏联在贵国的北部边境摆着百万军队压境，威胁着你们的生存，美国是不能坐视不管的，那是霸权主义表现。"周恩来驳斥黑格："我们反对霸权主义是中国政府的一贯立场，但中华人民共和国的生存不需要任何国家和集团来保护。这是一种帝国主义观念的反映，你们不能使用这样的词，否则将是对中国尊严的侮辱。"黑格心悦诚服地对陪同他的翻译章含之说："久闻周恩来的大名，今晚听他一番谈话真使我佩服之至！"

广博的文化知识

著名的口译专家Jean Herbert曾说过，做一名好的译员要做到"know everything of something and something of everything"（好的译员应既是专才，又是通才）。译员翻译的内容涉及面宽，如政治、经济、文化、科技、人文、环境、卫生、国际关系等，因此译员要做一位通才。

良好的心理素质

新手译员经常会觉得翻译时心发慌、嘴发紧,平时熟悉的内容也有可能会译得一塌糊涂,这主要是因为心理素质欠佳。译员要有良好的心理素质,能做到处事不惊,遇到临场问题也要平稳应对;要有较强的情绪控制能力,在任何情况下都要保持镇定。

强烈的求知欲望

口译技能包括三大板块:口译技巧、专业知识和语言基本功,后两个板块要求译员不断地学习积累。如果译员对新知识的学习缺少兴趣,就很难应对日新月异的翻译题材。翻译是一个终身学习的职业。

团队合作精神

在口译工作中,不仅仅要求译员个人素质好,还要求译员与其他译员、讲者和工作人员互相配合,团队在整个过程中,要互相体谅、互相支持,才能做好整个翻译工作。翻译工作本身经常是团队协作,比如不同人负责同一个会议的不同稿子,需要统一术语、协调工作进程和节奏,各司其职,最后呈现出统一的翻译风格和质量。

模块七　译员风采:中国外交部翻译的成长历程

我国外交部的高翻队伍是在周恩来总理等国家领导人的直接关怀下成长壮大的。周总理过去曾经说过,"外交人员是文装解放军",并提出 16 字工作要求,即"站稳立场、掌握政策、熟悉业务、严守纪律"。1949 年 9 月,开国大典还未举行,在周总理的指示下,外交部的组建就提上了议程。彼时中国根基尚浅,需要得到国际社会的认可,因此外交战线的建立十分重要。中国在对外交往过程中坚持使用自己的翻译,建设一支能力过硬的外事翻译队伍迫在眉睫。

1949 年 11 月,一支多语种口笔译队伍组建起来,当时叫作编译科,主要是负责英语、俄语的翻译定稿工作。那时的定稿人员并不在编译科上班,他们都有自己的工作,有需要时才会到编译科来工作。随着中国政治、经济等方面的发展,同我国建交、半建交的国家不断增加,翻译力量不足的问题日益突出,而外交翻译队伍的扩大与中国历史上的三件外交大事息息相关。

第一件大事是抗美援朝战争。1951年，朝鲜停战谈判开始，中国派遣十多位朝、英文口笔译人员前往朝鲜半岛做翻译和速记。这十多位翻译人员苦练翻译和速记能力，最终圆满完成了停战谈判的翻译和速记任务。归国后，这些人成为外交部翻译队伍的骨干。自此，外交部也有了专职的翻译部门，当时称为办公厅一科（翻译科）。外交部的翻译不仅为中央领导提供口译服务，还负责中共重要文件的笔译工作。

第二件大事是日内瓦会议。1954年4月26日，周恩来总理率领中国代表团出席日内瓦会议，为此外交部从各地召回正在工作或留学的擅长英、法、俄语翻译工作的中国人，经过严格的选拔和培训，组成了一支优秀的翻译队伍随行前往日内瓦。这支翻译队伍有力地补充了外交部翻译人才。

第三件大事是恢复联合国合法席位。1971年10月25日，中国凭借着76票赞成、35票反对、17票弃权的压倒性胜利，恢复了其联合国合法席位，自此中国在联合国的影响力和话语权逐步提高，在国际多边舞台上日益发挥重要作用。而在这漫长的22年的交锋过程中，外交以及外交部的翻译队伍都贡献出了巨大的力量，翻译队伍随着需求的提高不断扩大，翻译人员的能力历经考验也越来越出色。

外交部翻译的严谨作风和扎实功底与周总理的关怀和亲自指导密切相关。周总理多次批示，要求外交部译员每天要有3个小时练基本功（听、说、写、读、译），做外语对话练习。翻译要实现专有名词翻译的统一性。在解决各种问题的过程中，外交部逐步形成了有效的工作分配与管理程序，如译初稿的同志必须查核所有的人名、地名（由新华社编著的英、法、俄、日等人名地名字典）、国名、引语、政治术语的固定译法等；出手前必须"三合一"，即中文定稿、外文译稿、外文最终清样必须是一致的。因为当时没有电脑，文件的每次改动，都是用手在初稿上改外文，改动多时，外文稿会显得很乱，难免有错漏，三份稿子同时核对，就避免了这个问题。这些规定一直延续至今。有了电脑，不必一遍一遍地重打，但也免不了漏译、漏改，"三合一"等严格的程序保证了译文的严谨性与高质量。

改革开放以来，中国越来越频繁地参与国际事务。随着多边外交的开展，外交翻译的工作量激增，为了适应需求，外交部各语种都加强了口笔译翻译的培训，培养出一大批高级翻译人才，完美完成了国际性活动的翻译工作，受到了国内外参与人士的一致好评，让世界听到了中国翻译的声音。

现在，外交翻译的选拔和培训都已形成了一套严格系统的制度，每年招募一批优秀人才，经过全面培训和锻炼，培养高级翻译人才，充实外交部的翻译队伍，助力中国的外交事业，让世界听到中国声音。

第二章

电子商务
E-commerce

模块一   技能概要：听辨关键词

我们在第一章听辨逻辑讲解中提到过，译中听辨有三大要点。一是听结构，要注意衔接词和线索词，把握话语的句子结构和逻辑关系，实现对信息的明确把握。二是听意图，根据发言人的认知语境，结合发言人的角度，运用预测（anticipation），对发言的真实意图进行揣摩，预测发言内容，在听辨过程中有的放矢。三是听关键词，听辨中要基于语言冗余性的特点，提取关键词，即承担句意的实词，如名词、动词、形容词和副词，抓住主干信息，锁定主要意图。

本章重点学习"听辨关键词"，即什么是关键词，如何寻找关键词。一般而言，关键词的出现往往会有提示语，我们可以通过以下14个角度的语境提示来抓取关键词：

1. 段首段尾句：在段首、段尾常见总结性语句。

2. 总结性信息：如 in conclusion、in a word、to sum up、generally speaking。

3. 重复性信息：当某个单词重复出现时，往往较为重要，能体现出文章的中心，特别需要注意重复出现的实词。

4. 引用处：要注意专有名词的出现，可以在人名、机构或职位等专有名词上重点做标记。

5. 因果关系处：可以分为明显因果和隐含因果。表示因果关系的词有 because、for、as、given、considering、so that、therefore、consequently、as a result 等；表示隐含因果的词有 lead to、cause、reflect、derive from、result from、be based on、rely on、underlying 等。

6. 对比转折处：可以分为明显转折、隐含转折和特殊含义词转折。表示明显转折的词有 although、though、even though、despite、in spite of、however、but、yet、while、whatever；表示隐含转折的词有 not... but...、instead、in contrast、on the contrary、far from...、on the other hand、rather than、more... than...、otherwise、unlike、not so much... as...；特殊含义转折词有 unexpected、unexpectedly、surprisingly、unfortunate、unfortunately 等。

7. 设问句：如果是一般疑问句，发言者的语调往往是上扬的。而听特殊疑问句时，要注意"5W + 1H"，即 when、where、what、who、which、how 等。

8. 定义处：要注意下定义的线索词或线索句，它们往往会引出主题，比如 we call it sth.、sth. be defined、that is sth. 等。

9. 建议意见处：常见表示建议的词或句有 you should、suggest、recommend、tips、advice、had better do、How about、What about、Why not、Why don't you、If I were you、How does... sound 等。

10. 强调处：常见表示强调的词有 especially、indeed、certainly、just remember、and again、most importantly 等。

11. 举例处：常见表示举例的词有 for example、for instance、such as、take sth. as an example、say 等。

12. 解释处：常见表示解释的词有 which means、that is to say、meant that、known as、for short 等。

13. 实词重读处：听力中的停顿、重读部分，往往提示重要信息将出现。在一句话中，如果没有任何特殊的重读，其重音往往落在这句话最后一个实词的重读音节处。

14. 数字信息处：要记录数字，听清单位，注意数值之间的比较关系。

综上所述，听辨技能离不开准确抓取关键词的能力。而要掌握这一能力，除了要掌握好以上14个提示原则之外，在口译技能训练过程中，还要会"抓大放小"，抓住主干部分，切记不要"因小失大"。除此之外，在练习笔记法时，适当对它们进行符号编码，以求口译时能够快速记下来。最后，要找寻各种真实文本，进行大量的练习。本章以电子商务文本为中心，这类文本涉及企业在经营运转、贸易往来、业务开拓等一系列商务活动主题，往往会突出重点，以便更好地传递出讲者意图，达到商业目的。因此，学生若能快速准确抓取关键词，将更容易抓取主题中心思想和文章结构脉络，为商务口译任务打下坚实的基础。

模块二　译前准备

◎ 1. 背景知识

电商已然成为人们日常生活中必不可少的部分，在商务活动中不免会遇到电商类

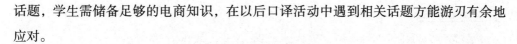

话题，学生需储备足够的电商知识，在以后口译活动中遇到相关话题方能游刃有余地应对。

本模块涉及的概念包括电商的多个场景，如现场直播、虚拟货币、技术问题等。

现场直播（live stream）：指随着现场事件的发生、发展，进行同步制作和播出的一种节目播出方式，是充分体现广播电视媒介传播优势的播出方式。

主播（live streamer）：指在节目或活动中，负责参与一系列策划、编辑、录制、制作、观众互动等工作，并由本人担当主持工作的人或职业。

电子商务（E-commerce）：简称电商，是指在互联网、内部网和增值网上以电子交易方式进行交易活动和相关服务活动。

虚拟货币（virtual currency）：指非真实的货币。市场上的虚拟货币主要有四类：游戏币、专用虚拟货币、交互式虚拟货币和网络密码币。

电子货币（electronic money）：指以金融电子化网络为基础，商用电子化工具和各类交易卡为媒介，计算机和通信技术为手段，电子信息传递形式实现流通和支付功能的货币。

供应链（supply chain）：指生产及流通过程中，涉及将产品或服务提供给最终用户活动的上游与下游企业形成的网链结构。

电子交易市场（electronic market）：指运用通信技术，通过应用程序把交易的买卖双方集成在一起的虚拟交易环境，如淘宝、京东、抖音和阿里巴巴等平台。

网络营销（E-marketing）：也叫网上营销或者电子营销，指的是以现代营销理论为基础，借助网络、通信和数字媒体技术等实现营销目标的商务活动。

在线事务处理过程（online transaction processing）：也称为面向交易的处理过程，指前台接收的用户数据立即传送到计算中心进行处理，并在很短的时间内给出处理结果。

电子数据交换系统（electronic data interchange）：指能够将如订单、发货单、发票等商业文档在企业间通过通信网络自动传输和处理的系统。

存货管理（inventory management）：指对存货的信息管理和决策分析进行有效控制，达到提高经济效益的目的。

自动数据收集系统（automatic data collection system）：分为设备类和网络类。设备类是指从传感器和其他待测设备等模拟和数字被测单元中自动采集信息的过程。网络类用来批量采集网页、论坛等的内容，直接保存到数据库或发布到网络的一种信息化工具。

◎ 2. 核心词汇

现场直播	live stream	在线事务处理过程	on-line transaction processing
主播	live streamer	电子数据交换系统	electronic data interchange
电子商务	E-commerce	存货管理	inventory management
虚拟货币	virtual currency	自动数据收集系统	automatic data collection system
电子货币	electronic money	疫情	pandemic
供应链	supply chain	物流	logistics
电子交易市场	electronic market	配送	distribution
网络营销	E-marketing		

模块三　　语料实训

 任务1. 英译汉
难度级别：★★★★

> 训练要点：本文介绍了电商活动进行的一种方式——直播。介绍了直播如何应用于电商界、直播的运作方式、国内直播平台、直播带来的收益以及疫情对于直播的影响。本文偏向口语化介绍，信息多且零碎，是训练听辨能力、准确抓取关键词的绝佳材料。

Live Streaming

　　Live streaming is not a new thing, and it started in China in 2015 with the roll out of 4G. And it was first used for entertainment and socializing. Many live streamers performed for their followers or chatted to them, making money by receiving virtual currency and gifts. In the West, live streaming is mainly the domain of avid gamers. And China is broken into E-commerce. China actually has a very big E-commerce empire. So it uses these "Super Apps", what we call that you have payment, you have search of information, you have recommendation system, and you have huge amount of goods available on the platform, and as well as a lot of consumers. So with this advantage, they merge these features of live streaming to make the influences actually sell goods. Traditional TV shopping involves in one way direction, whereby a host introduces a product, demonstrates the things, and they call its number or something. But the live stream shopping is live that means sell with a very, very big difference. They call this "different psychology". And live stream shopping is a very entertaining way of engaging someone else. When you shop, actually, this live streaming video will continue. It will minimize into a corner, and you can, like, buy the items and pay all on the same app. After that, the live streaming screen will just enlarge by itself, and the promoter will come back to screen. So it's like, very convenient. Taobao, one of China's biggest E-commerce platforms, owned by tech giant Alibaba, added a live streaming function in early 2016. In the following years, other E-commerce and social platforms like JD and Douyin also integrated this feature. Over $70 billion worth of goods was sold via live stream on Taobao in the year through March 2021. Latest surveys show that over 60% of live stream users in China were watching shopping shows, and over 65% of them shopped at least once via live stream. In 2020, live stream shopping got a huge boost during the pandemic, when millions of people were in lockdown, and many retailers were pushed online. People during the lockdown felt like there's a need for more social interactions. This live platform creates an interesting kind of environment. And live stream shopping brings in a lot more variety of things that people could buy and satisfy the sense of losing control, especially in the pandemic.

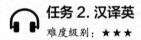

> 训练要点：本文对电子商务进行了简单的介绍，专业术语较多，听辨过程中译者要对专业术语关键词进行把握，在把握关键词和框架的基础上听辨其他细节信息，尽量避免关键信息遗漏。

电商简介

电子商务是以网络通信技术进行的商务活动。即使在各国或不同的领域有不同的定义，但其关键依然是依靠电子设备和网络技术进行的商业模式。随着电子商务的高速发展，它已不仅仅包括其购物的主要内涵，还应包括了物流、配送等附带服务等，包括电子货币交换、供应链管理、电子交易市场、网络营销、在线事务处理、电子数据交换、存货管理和自动数据收集系统。电子商务是因特网爆炸式发展的直接产物，是网络技术应用的全新发展方向。因特网本身所具有的开放性、全球性、低成本、高效率的特点，也成为电子商务的内在特征，并使得电子商务大大超越了作为一种新的贸易形式所具有的价值。它不仅会改变企业本身的生产、经营、管理活动，而且将影响到整个社会的经济运行与结构。以互联网为依托的电子技术平台为传统商务活动提供了一个无比宽阔的发展空间，其突出的优越性是传统媒介手段根本无法比拟的。

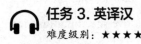

> 训练要点：本文介绍了电子商务发展的未来趋势。本文着重探讨了随着线上交易越来越普及和便利化，电商兴起的消费模式下企业应何去何从；从背景信息引入介绍电商发展的趋势，并从竞争和个性化定制两个角度展开叙述。文章结构清晰、框架分明，有利于增强听辨能力、准确抓取信息关键词、获取文章主旨。

The Future of E-Commerce

Buying and selling online is easier than ever, even as in person shopping resumes, E-commerce sales continue to grow along with the competition. How do you win when advertising costs are sky high? And trust and attention are getting harder to earn. To answer this question, we commissioned a brand-new research and dug into data from Shopify merchants across the globe. The result, a trend report unlike any other. This is the future of E-commerce.

Competition will be the biggest obstacle to growth in 2022 with a record number of companies moving online. Digital marketing is more expensive. Endless lucrative than ever before. Today most businesses are focused on converting people who are ready to buy. But by that time, most consumers already have a brand in mind. And in a saturated market, a strong brand not only makes performance marketing more effective in the short term, but it's also the foundation for sustainable growth. To combat rising acquisition costs in 2022, develop a brand measurement methodology that demonstrates the impact your top level brand goals; strengthen your brand by investing in both short term performance marketing and long-term brand building; diversify your advertising and sales channels to lower the cost of acquisition; and finally highlight your unique differentiators and values at every touchpoint.

Personalization, as we know it, is getting harder. As governments and operating systems introduce new data and privacy regulations, the biggest players are phasing out support for third party cookies. And consumers are more privacy-aware than ever. Nearly a third of technology decision-makers expect those changes to hinder their growth in 2022. That doesn't mean personalization is beyond and end all. People are over 3 times more likely abandoning brands that over personalized compared to brands that fail to personalize enough. But there is a nuance. Almost half of consumers say they are OK with brands they like using their data. If your business wants access to personal information, you have to get it and use it in a way that builds trust. By fostering a healthy community and appealing to shared values, brands can achieve the relevance customers want, without the privacy concerns of one-to-one personalization.

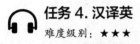

任务 4. 汉译英
难度级别：★★★

> **训练要点**：本文对电子商务进行了详细介绍，着重对为何发达国家不支持电商这一现象进行了原因陈述。听辨过程中译者要对专业术语、关键词进行把握，在此基础上听辨其他信息。

为何越发达的国家越不支持电商？

电商全称电子商务，是以新兴网络技术为手段，以商品交换为中心的商务活动。而在发达国家，电商的发展却非常慢，这究竟是怎么一回事呢？

近几年，各大电商平台纷纷崛起，其势头早已赶超实体经济。每年的"双 11"当天，淘宝平台的成交量就达到了上千亿元，这只是一天的销售额，数值非常惊人。而相较之下，实体店的经营就明显萧条很多。尤其是近两年的新冠疫情的侵扰，一大批的实体店纷纷倒闭，就连一些连锁的大型商超也支撑不下去了。

虽然中国的电商发展非常成熟，但是要知道电商的起源地并非中国。最新发展电商的几个国家，其电商的发展水平并不高，甚至是越发达的国家，电商发展起来越吃力。其中的原因跟西方的人口特点有关。发达国家非常看重实体经济，因为实体店可以提供更多的工作岗位。如果实体店纷纷倒闭，那会有一大批的员工失业，也就失去了经济收入。所以对于西方人而言，更注重于实体经济。

外国人更注重产品的质量问题。而网上购买的物品质量是难以保障的，外国人更喜欢亲眼所见到的商品，并亲身体验之后才会做出购买与否的选择。而网上购物的产品常常是照片和产品并不相符，即使是直播的产品也会出现不小的差别。另外，网上购买的产品价格会比实体店便宜得多，所以即使存在质量的瑕疵，也很难去苛责它。在国外，对于电商的发展并没有优惠政策，实体店和电商需要缴纳同等的税费。而在中国，国家给予电商不少的税收优惠政策，可以说是从国家层面就鼓励电商的发展，所以中国的电商发展要快于其他国家。

模块四　　技巧点拨：何谓"关键词"与如何寻找关键词

 任务1. 英译汉
难度级别：★★★★

In this video, we're gonna talk about the five best items to sell on **Amazon FBA** from E-bay to Amazon in my personal experience. And for each of these, we're going to talk about how to actually find them profitably. And in general, these are going to be items that are small and easy to ship and are worth a good bit of money that way, actually worth your time in order to actually sell these. So make sure to stick around to the end, because one of these categories I sold over 50,000 dollars worth of this one category alone. Not just in sales, but profit. So, the first type of item that you can sell profitably E-bay to Amazon is **calculators**. Calculators are great because they're small. They are often sold very quickly and they're worth a lot of money and a lot of cases. So the way that you can actually find these profitable is first by finding the **ASIN** on Amazon that actually have a lot of demand. You can just do this by typing "calculator" on Amazon, and then taking a look at the keeper graphs, and seeing which ones are selling fast and for a lot of money. And then you put these ASIN into your **replenishable sheet** and track them, and check back regularly on E-bay, to make

词汇

Amazon FBA
亚马逊物流，FBA（Fulfillment By Amazon），是指卖家将商品批量发送至亚马逊FBA仓库，随后由亚马逊负责进行存储、订单分拣、包装、配送和售后

calculator
计算器

ASIN
亚马逊标准识别号（每个产品的唯一代码）

replenishable sheet
补货表

sure that you can purchase them at a profitable price. So the second type item that you can sell successfully from E-bay to Amazon are DVDs. So this is a category that I personally have sold less of. I have sold some of these, but this is a category that my good friend Steve Raiken has sold lots of. The good thing about DVDs is that they're really small. Just think of a DVD, it's tiny. It's right here. They can oftentimes be valuable, and they can sell moderately quickly depending on what DVD you're purchasing. And so again, you find these products profitably, just like any other product you find an item on Amazon that is selling for a lot of money and relatively quickly. You put it in your list and then you make sure to check back regularly. You check. The more you check, the more you're gonna find, and then you purchase those items, and send them into Amazon to sell for a profit.

译文

在这个视频里，我们将探讨以我的经验看来，从易贝进货，转而在亚马逊上最畅销的5种商品。对于其中的每一个商品，我们将讨论如何从中获利。总的来说，这些都是小而容易运输的物品，这就能节省一大笔钱。换言之，值得我们花时间去卖这些东西。所以一定要坚持到最后，因为就其中一个产品，我就卖到超过5万美元。不仅销量高，利润也高。第一种商品我们能在亚马逊上获利的是计算器。计算器很好是因为其很小，用途众多，通常卖得快，带来巨大利润。你如果想确定其是否有利可图，首先可以在对计算器有很大的需求的亚马逊上检索，直接在亚马逊上搜索"计算器"即可。看看图表，哪些卖得快，卖得多？然后你把检索的信息放进你的可替换清单里。请定期查看易贝，确保你买进的价格很优惠。因此，第二种商品是DVD。这是我个人销售较少的类别。我卖了一些，但这是我的好朋友史蒂夫·不列颠卖了很多。DVD的好处是它们真的很小。想想看，DVD很小，就在这里。它们通常很有价值，而且卖得相当快，当然这取决于你售卖的DVD类型。所以你会发现这些产品就像亚马逊上那些获利多、卖得快的产品一样有利可图。你把DVD放在你的易贝清单上，然后时常来看看。来看吧，看的次数越多，你越可能找到并购买到这些商品，并把它们卖到亚马逊上，获得利润。

关键词标记

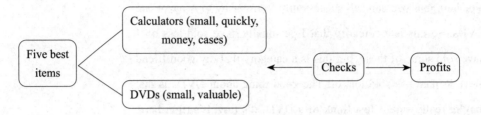

标记分析

基于关键词抓取全文关键信息：讲话人分享了亚马逊上最畅销的两类商品，主要包括商品名称和卖得好的原因。段落的中间和末尾都讲述了个人应如何确信该产品确实有利可图，两处重复，因此可以对其进行整合。

标记要点

1. 根据模块一口译技能概要中的 14 个原则，定位开头，学生便能知道段落的中心就是最畅销的 5 种商品；定位逻辑衔接词，如 first 和 second，厘清主题下的大分支。所以一定要熟记这 14 个原则，并能融会贯通。
2. 正如标记分析中所言，学生要合并处理重复的部分。

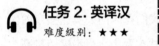

任务 2. 英译汉
难度级别：★★★

Cross-border E-commerce as a means to enter the Chinese market may have never been as appealing for foreign brands as in 2022. In this video, I will explain what foreign investors need to know about cross-border E-commerce to China in 2022, and what pitfalls they need to be aware of when **tapping into** the Chinese market solely through cross-border E-commerce. But first of all, a quick introduction. Cross-border E-commerce to China is a unique business model that allows foreign brands to sell their products to consumers in China as they are, that means, without having to set up an entity of finding a distribution partner in China, without having to register their products in China, without any Chinese labeling, and on top of all, with preferential policies that allow for

词 汇

tap into
挖掘，利用

lower duties and taxes when the products are imported into China. Now from this introduction, it can already be seen that cross-border E-commerce offers a lot of advantages over general or traditional trade, in particular, for foreign brands that do not yet have a presence in China, and that do want to test the Chinese market first, before they enter it. But there are, of course, also certain risks and challenges that come with this business model, some of which are new in 2022, and some of which are particularly important for foreign brands that really rely on cross-border E-commerce to enter the Chinese market.

译文

作为进入中国市场的一种手段，跨境电子商务对外国品牌的吸引力可能从未像2022年那样大。在这个视频中，我将解释2022年外国投资者要想在中国从事跨境电商，需要了解什么，以及会遇到哪些意想不到的问题。首先，快速介绍一下什么是跨境电商。这是一种独特的商业模式，允许外国品牌商向中国消费者销售他们的产品。这意味着不必在中国拥有实体店来寻找分销合作伙伴，不需要在中国注册，不需要贴上中国的标签，还有优惠政策，允许产品进口到中国时降低关税和税收。我们已经可以看到，跨境电子商务提供了许多优于一般或传统贸易的优势。尤其是那些还没有进入中国市场的外国品牌，他们确实想在进入中国市场之前先测试一下。当然，这种商业模式也会带来一定的风险和挑战，其中一些是2022年新出现的，其中一些对于真正依靠跨境电子商务进入中国市场的外国品牌来说尤为重要。

关键词标记

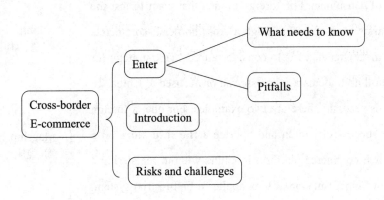

标记分析

本段主要讲述了外国投资者要想在中国从事跨境电商，需要了解什么，以及会遇到哪些意想不到的问题。然后给出在华电子商务的定义，并提出外商在华做电商存在的风险和挑战，引出下文。文段中标记的衔接词 now from、but 需重点注意，提醒学生中心词的转变或更重要的信息出现了。

标记要点

1. 本段篇幅适中，但真正重要的内容很少。听辨时，部分小细节可以放弃。
2. 注意衔接词对关键信息的提示，如 first。

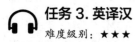

任务 3. 英译汉
难度级别：★★★

Now, as for the new challenges, in 2022, foreign brands engaged in cross-border E-commerce to China must pay increased attention to data and consumer protection. For one, ***Personal Information Protection Law***, which came into effect in September 2021, now also regulates data processing activities that occur outside of China, for example, between the foreign brands and their foreign cross-border E-commerce consulting firm. For another, many of the newest trends used to market foreign brands in China, such as social commerce or live-streaming, have been subjected to new regulations that now require more transparency for the protection of consumers. For foreign brands that want to test the Chinese market from abroad through a cross-border E-commerce, one of the main challenges is to consider a trademark strategy for China. Even if no trademark is transferred or licensed to China. To highlight this necessity, here are two examples. For one, a foreign brand may successfully open and operate a **flagship store** on a cross-border E-commerce platform in China without registering a trademark in China. But since China applies a first-to-trial system, if someone else registers the trademark first, it will likely be too

词汇

Personal Information Protection Law
《个人信息保护法》

flagship store
旗舰店

late. On the contrary, a foreign brand may have already registered its trademark in China, but someone else may have opened the store on a cross-border E-commerce platform under the brand's name. Therefore, foreign investors should always develop an independent trademark strategy for China, even if they solely enter the Chinese market from abroad through cross-border E-commerce.

译文

至于2022年出现的新挑战,在中国从事跨境电商的外国品牌必须更加重视数据和消费者保护。首先,2021年9月生效的《个人信息保护法案》现在还规定了中国境外的人的数据处理活动,比如,外国品牌与其外国跨境电子商务咨询公司之间的数据处理活动。再如,许多中国营销外国品牌时的新趋势,如社交商务或直播,都受到了新的规定,现在要求更透明地保护消费者。对于那些在国外想通过跨境电商来测试中国市场的外国品牌来说,主要挑战之一是考虑中国的商标战略,即使没有商标转让或许可给中国的品牌也是一样。为了强调这种必要性,这里有两个例子。首先,一个外国品牌没有在中国注册商标,可能也跨境成功开设和经营了旗舰店。但由于中国实行先注册先得的政策,如果这时其他人注册了他们的商标,就为时已晚了。相反,一个外国品牌可能已经在中国注册了商标,但其他人可能已经以该品牌的名义在中国的电子商务平台上开设了商店。因此,外国投资者应该始终为中国制定独立的商标战略,即使他们通过跨境电子商务从国外进入中国市场,也要如此。

关键词标记

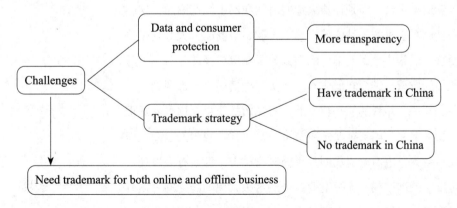

标记分析

通过标记出的关键词和导图,学生可知本段就challenge展开论述,主要有注重保护数据和消费者及商标策略这两大挑战。前者通过 for one 和 for another 这两个衔接词，引出数据处理活动中的隐私保护和保护消费者的方式更透明化；后者也举了两个例子，也是通过衔接词 for one 和 on the contrary 引出，分别列出在中国已有商标和无商标进行电子商务贸易的情况，最后，以逻辑衔接词 therefore 引出在华进行注册商标的重要性。

标记要点

1. 本段的逻辑十分清晰。在听辨过程中，要抓住各逻辑词，掌握全段逻辑。
2. 联系任务 2，可以得出整篇文章以"总—分"的形式贯穿全文，是英文演讲常见的布局模式。平日训练积累时，多注意这种文章本身的逻辑线索，形成对线索敏感的听辨习惯。
3. 文中提及外商在中国从事跨境电商应注意的事项，且涉及专业知识，建议学生在听前积累背景知识。

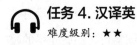

任务 4. 汉译英

难度级别：★★

更低的价格买到心仪的产品，可以打破信息壁垒，避免花冤枉钱吗？确实电商发展的好处有很多，但是我们也不能忽略电商的弊端。电商的发展让越来越多的国人出现"懒癌"。在家里，躺着刷刷手机就什么都有了，还出去干啥呢？这会对身体健康产生一定的影响。一方面，电商购物，往往不是买到想要的就退出平台，而是耗费大量的时间在网上浏览商品，这会加深我们对手机的一种依赖。另一方面，电商的一大好处是价格便宜，但是这会促使不少的商家为了获取更高的收益率，降低产品的质量，进而降低成本。其实这种情况大家都遇到过，明明是同一个品牌的同一款产品，实体店的质量要比电商好很多，长久下去，国家企业的声誉将不复存在。我国的电商发展是**如日中天**，电商解决我们大半的购物需求，但是有人发现，越是发达的国家越不支持电商，当然这跟其他的国家的习惯有关。但是，我们在享受电商带来便利的同时，也不能忽略电商带来的负面影响，应当采取措施予以防范。对于我国电商的发展，朋友们有何看法？

◇ 词汇

如日中天
in full swing

译文

Can you break down information barriers and avoid wasting money by buying your favorite products at a lower price? It is true that there are many advantages of E-commerce development, but we can't ignore the disadvantages of it. With the development of E-commerce, more and more people in our country are overwhelmed with laziness. You can have everything with your mobile phone just lying down at home. Therefore, there is no reason to go out. However, this will have a certain impact on health. On one hand, when you shop on E-commerce platforms but not find what you want, you will waste lots of time browsing products online instead of exiting, which will deepen our dependence on mobile phones. On the other hand, one of the advantages of E-commerce is its low price, which, however, will encourage many businesses to obtain higher yields by reducing the quality of products and consequently reducing costs. In fact, everyone has encountered this situation: the quality of a same product of the same brand in physical stores is obviously much higher than that in E-commerce platforms. In the long run, the reputation of national enterprises will cease to exist. China's E-commerce development is in full swing, and E-commerce meets most of our shopping needs. However, someone finds that the more developed countries are, less support will be given to the development of E-commerce, which, of course, is related to the habits of these countries. However, while enjoying the convenience brought by E-commerce, we should not ignore the negative impacts brought by it, and take measures to prevent. What do you think of the development of E-commerce in China?

关键词标记

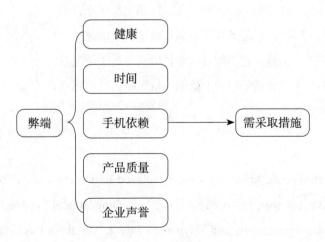

标记分析

本段主要讲述了电商发展的弊端，即对身体健康产生影响、耗费时间、加深对手机的依赖、影响产品质量和国家企业的声誉，最后以呼吁采取措施结尾，逻辑结构清晰明了。相对几个关键词，整段篇幅较长，但若仔细分析，会发现很多话术都是围绕一个主题展开。比如，在谈起电商"影响产品质量"这一弊端时，文中先谈"价格便宜"这一好处，进而用"但是"进行转折，突出重点。

标记要点

本段逻辑清晰，根据模块一口译技能概要的 14 个原则，学生要注意语篇的句首，主旨句往往就出现在句首。因此，若掌握这 14 个原则，学生便能快速识别文章主题，因为它们不仅能帮助学生进行有效预测，还能快速抓住关键词和全文重点。

任务5. 汉译英
难度级别：★★

今年6月底，每日优鲜分别关闭苏州、南京，7月1日关闭杭州、青岛、深圳，以及7月2日关闭广州、济南、石家庄、太原等九个城市的业务。生鲜行业本来就面临着高成本、高**库存**等压力，疫情带来的流量红利毕竟不是长久的。由于平台上的货品种类越来越少，订单量也在持续下滑。每日优鲜陷入这次危机，主要原因就是长期亏损。曾经火爆的生鲜电商为什么短时间内几乎已被市场遗忘？上海财经大学电子商务研究中心主任劳帼龄说，这不是一个暴利行业，这是一个辛辛苦苦起早贪黑的行业。同时，它的毛利又不高。数字化赋能之后，这个行业更加高效。但是，也不能盲目地觉得只要搭上了互联网的快车，我们今天这卖菜的路途上就能一帆风顺。没有那么简单。对此你怎么看？

词汇

库存
inventory

译文

The retail enterprise, Missfresh Limited, closed its business in Suzhou and Nanjing at the end of June this year, followed by Hangzhou, Qingdao and Shenzhen on July 1, and Guangzhou, Jinan, Shijiazhuang and Taiyuan on July 2. The fresh food industry is already facing the pressure of high cost and high inventory. After all, the flow dividend brought by the epidemic is not long-term. The order quantity continues to decline as there are fewer and fewer kinds of goods on the platform. And the major contributor of this crisis lies in long-term losses. Why has the fresh E-commerce platform craze been almost forgotten by the market in a short time? Lau Guoling, the director of the E-Commerce Research Center of Shanghai University of Finance and Economics, said that this is not a profiteering industry, but an industry where people work from dawn to night. At the same time, the gross profit is not high. With digital empowerment, this industry will be more efficient. However, I can't say that we blindly think that as long as we take the high-speed railway of Internet, we can easily sell food nowadays, which is not so simple. How do you think of this?

关键词标记

标记分析

通过标记出的关键词，学生可以给出相应的思维导图，即首先由每日优鲜门店的相继倒闭这一事实，引出表面原因和深层原因。表面原因分别有行业成本高、库存多、平台种类少和订单量下滑；深层原因主要是生鲜行业本身并非能获得暴利的行业，而且它并未能从互联网数字化中获利。在口译实践中，输出的译文可以进一步简化，学生甚至可以将表面原因中的标记点缩减为行业成本高和平台订单量下滑，任选其中两种即可，以求做到"抓大放小"，即抓住文章最主要的内容，忽略细枝末节。

标记要点

1. 本段逻辑结构不是明示的，但是逻辑线条仍然很清晰，能够立刻把握逻辑并不容易，学生要有大量的训练基础才能敏感地捕捉非明示的语篇逻辑框架。
2. 做到"抓大放小"的前提也是要理解全文脉络，学生在听辨环节中，仅靠一遍就记住的东西无法太多，所以学生要学会抓住最要紧的部分，以求传递出源语的中心内容。
3. 在口译实践中，如果时间紧或者没有笔记，只能通过无笔记交传进行翻译，学生可以进行删减式的口译，保证不遗漏关键信息。

任务 6. 汉译英

难度级别：★★★

不同于往年的各自为战，今年各大互联网平台携手拆墙，内容与电商的边界愈发模糊。传统的货架电商在补齐自己的内容短板，除了此前内嵌小游戏、开发短视频内容之外，淘宝近期还挖来了罗永浩、俞敏洪等个人 IP 的头部**主播**入驻。内容平台也在完善自己的**交易闭环**。抖音、快手等短视频平台均针对商城做了一系列革新升级，加大货架电商占比。

○ 词汇

主播
streamer

交易闭环
trading loop

译文

Different from previous years, this year's major Internet platforms have joined hands to tear down the boundary, making it hard to tell the difference from the E-commerce. Traditional shelf E-commerce companies are making up the difference. In addition to embedding small games and developing short video content, Taobao recently recruited some top streamers with huge online influence from TikTok such as Luo Yonghao and Yu Minhong. The content platform is also improving its own trading loop. Short video platforms, such as TikTok and Kuaishou, have made a series of innovations and upgrades for its shopping, increasing the proportion of shelf E-commerce.

关键词标记

标记分析

本段主要讲述了各大互联网平台如何扩大营销渠道。通过上文标记出的关键词，段落的总体逻辑浮现眼前。若学生在复述或翻译时，漏掉了某互联网平台类型或平台类型的具体例子，也不会影响对本段的整体输出。

标记要点

本段的例子较多，学生可以采用"抓大放小"的策略，抓大点，漏掉了几个例子对整体影响不大。学生要切记，字多不一定代表内容重要，这要求学生平时多加练习，将听辨意识放在第一位，随时分析和理解段落中的逻辑关系。

模块五　拓展练习

任务：电子商务口译练习

语篇 1
难度级别：★★★

请根据关键词串联文章，对音频进行复述[1]。

E-commerce Platforms

Hey everybody. Today, we're going to go over the top E-commerce platforms for 2020. First, let's take a look at the entire web and see which E-commerce platforms are dominating the marketplace. We use a site called Builwith that scans the entire web and looks at what E-commerce platforms these websites are using. The scan is global, so it takes all websites throughout the world into account. As you can see, the No.1 E-commerce platform in the entire world is Shopify. They have 22% of the market and have been one of the fastest growing E-commerce platforms in recent years. Second, we **have a tie with** 15% each, Wix and WooCommerce. This is surprising for Wix. Wix is more of a general website builder. They have built some E-commerce functionality into their platform, but they are by no means a fully functional E-commerce platform. WooCommerce is open source, so it's free and is tied into WordPress. WooCommerce has grown quickly. They have a fully functional E-commerce back end and keep coming out with new features. We see them continuing to

词汇

have a tie with...
与……有关系

1　全文涉及很多商家，这种专有名字如果不是特别重要，可以不用翻译，在目标语中直接复述原词发音。本文涉及的商家有 Builwith、Shopify、Wix、WooCommerce、WordPress、Opencart、PrestaShop、Ecwid、Zen Cart、Magento 和 Alexa Rankings。

grow internationally, because they are open source, and anyone using their platform can modify anything they want. So, if you need specialized shopping somewhere in the world, you can add this type of shopping method through WooCommerce that you may not have been able to do through Shopify or Wix. WooCommerce is a big contender. Keep an eye on for them. Forth, we have Square with 7 %. They provide a basic website builder, and have started tying in E-commerce functionality on their back end. They have been growing by attracting the small E-commerce shops because they're easy to get up and running. Fifth is Opencart, with 5% of the market. There are another open-source platform, and continue to compete as a global E-commerce player. Sixth, we have PrestaShop with 4% of the marketplace. Seventh, we have Ecwid with 4%. Eighth is Zen Cart, with 3% of the marketplace. And the nineth, we have Magento, with 3% of the marketplace. Magento was the No.1 platform in the world for the longest time. They don't promote their open source solution as much anymore, so their numbers have dropped with their smaller sites. They are now focused on the enterprise E-commerce players that are doing tens of millions of dollars and more online. Magenta 1 will also no longer be supported in June 2020. So merchants who do not have the need to upgrade to an enterprise level are switching to other E-commerce platforms instead. Now, let's move onto the top million sites. Remember, there are billions of sites on the Internet, so if you're in the top million sites online, this is actually really good. We look at these rankings through a site called Alexa Rankings, which is owned by Amazon. They rank sites from one to a billion, and where the site ranks based on the amount of traffic received to that site. If you ranked in the top million, you're getting a pretty heavy amount of site visits. For example, a brand like Tabasco ranks around the 300,000 mark on Alex rankings. They are not on the top end of the million, but they are **a reputable** site

> 词汇

reputable
名声好的

that still gets a lot of traffic. Sites ranked on the top million are probably doing about a million in E-commerce sales each year. Let's check out which E-commerce platforms have the largest slice of the pie in this top million. Number one, WooCommerce, with 20% of the market. This is surprising that WooCommerce has taken the lead over Shopify. Shopify was No.1 just a couple months ago. WooCommerce is seriously becoming a true player in the E-commerce world. And No.2, right behind them, we have Shopify with 21%. No.3, we have Magento with 7% of the market. This is where Magento starts to become more competitive in the scene, where we're looking at enterprise type sites. The sites that are doing more complex E-commerce and that needs more fully functional E-commerce systems. No. 4 is Opencart, with 4% of the marketplace. And No. 5, with 3%, is BigCommerce. BigCommerce is based out of Austin, Texas, and as another enterprise focused E-commerce player offering a fully functional platform, they are an exciting, up and coming E-commerce platform which is contending with the Shopifies, Magentos and Woocommerces of the world.

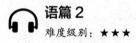

电商不倒，实体不活？

"双 11"购物节又来了。过去十几年，我国电商发展迅猛，从网店到直播，带货形式是越来越多样化。与此同时，实体店的日子却越来越难了。因为大家都在网上买东西，逛实体店的次数越来越少，所以就有了"电商不倒，实体不活"的说法。客观上来说，电商确实抢走了不少实体店的生意。比如，以前大家都去服装店买衣服，现在网上买了，以前家里缺点毛巾、牙刷、衣架、插座之类的，都会去超市或小卖部买，现在动动手指就搞定了。但另外，电商和实体又不完全是竞争的关系，其中也有承接和促进。

那什么是承接呢？2015 年，因为我国产能过剩，小商品堆积严重，国家就提出了供给侧结构性改革。在这个背景下，以前街上经常能见到两元店、五元店后来基本消失了。一边是库存积压太严重，另一边是本地消费者范围太小，东西卖不出去，再加年年上涨的租金，这些小店难以为继。于是就大批开始转战线上，直接通过厂家和全国消费者对接，等于电商承接了部分实体店。

那什么是促进呢？实体店有很多种，比如，一些餐饮店、水果店和超市，它们既有店面，同时也送外卖，线上线下"两条腿"走路。尤其是在疫情期间，大家购物不方便，线上这条"腿"变成了存活的保障。除了承接和促进外，还要考虑一种现象，就是一些人有好产品，但没条件开店。比如，远在农村的农民或者临海的渔民，有好的农产品和水产品，以前只能通过一层层中间商运到城里去卖，拿到微薄的利润。现在通过直播电商自己就可以发货到全国了。所以电商和实体店不完全是竞争关系，当中还有承接和促进。并且在实体店之外，电商还开拓了一些生意。那我国电商还会继续发展吗？答案是一定会的。

模块六　　译海拾贝：译员的职业道德

如果说准确且流畅地翻译是一名译员的基本业务素质，那么遵守职业道德就是一名译员的行为准则。在工作中，译员应该遵守职业道德规范，如保守秘密、保持中立、准确翻译、不发表任何针对会议发言人的评论、不接受超出自己能力范围的翻译任务。一旦接受了翻译任务，就要按时按质完成，要表现出良好的业务水准。一位真正有职业道德和职业素养的译员会将客户或服务对象的利益和感受放在第一位。

试着思考一个问题，你受聘于 A 公司，为其与 B 公司的合作谈判提供口译服务，你认为做到以下哪点是真正完成了译员的工作呢？

A. 客观公正地为 A 公司传达信息。

B. 积极地帮助双方充分交流，促成合作。

C. 积极地帮助 A 公司达成目标，维护雇主的利益。

这个问题并没有标准答案，我们可以从下面两个案例中体会一下。

>> 案例一

一家外商企业与一个中国制造公司谈判，译员甲受雇于该外企，中方也有一名译员。此次谈判是为了决定该外商企业是否要采购中国制造公司的产品。该外资企业非常重视环保问题，制造公司代表也深知这一点，因此在谈判中不断强调自己非常重视环保问题，想要以此打动外资企业代表，然而中方的译员却将这译成了"We have attached great importance to the problem of environment protection in our company."。外资企业代表听到之后误以为这家公司在环保方面出现了问题，着急地连连追问。这时译员甲及时指出了对方译员出现的错误，这里的 problem 应改为 issue，或者直接省略范畴词不译，向外资代表解释清楚了事情的原委，这次谈判才没有功亏一篑。

>> 案例二

译员乙陪同一家中国企业到中东某地区会见经销商，商谈该企业产品在中东地区的代理销售事宜，双方很快就价格问题达成了口头意向，并当场拟了一份简单的英文书面协议。就在中方企业负责人准备在协议上签字时，细心的译员乙注意到关于价格的条款过于模糊，未区分离岸价格（FOB）和到岸价格（CIF），而违约条款却十分详尽明确，他及时阻止了签字，告知了中方负责人这一信息。在译员乙的提醒下，中方负责人随即向经销商提出了这一问题，双方又经过一番讨价还价，最终明确了价格类型，维护了中方企业正当利益的同时，合同也签署了。

上述两位译员的行为都是他们优秀职业道德和业务素养的体现，如果做过了头，或许会产生喧宾夺主的效果，毕竟译员的本职工作还是翻译，但为自己的雇主提供有价值的建议和信息，让雇主自己做判断下决定，这是一个值得参考的做法。

译员在具有客户意识和服务意识的同时，也要保证翻译的质量。对于职业译者而言，翻译质量是最核心的竞争力，保证翻译质量也是译员应当承担的首要职业道德。为了保证自己的翻译质量，译员需要不断地提高自己的双语语言水平，关注时事新闻，掌握世界的发展变化，不断更新自己的知识结构；同时，也要做好充足的译前准备，这样才能在翻译时表现出自己最好的水平。

模块七　　译员风采："红墙内第一翻译"冀朝铸

"生于中国，长在美国，外交先锋，鞠躬尽瘁"，这短短十六字，凝练了"红墙第一翻译"冀朝铸的一生，他又被称为"站在毛主席右边的人"（出版了 *The Man on Mao's Right* 一书，回顾译员和外交官生涯）。正如联合国的刊物所说，冀朝铸是"了解中国过去四十年发生的大事"的人。"冀朝铸是外交部翻译圈的标杆和榜样"，曾担任外交部翻译室主任、出任过中国驻新西兰和比利时大使的张援远说。作为一名翻译官，他的身影曾出现在"日内瓦会议"、"万隆会议"、中美建交和谈、尼克松访华等一系列重大事件当中，见证历史和中国的发展。

冀朝铸于1929年7月30日出生在太原。他9岁时因父亲冀贡泉和大哥冀朝鼎受周恩来总理派遣赴美国工作，他就随家人到美国生活和学习。1950年，他毅然决定中断在哈佛大学的学业，离开美国返回祖国，他说："我是一个中国人，我要回去为自己的祖国服务！"

1952年，冀朝铸随团前往朝鲜开城，进入志愿军代表团谈判组工作。工作中，中美双方代表言辞激烈，气氛有时候剑拔弩张。现场的发言需要被全文准确记录，但是当时中方缺乏英文速记员，冀朝铸和三个同事经过赴美短期美国速记学习后，他可以每分钟记165个单词，足以跟上美方在谈判桌上骂人的速度。"中华人民共和国第一英文速记员"的美誉由此而来。

1956年，周恩来英文翻译浦寿昌已年过40岁，冀朝铸被外交部选为周总理翻译接班人。9月，总理在北京饭店为尼泊尔首相阿查利亚举行国宴，这是冀朝铸首次以周恩来译员的身份露面。他本来坐第50桌，突然被礼宾司安排到首桌，为周恩来的祝酒讲话作翻译。致欢迎词时，周恩来即兴脱稿增加了一大段内容，而冀朝铸仍按原稿译出，周恩来立即发现了，回过头来很严肃地对冀朝铸说："不对，不对，小冀你太紧张了，换一个翻译吧！"就这样，冀朝铸又被从第一桌换到最后一桌。但是第二天，周总理仍提出要他当翻译，而且一干就是17年，并见证了诸多历史性场面。

1970年，当周总理了解到冀朝铸已40岁时，对他说："口译在40岁后就应该转行"，并说，"口译工作非常辛苦，年纪大了，身体也受不了。另外，当了一段时间的翻译，也可以做更多的事情了。"此时中美关系有了转机。1971年7月美国国务卿基辛格访华、1972年2月美国总统尼克松访华等一系列的重大外事活动，毛泽东主席、周恩来总理等中央领导人的翻译工作，都是由精通英语又熟悉中美关系的冀朝铸担任的。1972年，尼克松访华，冀朝铸近距离见证了"跨越太平洋的握手"。尼克松走下专机，向周恩来伸出手。周恩来迎了上去，冀朝铸也马上跟了上去。此前，周总理特地要求，"小冀近一点，每句话都得准确地听清楚，准确地翻译"。于是，冀朝铸替尼克松翻译出了那句著名的话："我是跨越太平洋与中国人民握手。"尼克松后来在他的回忆录里写道："当我们握手的时候，意味着一个时代结束了，另一个时代开始了。"

1973年，周总理亲自安排44岁的冀朝铸去当外交官。冀朝铸被任命为中国驻美国联络处参赞，后被调回外交部担任副司长。

中国和美国于1979年1月1日建立外交关系，实现两国关系正常化。同年1月28

日至 2 月 5 日，邓小平副总理应邀访问美国，美国以接待国家元首的规格接待邓小平副总理。50 岁的冀朝铸全程担任翻译。美国各家媒体都很关注这个曾经的哈佛大学的高才生，美国《纽约时报》以"不可或缺的冀先生"为题发表社论，感叹"美国缺少这样的人才"。

1987 年，冀朝铸被任命为驻英国大使。在谈起当外交官的体会时，冀朝铸说："关键的关键，是要忠于自己的国家。"从"红墙内第一翻译"到杰出外交官，冀朝铸切身履行了为祖国服务的豪言，是广大译员学习的典范。

第三章

商务礼仪与文化
Business Etiquette & Culture

模块一　　　　　　　　　　　　　　　　　　　　　　技能概要：源语复述

听辨源语信息是口译能力培养过程中最初也是最重要的一步，不管是同传、交传还是陪同口译、联络口译，听辨都能帮助学生形成对原文的主要信息和逻辑框架的正确把握。在此基础上，学生需要进行复述训练，形成口译能力金字塔的第二步。源语复述是口译能力培养过程中听辨与笔记能力之间的过渡阶段，让学生从被动听力到主动认知加工，平衡听、辨和脑记，任务处理相对简单，但却是精力匹配和多任务处理的基础。在口译学习的基础阶段，学生需要从被动性的听力听解模式转换成多任务处理模式，听辨和源语复述能够为这种输出转换奠定坚实的基础。很多 MTI 专业招生复试题目中会包含源语复述题目，以考查学生的口译基础是否牢固。

所谓源语复述是指在听完源语信息后，学生将原文的语言要点按照源语的行文顺序进行口述。源语复述不是原文的完整折射，学生尽量保全源语的逻辑框架和关键信息即可。在保全重要信息的前提下，学生可以逐步填补细节信息。

源语复述一般按照下面的方法和步骤来练习。

1. 选择合适的源语音频

学生在训练起步阶段不要选择语速快、语篇长的语料，源语的选择还要兼顾汉英。

2. 打破复杂结构

复述过程中，学生要打破源语的复杂结构，用简单结构和简单词汇取代源语的复杂长句、复杂结构和复杂词汇。

例如：We have decided to cancel our order with you. As you know, the packing in the last order wasn't up to standard. This resulted in a high percentage of breakage, which meant we couldn't supply our customers on time. As a result, they were dissatisfied with our service and threatened to go elsewhere. Therefore, we really had no alternative but to look around for another supplier.

在听到这段话的时候,学生要边听边识辨逻辑和重要信息:

cancel order ← not standard (breakage → unable on time, dissatisfied)
↓
look for another supplier

巴黎释义派的脱壳理论认为,口译是信息映射而非鹦鹉学舌。因此,学生在源语复述时,要学会传递信息,不要被源语的外壳束缚,重视意义传递而非按照源语的句式结构来进行表述。根据该原则,源语口译可以被简化表述如下:

We have decided to cancel the order, because your last order is not qualified. It has high rate of breakage, so that we cannot deliver to our customers on time. Our customer is very angry with us. We need to find other suppliers.

如果学生觉得将每句话的要点都复述出来容易导致后面的信息遗漏,就可以先顾全大局,正确复述关键信息,之后再逐步过渡到填补细节。

例如:8月28日,商务部部长王文涛在京与来访的美国商务部部长雷蒙多举行会谈。双方围绕落实中美元首巴厘岛会晤重要共识,就中美经贸关系和共同关心的经贸问题进行了理性、坦诚、建设性的沟通。王文涛表示,经贸关系是中美关系的压舱石。两国的贸易对各自经济和世界经济都很重要。中方愿与美方共同努力,秉持相互尊重、和平共处、合作共赢的原则,为两国工商界合作创造良好政策环境。

初学者版:中国商务部部长与来访的美国商务部部长会谈。沟通的内容是中美经贸关系和经贸问题。经贸关系是双边关系最重要的基础。两国和平相处,才能发展经济和贸易以及投资。

上述复述过程表明,流畅准确的复述建立在良好听辨能力的基础上,准确地把握源语的关键词和逻辑关系能够帮助学生全面掌握原文内容。

3. 流畅复述,正确输出

学生需要重视输出语的流畅度,逐步控制"嗯""啊""哈"等语言填充词(language filler)、重复、自我纠正等影响流畅度的表达方式,也要重视输出语的语法正确性和语言得体性。如果源语是比较正式的语体,学生在脱壳复述中也不可过于违背源语的语言风格。

4. 均匀平衡地覆盖全文内容

复述要避免头重脚轻的现象。学生的复述问题集中在头重脚轻、源语头部信息保全较多、后面的记不住。出现这种情况，可以缩短源语长度、重视听辨训练。

5. 改述（paraphrase）练习

改述能够加快学生的反应速度和增强语言表达能力，为日后的翻译输出奠定基础。所谓改述，就是不拘于源语的语言结构和用词，换一种方式来表达。通常改述后的句子更加简单。

例如：Are you tired of feeling like you're constantly falling short on your self-improvement aspirations? Frustrated by the lack of progress you've made on your personal development journey? It's more common than you might think.

该例句为了使语言富有变化，比如 tired of 和 frustrated 其实是一样的效果，可以在源语复述训练中用同样的结构表述出来，减少转换带来的麻烦，以下改述答案可供参考：

If you are lack of self-improvement aspiration or personal development journey progress, this kind of things happen more than you think.

在充足的源语复述训练的前提下，学生的听辨、记忆、表述能力和反应速度等基础能力都会得到较大的提升。

翻译的本质并不是词对词、句对句的对等直译，而是对语篇层面信息的传达。口译学习的起步阶段，学生对接收到的信息进行快速的分辨和复述，能够对源语的语法、语义、语篇、文化层面等形成源语熟悉度，为后期的口译学习精力匹配奠定重要基础。

模块二　　　　　　　　　　　　　　　　　　　　　　　　译前准备

◎ 1. 背景知识

除了不同的语言差异外，国际商务也会涉及非语言差异。在商务交际中，行为差异往往是双方的文化差异所导致的，而文化差异也必然会导致不同的商务礼仪。不同文化之间的习俗和禁忌的差异很多时候会造成商务会谈的尴尬和紧张。所以在国际商务中，了解相关文化的礼仪习俗与禁忌，可以避免误解和冲突。本章主要围绕文化差异在商务礼仪中的体现，商务礼仪是在商务活动中体现相互尊重的行为准则，规范和约束着人们的交际行为。

本模块涉及的概念包括中西方的隐私观念、面子文化、跨文化敏感性等。

隐私（privacy）：不愿公开的信息。隐私具有一定的文化基础，不同的文化对于隐私的理解和认知也不同。跨文化交际双方对隐私权利的尊重是交际顺利进行的前提。西方人，尤其是美国人，十分注重隐私；而中国传统文化中并没有隐私的概念。跨文化交际是以对私人权利的相互尊重为前提的。隐私观念的差异是造成文化差异的重要原因，涉及收入等多方面。

面子文化（concept of honor）：面子是一个人自尊与尊严的体现，根植于文化的社会心理建构，具有情境性和可变性。面子文化是中国传统文化的重要组成部分。中国人的面子观念比西方人强，做事情时首先考虑别人会怎么看，所以中国人重面子。而美国人极其崇尚个人主义，做事以自我为中心。

跨文化敏感性（transcultural sensitivity）：跨文化敏感性是指在不同文化交汇的情况下用灵活的方式应对文化差异的能力。跨文化敏感性是跨文化商务一个重要的纬度，目的是让来自一个国家的人了解另一个国家的文化，理解他们的价值观和文化习俗。

◎ 2. 核心词汇

faux pas	失态，失礼	OSHA	（Occupational Safety and Health Administration）美国职业安全卫生署
offense	冒犯		
entrepreneur	企业家	UAW	（United Automobile Workers）全美汽车工人联合会
pointer	提示，建议		
protocol	礼节，礼仪	egalitarian	平等主义
showboat	卖弄，炫耀	priority	优先，重点
off-limits	禁止的	dispassionate	冷静的
cultural conflict	文化冲突	undermine	破坏

模块三　　　　　　　　　　　　　　　　　　　　　语料实训

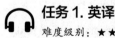
任务 1. 英译汉
难度级别：★★

训练要点：本篇谈论中美文化涉及收入等隐私方面的差异，并解释这种文化禁忌的原因，有助于学生了解跨文化商务和交际中文化禁忌。本篇语料

> 内容简单，但是对话形式展开的内容不容易记忆，话轮的转换相当于增加了记忆干扰，对于提升源语复述和记忆能力非常有帮助。

To Say and Not to Say

对话背景：晚宴结束，Jason 跟同事 Harold 一起往外走。

Jason: That was a lovely party, wasn't it?

Harold: Yes, it was. The food was pretty good, too.

J: I was a little puzzled about something, though.

H: What was that?

J: At one point in our conversation, Mr. Jones gave me a really funny look... it was almost like I'd broken some sort of a rule.

H: Oh, yes... well you did ask him how much he paid for his apartment.

J: And? What's wrong with asking someone how much they paid for a piece of property? Back in China, everybody talks about buying and selling apartments.

H: Yeah, I know... but in many Western societies, talking about money in public is a faux pas.

J: What's a faux pas?

H: It's a French term that means a social blunder. Questions like that are considered a little bit impolite.

J: Really? I had no idea. Back in China, it's not generally a problem to ask about how much something costs.

H: I know you meant no offense. When I was assigned to Guangzhou for 6 months, people frequently ask me how much my monthly salary is.

J: That's funny, because Western society seems so open. People talk about all kinds of private things that we wouldn't bring up in China. But money is a no-no, huh?

H: If your Western friend buys something for a really good price, he or she might mention it to you by saying something like, "Take a look at this camera that I got on sale for only $99 dollars." But unless the person is a close friend, we almost never ask how much something costs.

J: So, do you avoid talking about money so that people with less money don't feel bad?

H: Yes, I think you hit the nail on the head. Also, I think many Westerners believe that if you're rich, you should be quiet about it. In fact, I believe many wealthy people in the West feel a little bit guilty.

J: Why would they feel guilty?

H: Because so many other people work very hard, but never become successful. When the wealthy turn on TV, they see so much pain and suffering... but their own lives are so comfortable.

J: Ah... I can understand that. If I were a wealthy person I think I'd feel the same way.

H: It's interesting that some of the most successful entrepreneurs such as John D. Rockefeller and Bill Gates ended up setting up charity organizations and giving away a large portion of the money they made.

J: So you're saying that Bill Gates, for example, doesn't necessarily think he deserves all the money he made... he knows a part of it was luck, right?

H: Yeah. Bill Gates is a computer genius, but he was there at the right place and the right time.

J: That's a good attitude. It's good to remember that hard work and good luck often go hand-in-hand. Okay, so one more time... what's the etiquette when it comes to talking about money with Westerners?

H: If the person doesn't volunteer information about how much something costs, don't bring it up. Don't ask about personal savings or salary.

J: Is it OK to comment on or praise someone's possessions? If you have a really nice car, can I say, "Wow... nice car?"

H: Yes, that's fine. It only gets complicated when you start talking about specific prices.

J: I see your point. Topics like that could lead to embarrassment.

H: Exactly. Maybe Mr. Jones' apartment was really expensive, but his company paid for it... or maybe he overpaid and got a bad deal... in either case, it's easier for everyone if we don't discuss it in public.

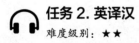

> 训练要点：本篇语料探讨中西方关于面子文化的差异，以及如何做到入乡随俗，了解和适应不同的文化。

Face Culture

背景：Jerry 要去中国出差，找同事 Amy 请教。

Jerry: Hey Amy... your family is from China, right?

A: Yep. I was born and raised in Shanghai. Why do you ask?

J: Well, I hope you don't mind... but I'm planning a business trip to China soon and I was wondering if you could give me some pointers.

A: You mean like where to go for food or shopping?

J: That would be good, too. But I'm actually hoping you might give me some insights into doing business in China.

A: Ah... sure! I think I can help. Do you have a specific question?

J: Well, for starters, what do they mean by "saving face"?

A: "Saving face" is a catch-all term for the concept of honor. In China there is a protocol to everything and it should be followed, otherwise you and the other party might be embarrassed.

J: So, in short... saving face is about avoiding embarrassment?

A: Exactly. Say you're late to a meeting. This would cause you to lose face.

J: How can you go about regaining your "face", or your honor?

A: It depends on how serious the offense was. If you were late, you can repeatedly apologize and the other person will probably forgive you.

J: But I would need to apologize more times than I would if I was late here in America?

A: Yes. Make many apologies. The person will probably say it's not a big deal, but in fact it could be a pretty big deal to them, so make sure to say sorry if you make a mistake.

J: My book on Chinese culture says that the idea of shame is a big part of how society works.

A: That's true. Chinese culture places more value on the group and less on the individual.

J: Pretty much the opposite of the US huh?

A: Yeah. In China your actions at work reflect on your employer and your daily conduct reflects on your family.

J: So if you shame yourself you're also shaming your employer?

A: In some cases, yes. Chinese culture doesn't encourage showboating or aggressive self-promotion.

J: Ha! In America, we promote ourselves all the time! It's the only way to get noticed.

A: But in Chinese society, you might have a better chance at getting a promotion at work by being a real team player. The best advice I can give to a foreigner who wants to do business in China is this: be sincere, try not to offend and tone down the volume.

J: What do you mean when you say, "turn down the volume"?

A: Well, for one thing: don't talk so loud! Americans are loud and although China is a very noisy country. People don't like it when you draw attention to yourself.

J: Would that include how I dress as well?

A: Certainly. Try to blend in as much as possible. The locals will appreciate the effort.

J: Wow, Amy... I'm so glad I talked with you! You've been a great source of information.

A: Sure. Let me know if you need more specifics.

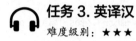

任务 3. 英译汉

难度级别：★★★

> 训练要点：本篇语料是关于跨文化敏感性的，跨文化商务活动和行为要求参与者有一定的文化敏感性，可以在不同的文化中自由穿梭，不触碰文化壁垒和禁忌。本篇语料仍需要跨越话轮切换的障碍来复述源语，这比起复述一个话轮之下的内容显然更具有难度。

Culture Shock

P: Hello and good morning. I'm Paul Higgins and I've been asked to help prepare all of you for your new positions.

J&E: Good morning.

P: Well, let's get right down to business, shall we? Each of you will be traveling to business meetings, attending fairs and exhibitions as well as receiving clients from abroad. It's therefore very important that you make a good impression. Let's start with how to greet people.

P: Yes, Emily?

E: Why do some Europeans kiss each other when they say hello? I've even seen men kiss each other!

P: Yes, in some places in Europe such as France, people do give each other a light kiss on the cheek. It's considered friendly and is not sexual in any way.

J: But Americans wouldn't do that, would they?

P: No, it's highly unlikely that an American would offer a kiss.

J: But Americans seem to like to hug each other frequently.

P: That's true. In recent years it has become more popular to hug. But usually, it's people who have met before and perhaps haven't seen each other in a while that might hug. At a first meeting, a hug would be very unlikely.

E: Hugs kind of creep me out! I don't really like to be touched by strangers.

P: Fair enough. I'd say hugging is not usually appropriate in a business situation. Some people are a bit overly friendly. But if the person initiates it, I'd recommend you grit your teeth and go along with it, otherwise people might think you are rude.

J: So the same rule would apply to getting a kiss from a European: if they initiate it, just go along and be friendly, right?

P: Yes. As the saying goes, "When in Rome, do as the Romans do." In other words, follow the local customs.

E: I know that we will be expected to chat and make small talk with our customers, but I'm worried I'm going to put my foot in my mouth.

P: There are a couple of topics that are considered "no-nos" in Western culture. It's best to avoid discussions on politics, religion and money.

J: Why is religion a sensitive topic?

P: Well, there are a lot of religions and each one thinks very differently. Overall, it's an area that could cause trouble; so, it's best to stay away from it.

J: When I visited Italy last year, I noticed a sign at a church asking people to remove their hats. Why is this necessary?

P: In some religious centers, it's considered impolite to wear hats. Many Western people also think you should remove your hat when dining or in a more formal setting.

J: You said money is off-limits as well. Can you explain?

P: In some parts of Asia, discussing salary amounts or how much you paid for something is an acceptable conversation topic, but in the West, people get very uncomfortable when discussing money.

E: That makes sense. Money can be a tricky subject.

P: OK... a couple more important points: in some Asian societies, when you meet someone and you notice they have put on weight, you might say "Hey! You've gained weight!" But in the West, it's almost never appropriate to comment on someone's appearance.

J: But why? It's not a criticism; it's just an observation.

P: In the West, it is viewed as a criticism. So don't comment on age or weight.

E: I think it's best to simply say, "You look well."

P: Yes... that would be perfect. Thank you all for your attention and we will meet again next week.

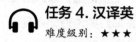

> 训练要点：《美国工厂》是美国前总统奥巴马担任制片人的纪录片，讲述中国企业福耀玻璃在美国创建工厂的故事。企业文化反映了中美两国的文化差异。本文语速适中、思路清晰。听辨过程中，注意抓住关键词，厘清文章的结构层次。

曹德旺美国工厂的官司

最近被称为"玻璃大王"的福耀玻璃集团创始人曹德旺又成为舆论的焦点，本月12日《纽约时报》发表了一篇题为《中国工厂遇到了美国工会》的文章，报道了曹德旺在美国建厂时遇到的困境以及车间里的文化冲突等。那么，《纽约时报》所说的文化冲突到底是指什么呢？

据美国《纽约时报》报道，曹德旺的福耀玻璃美国工厂设在俄亥俄州，成立于2014年，为当地创造了1 500多个工作岗位。随着工厂的发展，中美之间的文化冲突也日益凸显。工厂的一名前任副总经理提起诉讼，自己因为不是中国人而被辞退。有员工抱怨，"如果没有足够早地提前申请带薪假，福耀就会以旷工为由对工人进行纪律处分。"还有一名前雇员表示，"公司让他暴露在刺鼻的化学物质中，令他的双臂起泡，肺活量变小。"这名雇员于今年1月在补休期间丢了工作，理由是旷工记录太多。除此之外，去年11月美国联邦职业安全与卫生署（简称OSHA）对福耀的一些违规行为处以22.5万多美元的罚款，而全美汽车工人联合会也发起了激烈的工会运动，开始抵制福耀玻璃。据报道，曹德旺表示，他解雇工厂总裁和副总裁是因为他们不尽职、浪费钱。他还称，工厂的生产效率没有我们在中国的工厂高，还说有些工人是在消磨时间。据《纽约时报》报道，美国工会似乎应该是福耀遇到的大问题。全美汽车工人联合会（简称UAW）是美国最大的工会之一。2016年，UAW正式宣布支持福耀工人争取安全生产的权利，认为OSHA开出22.6万美元的罚款是合法的。2017年4月，在UAW的支持下，福耀的工人举行集会，抗议福耀忽视工人的行径。5月，UAW的行动达到高潮，直接在网站上要求民众联手请愿，希望劳方工人能够和资方进行联合谈判，对抗福耀不安全生产的行为。

以前曹德旺认为成本比较低，这些确实是。从煤气、水电、土地，还有税收成本来说，当初曹德旺去的时候是比较低，而且当地政府当时也是欢迎的。但是从现在的工人，包括一些政府部门的处罚来看，曹德旺必须不得不提高他的成本。中国企业在用工制度这些方面往往跟西方的一些规则会起冲突，包括工人的薪酬、安全措施，以及需要买的仪器，这些方面的措施需要提升。另外，曹德旺要加强跟有关部门的沟通，而且要学习当地的法律和文化，比如他的法律成本，包括税收成本。美国是一个税收非常复杂的国家，而且也是个法律体系很复杂的国家。他这方面的成本必须提升。

模块四

技巧点拨：
语篇信息脉络与源语复述

任务1. 英译汉
难度级别：★★★

> 训练要点：本段音频中挑出两个实例来分析如何培养听辨能力。音频较长，听第一遍的时候，将全篇音频听完，尝试提炼全文主旨框架。第二遍复盘时，体会两处例子如何进行具体的框架提炼。

>> 例一

American white collar workers work longer hours, take fewer days off, and log more overtime than you might think. Although outsiders might perceive them as informal, casual and relaxed, US work culture takes full ownership of the saying, time is money. The American dream is built on hard work and a focus on getting things done. It is extremely hard to generalize about US business culture. It is a culture of contradictions and opposites. It is focused on money, but relationships are built on a **golf course**. **Egalitarian**, but status and rewards are high priorities. The US leads the way in direct financial services and legal business, based on a reputation for dispassionate decision-making, but both a

词汇

golf course
高尔夫球场
egalitarian
平等主义者；
平等主义

huge creative and media sector, where relationship building and instinctive judgments rule.

译文

美国白领工作时间更长，休假天数更少，加班时间比你想象的要多。虽然外人可能会认为他们非正式、随意、放松，但美国的工作文化完全信奉"时间就是金钱"这句话。"美国梦"建立在努力工作和专注于把事情做好的基础之上。概括美国的商业文化是极其困难的。这是一种充满矛盾和对立的文化。它关注的是金钱，但关系是建立在高尔夫球场上的。提倡平等主义，但地位阶层和给予奖励则更重要。美国在直接金融服务和法律业务方面处于领先地位，这是因为其具有公平决断的名声，但这两个都是巨大的创意性和中介性领域，人际关系的建立和基于本能的判断占主导地位。

源语复述

American white-collar workers work longer hours, take fewer days off and log more overtime. They are not informal, casual or relaxed, "Time is money". The American dream means hard work and a focus on getting things done. American culture is of contradictions and opposites. Money vs relationships built on the golf course; egalitarian vs status and rewards. Financial services and legal business are based on a reputation for dispassionate decision-making, but America values judgement rules.

策略分析

源语复述建立在良好的听辨基础之上。当抓住关键词和行文逻辑的脉络后，学生复述源语就相对轻松。本段的主题是美国的商业文化，讲话者是从美国工作文化过渡到商业文化，因为商业文化是基于工作文化的；再者，讲话者也是把美国工作文化和商业文化进行了对比。学生听辨时一定要把握这个结构，否则就会感觉思路很乱。这部分的第一句是主题句，是典型的"主题＋细节"的结构。听辨主题句中的关键词就能把握文章的走向，根据 hard、generalize、business culture、contradictions、opposites，就可以预测接下来讲话者肯定会具体阐释美国商业文化的矛盾和对立。讲话者从三个方面来阐释为什么说美国商业文化是矛盾和对立的。其中第一个句子中有两个点，但是因为用了省略句，所以可能会造成听辨的障碍，因此听辨过程中一定要注意文章的逻辑关系。"It is focused on money, but relationships are built on the golf course." 这句话理解没问题，but 表转折，学生就明白了前后两个句子表达的是矛盾对立。"Egalitarian, but status and rewards are high priorities." 这句也是同样的道理，but 揭示出前后的逻辑转折。

通过这种关键词和逻辑剥离过程，灵活使用复述技巧，学生可以把源语复述出来。这段复述答案表达的复述思维是：源语复述的原则就是不能面面俱到，需要"抓大放小"。

复述要点

1. 抓住关键词，厘清段落和篇章结构，推断和预测信息。
2. 不必拘泥于源语的形式，正确折射源语意思即可，长句可以化成短句，复杂单词替换成简单词，次要信息可以省略。

》例二

The American style of communication is direct and straight to the point. If you're meeting someone in person, a simple handshake and a hello will do just fine. And don't forget to look them in the eyes. Despite preferring straight talk, you should be more subtle giving criticism to a senior person. In a culture driven by success and ambition, criticizing your boss can be seen as a power play, or trying to undermine them. Try to avoid direct **confrontation** if you disagree, and deal with your objection in private on a one-to-one basis. Americans are very comfortable with relaxed, open body language, and they smile a lot. They have a keen sense of personal space, and can react defensively if you stand or sit too close. Hand gestures are muted and not overly expressive. For most first meetings in business, formal business suits are the norm. There are some exceptions, e.g. startup tech companies. However, unless told otherwise, formal **attire** will be expected initially. Punctuality is of the essence in the USA. If you are late, you are wasting both their time and money. Being somewhere on time, jumping quickly into work and sticking to the plans are common practice in the United States. Most formal meetings will **follow the agenda** quite closely. Topics will be allocated a specific time limit, and the chair is likely to end a discussion when the allotted time ends. Most meetings will start with a very short amount of social chat as people settle down.

◇ 词汇

confrontation
对抗

attire
衣服，装扮

follow the agenda
根据日程安排

This can transition quite abruptly to business. If you are the host, you will be expected to draw the warm-up to an end and introduce the topic. In a negotiation, both sides will expect to move from their initial position towards a mutually beneficial compromise.

译文

美国人的交流方式是直截了当、直奔主题的。如果你和某人见面，一个简单的握手和打个招呼就可以了。别忘了看着他们的眼睛。尽管你更喜欢直言不讳，但在批评高层时，你应该更加谨慎。在一个成功和雄心壮志驱动的文化中，批评你的老板可能被视为一种权力博弈，或者试图破坏领导权。如果你不同意，尽量避免直接对抗，并私下一对一地处理你的反对意见。美国人容易接纳放松的、开放的肢体语言，他们经常微笑。他们有敏锐的个人空间感，如果你站或坐得太近，他们会做出防御反应。手势要柔和，不要过度表达。对于大多数第一次参加商务会议来说，正式的商务套装是标准的。当然也有一些例外，比如一些新兴的科技公司。不过，除非另有规定，否则在开始的时候应该穿正装。在美国，守时是至关重要的。如果你迟到了，你就是在浪费他人时间和金钱。在美国，准时到达某地、迅速投入工作和坚持计划是很常见的做法。大多数正式会议将密切关注议程。每个讲话都被分配讲话时长限制，当规定时限结束时，主持人可能会结束讨论。大多数会议都会以简短的社交聊天开始。这可以很突然地转变为业务。如果你是主持人，你应该结束热身寒暄并介绍话题。在谈判中，双方都希望从最初的立场走向互利的妥协。

源语复述

The American style of communication is direct and straight. You should be more subtle giving criticism to a senior person, and deal with your objection in private on a one-to-one basis. They have a keen sense of personal space. On business occasions, you should wear a formal business suit. The USA attaches great importance to punctuality, so you should not be late and should follow the agenda closely.

策略分析

这段话涉及两个美国商务文化方面：一个是美国人的商务交际风格（直接＋不适合直接批评领导），另一个是守时观念（不迟到＋说话不延时）。每个部分都是"主题句＋细节分析"的结构。第一句主题句中抓住 direct 和 to the point，就基本抓住了这部分的主题；接下来讲话者转到美国人守时的商业文化。注意第一句中的 is of the essence 的用法，相当于 is essential。第二句是对主题句的进一步阐释。基于以上听辨信息，复述源语就只需将上述主要内容折射出来即可。初学者切记,源语复述不是西瓜芝麻一起抓,而是在不漏掉重点信息的基础上进行细节填充。

复述要点

1. 正说和反说是英语表达的两个不同方式,复述或者口译中如能正说,尽量不用双重否定或者倒装等结构。这种结构从文采性来看更优,但是表达更烦琐。本例的源语 don't forget to look them in the eyes 直接表述成 should look them in the eyes。

2. 如果遇到不会的生词,可以根据上下文的意思推断出其意思,用同义词替换即可。同样地,复杂词汇和复杂句式可以用简单的同义词和结构来替换。例如源语中,"Topics will be allocated a specific time limit and the chair is likely to end a discussion when the allotted time ends"其实就是说"Speech has to be delivered within time limit.",也可以换成更简单的说法,"You have to make your speech within the time limit."。

 任务 2. 汉译英
难度级别:★★★

> 训练要点:本段音频中挑出两个实例来分析如何培养听辨能力。音频较长,听第一遍的时候,将全篇音频听完,尝试提炼全文主旨框架。第二遍复盘时,体会两处例子如何进行具体的框架提炼。

》 例一

研究表明,在商务谈判中,人们的肢体语言对发挥双方的口才和谈判能力具有**潜移默化**的影响,甚至还能对谈判结果产生一定的作用。谈判就如一场激烈的**博弈**,一次次的过招决定着双方的输赢。在谈判的过程中,双方唇枪舌剑、各展神通。那么这个时候,观察谈判对手的肢体语言就会更容易地洞察其心理,同时如果巧妙地加以利用,也能很好地用来为谈判服务。所以在谈判中,无论面对的是什么样的谈判对手,我们都要善于察觉、搜集对方身体发出的诸多信号并加以巧妙运用。唯有如此,我们才能事半功倍,甚至收获出乎意料的效果。那么在谈判中我们应该从哪些方面着手来破解和运用肢体语言、掌握谈判优势呢?

词汇
潜移默化的影响 subtle effect
博弈 game

译文

Studies have shown that in business negotiations, people's body language has a subtle effect on the eloquence and negotiation ability of both parties, and even has a certain effect on the outcome of the negotiation. Negotiation is like a fierce game, and the success of both parties is determined by the repeated moves. During the negotiation process, both sides debated heatedly, each trying for all one is worth. Then at this time, observing the body language of the negotiating opponent will make it easier to gain insight into his psychology. At the same time, if it is used skillfully, it can also serve the negotiation well. Therefore, in negotiations, no matter what kind of opponent we are facing, we must be good at detecting and collecting many signals from the opponent's body and use them skillfully. Only in this way can we get twice the result with half the effort, and even reap unexpected results. So in the negotiation, how can we decipher and use body language to our advantage?

策略分析

本段结构层次清晰，开篇点题：肢体语言会对谈判本身以及谈判结果起到一定的作用。谈判是场博弈，如何能够获得优势，抢占谈判先机？学生根据主题句就可以推测肯定是需要观察对手的肢体语言。接下来，如何能够通过肢体语言洞察对手的心理？通过哪些肢体语言进行心理解读？不同的肢体语言反映了不同的心理活动。整个文章的逻辑走向就清晰了。这段话的难点不是结构或逻辑，而是各种成语。在口译中，学生经常会遇到汉语的四字成语，如何能够一方面准确无误地传递信息，另一方面还要符合英语的语言习惯，让英语母语者理解其意思。第一种情况，如果英语里有相对应的习语或者惯用语，直接拿来用。第二种情况，如果英语里没有相对应的成语可用，可以直译，也可以意译，即对成语的意思进行解释。本段中的"唇枪舌剑""各显神通"是学生非常熟悉的成语，但在英语里找不到对应的习语或者惯用语，这时学生就要对它们进行解释，力争让英语母语者理解它们的意思。如何应对汉语的成语等四字结构是汉译英中常见的挑战，学生需要适度训练，逐步积累应对这种语言架构的策略。

复述要点

1. 平时多积累与商务相关的词汇，听辨中就不会因为术语储备不足而造成输出失误。
2. 在平时的训练中，多积累一些英语谚语。遇到汉语的成语时，学生可以很轻松地找到英语中对应的习语或者惯用语。

例二

谈判的时候，如果对方一脸笑容地听从你的意见，且表现出"非常满意"的姿态，他有可能是在敷衍你，让你放松警惕，然后再出奇招制胜。如果谈判对手的眉毛变化明显，尤其是当你提出最后议案时，他突然双眉上扬或眉毛迅速上下活动，这就说明这个议案正中其怀，他感到非常惊喜并发自内心地赞同你提出的决定，那么接下来他要说出口的话很可能就是"合作愉快"了。谈判的时候，如果对方表情十分自信，并且嘴角不自主地扯动，则是高傲、占据优势的表现。在这种情况下，若同意对方的条件，将十分不利，所以你可以用凝重的表情予以回应，挫挫他的锐气。谈判的时候如果对方面无表情，则说明其内心正情绪波动，不过不想让别人察觉而努力克制，且其表情越淡漠，便说明其内心越不满。这样的谈判看样子是进行不下去了，倒不如见好就收。

译文

When negotiating, if the other party listens to your opinion with a smile on his face and shows a "very satisfied" attitude, he may be perfunctory, get you off guard, and then make a surprise move to win. If the negotiating opponent's eye brows change significantly, especially when you put forward the final proposal, his eyebrows suddenly rise or move up and down quickly, it means that the proposal is exactly what he wants, and that he is very pleased and sincerely agrees with the decision you propose. Most probably the next thing he will say is "this is a pleasant cooperation". When negotiating, if the other party appears very confident, and the corners of the mouth go upward involuntarily, it is a sign of arrogance and dominance. In this case, if you agree to the other party's terms, it will be very disadvantageous, so you can respond with a frozen expression to dampen his spirit. If the other party is expressionless during the negotiation, it means that his inner thoughts are fluctuating, but he does not want others to notice and tries to restrain himself. And the more indifferent his expression, the more dissatisfied he is. It seems that this kind of negotiation can't go on any longer, so it's better to stop at the right time.

策略分析

本段开篇点题，关于表情这种肢体语言。听到这个关键词，学生就可以推断接下来肯定是分成几种情况来解读肢体语言，做好准备，听辨出不同的表情分别反映了谈判对手什么样的内心活动和潜台词。本段由四个排比句构成，学生在复述源语的过程中，能够抓住中心词"表情"、关键词"满意""眉毛""自信""无表情",那么复述时就可以基本覆盖本段内容。

> **复述要点**

1. 听辨过程中,不能仅聚焦于听,而要把握主题和关键信息并分析话语脉络,并基于此对行文的信息和逻辑走向进行有效的预测。
2. 源语复述过程中化繁为简,"奇招制胜""正中其下怀""凝滞"等词汇都是比较书面的表达,复述过程中可以改成其他简单的表述方式。

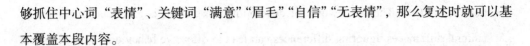

模块五　　　　　　　　　　　　　　　　　　　　　　　　　　　　拓展练习

 任务1:
源语复述练习

请用一分钟左右看完每个源语段落,然后进行源语复述。

1. This is a happy and memorable occasion for me personally, as well as for all the members of my delegation. I'd like to thank you for the gracious hospitality and the warmth with which we have been received. I am very happy with your arrangement. In accepting your gracious invitation to Shanghai, I have an excellent opportunity to learn about the investment environment here. It is my sincere wish that we should reach an agreement on the establishment of joint venture in this most promising city.

2. Cross-cultural communication is the process of respectfully engaging with people from other cultures. It involves verbal and nonverbal communication skills that consider the differences in beliefs and norms among cultures. Learning to interact with people from other cultures opens up people's life experiences, enabling participation as global citizens. Cultivating cross-cultural communication in a business setting is a key factor in a company's viability and revenue growth. Thus, it becomes essential for employees to gain the necessary skills to interact with people of cultural backgrounds outside of their own. Not possessing cross-cultural communication skills could lead to the loss of reputation, profits, and the ability to attract and retain good talent among a diversified

pool of workers. The framework for developing these skills is grounded in respecting cultural differences. Ignoring differences can lead to offensive behaviors. It matters what is said and done in acknowledging and embracing cultural differences to foster good communication.

3. 我非常高兴能在此会见来自大洋彼岸的加拿大商业界的朋友。"有朋自远方来，不亦乐乎"这句中国古话可以表达我此刻的心情。中国政府十分重视同加拿大双边经贸关系的发展，并且非常赞赏加中贸易理事会为加强我们两个国家商业界的联系而做出的努力和起到的桥梁作用。我感谢理事会所有成员为促进加中贸易所做出的努力。加拿大是个工业发达、资源丰富的国家，中国则是一个劳动力充足、拥有庞大市场的国家。我们希望看到加拿大的企业能够充分利用自己在技术和财力上的优势，赢得中国市场。

4. 在最近一次金融危机中，中国坚定不移地承担了对本地区和全世界的责任，帮助避免了又一个危险的货币贬值周期，我们必须继续携手合作，对付全球金融系统面临的威胁以及对整个亚太地区本应有的发展和繁荣的威胁。只要我们相互合作而不是互不往来，我们就能取得更大的成就。要做到这一点，我们就必须更好地相互了解，了解各自的共同利益、共同期望和真诚的分歧。我相信这种公开直接的交流有助于澄清和缩小我们之间的分歧。更为重要的是，允许人们理解、辩论和探讨这些问题，能使他们对我们建设的美好未来更加充满希望和信心。

任务 2:
商务礼仪与文化口译练习

语篇 1
难度级别：★★★★

In all the **exuberance** associated with negotiating new business relationships between China and the West, too little attention has been paid to managing conflict in those relationships, and conflict is inevitable as the story I'm about to tell you illustrates. Confronting conflict, by which I mean how you tell a person there is a problem that needs to be fixed, is handled very differently in the West than it is in East Asia.

词汇

exuberance
感情洋溢（或慷慨激昂）的言行；（感情等的）过度（或极度）表现

Jeff, one of my executive education students, told the story of the **rattling** bicycles. He had a contract with a German buyer for bicycles that he was having manufactured in China. Shortly before the bikes were to be shipped to Germany, Jeff went to the plant to check on them. When he got there, he and the plant manager took a couple of the bikes off the line, rode them around in the countryside. And Jeff's bike rattled, he thought the plant manager's bike rattled, too. When they got back to the plant, Jeff handed over his back and he turned to the plant manager and commented, "I think my bike rattled" and then he went back to Hong Kong, China.

When Jeff ended his story, there was a stunned silence in the room and then a flurry of questions, "You, just went back to Hong Kong?" "You did not check all the bikes?" "You did not tell the plant manager the Germans wouldn't accept bikes?"

"No", said Jeff.

Finally someone asked, "Well, why not?" Jeff explained that he knew the plant manager and why he had come, he was afraid that if he confronted the plant manager directly, the plant manager would lose face, he would feel disrespected and embarrassed. And in revenge, he might ship the rattling bikes. But Jeff thought if he was respectful, the plant manager would get the job done, fixed the bikes and shipped them on time to Germany.

Jeff understood the difference between direct and indirect confrontation of conflict. In the West, When we have a conflict, we tend to identify the problem, assign blame and responsibility for the fix and even tell what we think needs to be done. In East Asia, it is done much more indirectly. There is an assumption that the responsible party will fix the problem.

So if you are a Western manager working in East Asia, my advice for you is to be aware of subtle signals about problem in conflict. You might hear, for example, the term "that would be difficult" or when you ask questions, you might get a story back

> 词汇
>
> rattle
> 咔嗒声

in response where you might hear a **metaphor**. It is okay to probe what was the protagonists in the story thinking about what you say or how is this metaphor interpreted in China, but what you don't want to do is point fingers. In East Asia, people take roles and responsibilities very seriously. If for your peace of mind, you really have to make clear that there is a problem that needs to be fixed, state your problem in tentative terms. Don't be definitive. Engage your counterpart in defining the problem and solution.

> 词汇
>
> metaphor
> 比喻

Now if you are an East Asian manager working in the West, I advise you, be prepared for confrontation. Try not to take it personally, not to be defensive, and not to withdraw. Instead, engage the other party in understanding what the problem is; don't take the problem to the boss. In East Asia, it is very common to involve the boss very early in the conflict. But in the West, managers are supposed to resolve conflict themselves. So instead engage your counterpart, work together collaboratively to identify the problem and fix the problem. Just a little bit of cultural sensitivity to direct and indirect confrontation of conflict can really pay off. It did for Jeff. Those German buyers not only accepted the bikes but they reordered.

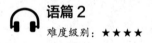

Negotiators all over the world fail to reach agreements or reach **sub-optimal** agreements because they don't know what to do when they come up against an **emphatic** "No". I learned to turn an emphatic "No" into a "Yes" by understanding my own interest and understanding the other party's interest when I was negotiating for pumpkins in France. Now interest is a term we use in negotiation and it means the motives, the concerns that are underlying emphatic "No". So let me tell you about negotiating for pumpkins

> 词汇
>
> sub-optimal
> 次优的
>
> emphatic
> 加强语气的

in France.

My husband and I were **on sabbatical** and we were writing. We had our daughters in the local school. The teacher there saw a couple of American parents as an opportunity to have a Halloween party for the French children. He wanted them to carve pumpkins into **Jack-O-lanterns** for their party, and my job was to find the pumpkins. I looked everywhere for the pumpkins. I could find these things called **courge**. They were about this big round; they weighed a ton and you need a **machete** to get into them. In negotiation terms, these courges were my **BATNA**, my best alternative to a negotiated agreement. The courge was my fallback, but it was actually terrible, so I kept looking.

Finally, I found a farmstand that had pumpkins. A woman, Madame Petite came out of the back, I told her I was interested in pumpkins. She gave me the price and I quickly accepted the price, because my BATNA in those courges was terrible. And then she asked me how many pumpkins I wanted, and I had 32 children. I quickly counted. She had slightly more than 32 pumpkins, but a lot of them were little. So I told her, I wanted all of them. And as soon as I did that, she turned and started walking away, going "No, no, no". So I had to think really quickly about what my strategic options were, to try to turn that emphatic "No" into a "Yes". One option was to offer her more money, but I didn't really think money was the interest underlying her "No", because she had given me a price and I had already accepted it. Another option would have been to ask her how many pumpkins she would sell me, but I wanted a pumpkin for each child. So I thought that option wasn't going to generate a solution that was going to meet my interests. I also thought of explaining to her what my interests were, that I wanted to do the Halloween party for the Vanassa children. But I also didn't think that was going to get to her interests, just mine. So my last option was to ask her, "Why not, why won't you sell me all

> 词汇

on sabbatical
休假

Jack-O-lantern
万圣节南瓜灯

courge
葫芦

machete
弯刀

BATNA
谈判方案

your pumpkins?" And then I thought lots of times negotiators don't like to reveal their interests. They are afraid that doing so makes them vulnerable to your exploitation, so I needed to fall back if she wouldn't answer my direct question. I knew I could make her an offer, and then maybe, if she said "No", we could engage in some conversation to understand what was behind that "No". A third option is to ask her "under what circumstances would you sell me all your pumpkins", so ask her to make me an offer. I decided to start with the first question asked her directly why. She explained if she sold me all her pumpkins, she wouldn't have any seeds to plant the next year. I, in turn, explained my interest to have pumpkins for the Vanassa children to turn into Jack O'lanterns. And I offered to bring all her seeds back November 1st, if she would sell me all her pumpkins. She agreed.

The negotiators often think that the only way to win a negotiation is for the other party to lose, but if you understand your own interest and you learn about the interests of the other party, you can often reach an agreement in which both parties win. Madame Petite and I did, she got her seeds and I got all the pumpkins.

模块六　译海拾贝：商务口译中的跨文化因素

不同的语言隶属于不同的文化，而文化之间的差异会导致跨文化交流障碍和误解。英汉口译过程中的文化差异大致可以归结为文化沉淀、认知体系以及思维模式等方面。

文化沉淀

不同的语言在长期形成和使用的过程中都积累了大量的习语。这些惯用语承载着丰富的文化内涵，蕴藏着浓厚的民族色彩，反映了不同文化和民族的生存环境、生活习惯、传统习俗以及宗教信仰等。口译工作者需要了解和沉淀不同语言承载的不同文化内涵和差异，才能保障在商务口译或谈判中准确传达双方的立场和诉求。

文化差异会导致语言含义不同：

例句：Exporting to some countries is greatly complicated by all the red tape.

译文：政府部分的繁文缛节使得向某些国家出口困难重重。

red tape 原指律师和政府官员惯用红带子扎捆文件，后引申为公事手续上的形式主义。如若直译为"红带子"，不仅没有将文化内涵传达出来，而且会让人感觉疑惑不解。

文化差异会导致理解不同。20世纪90年代时，中国代表团出访东南亚国家，印度尼西亚晚宴请柬着装要求为 black tie，我方将其理解为"黑色的领带"，因此穿着黑领结礼服来到宴会厅。礼宾官注意到中国的宾客穿了西装，为了避免电视新闻中出现印尼方与中方宾客服饰不一致的尴尬，让本国出席宴会的人员都回去将黑领结礼服换成西装。black tie 实际上是指半正式晚礼服。2009年傅莹大使与先生应英国女王伊丽莎白二世邀请到温莎城堡参加晚宴时，下午茶的邀请函写的是 lounge suit（商务套装），晚宴的请柬着装要求则是 black tie。而 white tie 则是最正式的礼服，也称为大礼服。

认知差异

人们感知和认识周围世界的方式是不同的。同属一个文化群体的人们也存在认知差异，但较少会产生理解障碍。因此，分属不同文化、不同语言的人们就会因为认知的差异而产生交流和理解障碍。

例句：我们会按时付款，不会给你们打白条的。

译文：We shall pay you on time instead of giving you an IOU.

汉语中"打白条"意指"欠条"，如果译成 blank paper，外国人很难明白，但其真实含义类似"开空头支票"，与英语中的 IOU 意思相近。

思维方式

不同的民族有着各自独特的思维方式。受到儒家思想影响，中国人趋于礼让谦逊，总说，"您先请"。但英语表达却不是我们想象的 you first，而是 after you。所以同一意思由于视点不一，英汉的表达方式完全不同，汉语用"先"表达的意思在英语中却是用"后"来表示。因此，口译中，切勿望文生义，务必要考虑到不同语言的思维模式差异。

综上，跨文化意识和能力在商务口译中极其重要。汉英语言在文化、认知以及思维方面的不同和差异意味着口译者不仅需要具备扎实的商务专业知识和语言能力，更需要具备文化意识和跨文化背景知识，只有这样才可能做到准确的交流。

模块七

译员风采："老虎书生"杨洁篪

六十甲子一轮回，一百二十载中华生巨变：1901年时值辛丑年，清政府代表李鸿章等与十一国列强签署了丧权辱国的《辛丑条约》；2021年，杨洁篪对美方拍案而起："我们把你们想得太好了，我们认为你们会遵守基本的外交礼节，所以我们刚才必须阐明立场！你们没有资格在中国的面前说，你们从实力的地位出发同中国谈话，我们中国人不吃这一套！"

这是时任中央外事委员会主任杨洁篪在2021年3月中美高层战略对话上对美方代表的不尊重行为的猛烈还击。被外媒称为"老虎杨"（Tiger Yang）的杨洁篪短短几句话，铿锵有力、掷地有声。他曾是我国最年轻的副外长、最年轻的驻美大使。让我们跟随本文的脚步，来回顾杨洁篪的成长经历。

左手持书，右手电笔

1950年，杨洁篪出生于上海市的一个普通工人家庭。从小他并没有像名字中的"篪"那样精通乐器，而是在祖父的严格要求下每天练字，写得一手漂亮的毛笔字。用"字如其人"形容成年后的杨洁篪的书法并不是吹捧之言。他的字俊秀儒雅，却又力透纸背。13岁时，他考入了大名鼎鼎的上海外国语学院附属中学，开始接触并喜欢上了学习外语。他同班40个同学里出了8个外交官。20世纪60年代，他不得不搁置学业，到上海浦江电表厂当一名电工学徒。然而，环境与条件的艰难并没有磨灭杨洁篪成为译员的执念；在工作闲暇之余，他拿起英语书、翻开单词本，不顾周围同事的不解与嘲笑，一直坚持外语学习并为工厂翻译资料。在外语人才稀缺的时代，他的翻译能力在上海市政府外语人才选拔过程中得到施展，借调成为政府翻译。1972年，周恩来总理积极培养翻译人才，将各大城市工厂和农村散落的英语人才择优送到英国深造，而年轻的杨洁篪抓住了这次机会。勤奋好学是他成功的秘诀之一。随身带小本子的习惯他一直带到外交部，王弄笙大使亲口夸赞他的用功。正如杨洁篪自己所言："我习惯用心观察领导人处理某些棘手问题的态度及选择，事后再反复琢磨，从中找到自身漏洞……"

英伦求学

1973年在外交部的资助下，杨洁篪到英国深造，与他同行的一批人包括后来成为中国常驻联合国代表王光亚、陈毅元帅女儿陈姗姗等人。杨洁篪在英国先后就读于伊林学院、巴斯大学以及伦敦政治经济学院。他勤奋刻苦，在各校均取得优异的成绩。

百炼成钢

1975年，杨洁篪回国后，凭借出色的外语能力和过硬的政治素质，如愿成为外交部翻译室的译员。在那里他曾两度工作超过十年（1975—1983年，1987—1990年），为时任的多位中央领导做翻译。这使他在年轻时就有了观察高层外交的有利条件，并结识了世界舞台上的关键人物。翻译经历中，他受益匪浅，历练蜕变，从一名普通译员升为二等秘书、一等秘书、政务参赞、外交部部长助理、副外长等职务。曾经那个稚气未脱的小电工，一步步成长为外交场合中能够独当一面的"老虎杨"了，直至外交部长、国务委员、中央外事工作委员会办公室主任。

砥柱中流，危机公关

2001年4月，在杨洁篪担任驻美大使仅三个月后，一架美国EP-3侦察机在中国海南岛领空与一架中国J-8拦截战斗机相撞，该事件导致中方机毁人亡，美国飞机被迫降落在海南岛。布什政府要求立即释放机组人员，但中方希望先正式道歉，而美方则拒绝道歉，坚持认为美方无过错。公众的对立情绪和民族主义情绪的浪潮席卷了两国。杨洁篪几天内多次访问国务院和国会交涉此事；他还每天两次出现在美国电视上，发表中国对该事件的看法。在接受CNN采访时，他巧用比喻暗讽，说道："一伙人总在你家门前转悠，家里有人出去查看，结果自家的车子被毁，人也失踪了。对此，家里人总该有权利做一点儿调查吧，对方至少应该道个歉，这非常重要。"

杨洁篪的努力对美国公众舆论产生了很大影响。在他上电视后，超过50%的民意调查赞成美国向中国道歉，而之前只有不到20%的人赞成。不久，布什政府公开表示歉意，危机升级被避免了。

从电厂小工到中央外事办主任，儒雅而坚定的杨洁篪正步履铿锵，在大国外交的舞台上展现自己，用能力和魄力见证着东方强国的崛起！

第四章

对外贸易
Foreign Trade

模块一　　技能概要：口译记忆

口译工作者的能力构成中，记忆思维能力极为重要。在口译过程中，译员必须具备强大的记忆策略，以完整、准确地还原源语信息。研究表明，信息进入人的感知系统后将历经瞬时记忆、短时记忆、长时记忆三种模式。其中，短时记忆+长时记忆的有机融合在口译活动中发挥着重要的作用。口译员依赖短时记忆对源语信息进行内容整合和逻辑连接；长时记忆则有助于语块加工、自动匹配输出语等。法国著名口译专家丹尼尔·吉尔（Daniel Gile）提出的认知负荷模型将口译过程视为以短时记忆为基础资源的多项认知操作。长时记忆包括信息存取系统和信息库，口译员依赖长时记忆提取贮存在大脑里的知识和经验，以减少口译现场的资源认知与处理负担。

在商务口译实践活动中，学生如果提前熟练掌握商务背景知识，那么就无须在这些内容上分配过多精力，只需记忆整体逻辑和内容要点。学生听到商务话语时，脑中存储的相关知识会被激活，大大缩短处理源语信息的时间，从而更快速地进行语言转换。长时记忆能力可以通过对商务领域文化和背景知识以及专业术语的学习加以训练。短时记忆依靠重复性的大量记忆训练以达到即时反应的目的。除此之外，掌握良好的记忆策略可以帮助学生在有效时间内最大限度地发挥信息加工能力，从而更准确、有效地处理信息。记忆策略包括逻辑梳理能力和要点提取能力等辅助记忆方法以及框架搭建、构图意识等记忆思维。学生要学会对源语信息进行整理、类化和组织，从而训练逻辑梳理能力，要有意识地从整体高度思考，整合提炼源语内容，以达到理解和记忆的目的。

模块二　　　　　　　　　　　　　　　　　　　　　　译前准备

◎ 1. 背景知识

外贸英语属于商务英语范畴，确切地说是针对外贸行业的英语。对外贸易主要分为进口与出口两个部分，其形式多样，如对等贸易、展卖贸易、加工贸易、补偿贸易等。改革开放后，中国全方位发展对外贸易，与全世界绝大多数国家和地区建立了贸易关系。对外贸易注重工作人员的跨文化交际能力。在中国企业开拓海外市场的过程中，消除沟通上的障碍可以避免双方合作分歧，维护长期合作关系。良好的对外贸易可以提升中国经济在国际经济大循环的质量，因此对外贸易的口译工作更加具有实践性与应用性。

本模块语料实训部分涉及的概念包括"一带一路"、通货膨胀、采购经理人指数等。

Druzhba pipeline（友谊输油管道）：俄罗斯向中欧和东欧国家输送原油的大型输油管道系统。

GasTerra（荷兰能源）：公司的总部位于荷兰的国际化天然气能源贸易公司，其运营范围跨域欧洲，是欧洲第二大天然气供应商。

"一带一路"（the Belt and Road, B&R）：是"丝绸之路经济带"和"21世纪海上丝绸之路"的合称。中国是该倡议的倡导者与推动者。"一带一路"不是实体和机制，而是合作发展的理念和倡议，依靠中国与有关国家既有的双多边机制，借助既有的、行之有效的区域合作平台，高举和平发展的旗帜，积极主动地发展与"一带一路"沿线国家的经济合作伙伴关系，共同打造政治互信、经济融合、文化包容的利益共同体、命运共同体和责任共同体。

通货膨胀（inflation）：在货币流通中，因货币实际需求小于市场上的货币供给，即现实购买力大于产出供给，导致货币贬值、物价上涨。通膨的实质是社会总供给小于社会总需求。

采购经理人指数（Purchase Management Index, PMI）：传统上是指美国的采购经理人指数，包括生产、新订单、商品价格、存货、雇员、订单交货、新出口订单、进口等八种指数。我国采购经理人指数是由国家统计局和中国物流与采购联合会合作发布，包括制造业和非制造业采购经理指数，与GDP一同构成我国宏观经济的指标体系。

◎ 2. 核心词汇

exemption	豁免	locked down	封锁
embargo	贸易禁运	lorry	卡车
watershed	分水岭	omicron variant	奥密克戎变体
shutoff	停止，装置关闭	closed loop	闭环
blockade	封锁	self-contained	自给自足的
deliberately	故意地	Tesla	特斯拉
freight	货运	harnesses	利用
nod	节点	nominal	名义上的
desultory chug	断断续续地发出轧轧声前进	exacerbate	加剧

The Belt and Road Initiative　　"一带一路"倡议
China's Customs Agency　　中国海关总署
purchasing manager　　采购经理人
China International Import Expo (CIIE)　　中国国际进口博览会（进博会）
pilot free trade area　　自由贸易试验区
Catalogue of Encouraged Industries for Foreign Investment　《鼓励外商投资产业目录》
Comprehensive and Progressive Agreement for Trans-Pacific Partnership (CPTPP)
《全面与进步跨太平洋伙伴关系协定》
Digital Economy Partnership Agreement (DEPA)　《数字经济伙伴关系协定》

模块三　　语料实训

 任务1. 英译汉
难度级别：★★★

> 训练要点：本文主要内容是欧盟与俄罗斯之间的外贸关系，介绍了欧盟对俄罗斯进口能源采取的措施以及所带来的影响。本文行文结构清晰、逻辑性强，音频速度较慢，有利于训练长时记忆能力。学生要注意运用听辨技能中的关键词听辨技能，在听解过程中要注意抓住关键词，运用要点记忆

> 技巧，然后根据要点信息进行逻辑上的组合。本文涉及多个国家的名称、国家领导人的名字，需要学生查阅并熟悉这些背景知识。

EU Bans Most Russian Oil Imports

The European Union (EU) has agreed to ban the majority of Russian oil imports. The agreement marks the biggest move yet to punish Russia for its conflict with Ukraine.

Since Russia's conflict with Ukraine on February 24, Western nations have sought to punish Russia economically. But targeting the energy sector has proven difficult. The EU depends on Russia for 25 percent of its oil and 40 percent of its natural gas. European countries that are even more heavily dependent on Russia have been especially resistant to act. EU leaders agreed late Monday to cut around 90 percent of all Russian oil imports brought in by sea over the next six months.

The ban permits a temporary exemption for imports delivered by pipeline. The exemption was critical in bringing Hungary on board with the decision, which required approval from all EU leaders. Hungarian Prime Minister Viktor Orban had made clear he could support the oil ban only if his country's supply was guaranteed. Hungary gets more than 60 percent of its oil from Russia through the Druzhba pipeline.

Belgian Prime Minister Alexander De Croo on Tuesday called the oil ban, or embargo, "big step forward". Irish Prime Minister Micheál Martin called it "a watershed moment". A watershed moment describes a major event that changes the direction of a situation. Both leaders also noted that Europe would need time to get used to the effects of the ban. They said any additional bans on Russian energy could only come slowly, if at all.

Dmitry Medvedev is the deputy head of Russia's Security Council. Medvedev is also a former Russian president and prime minister. He said Tuesday that energy sanctions against the country were meant to hurt Russian citizens by making it harder for the government to fund social programs. "They hate us all! The basis for these decisions is hatred for Russia, for Russians, and for all its inhabitants," Medvedev wrote on the Telegram messaging app. Simone Tagliapietra is an energy expert and research fellow at the Brussels-based organization Bruegel. She said Russia would likely have to sell its oil at a lower cost to other buyers. She called the embargo "a major blow".

Russia has also made moves to withhold its energy supplies, even with the economic damage it could suffer as a result. Russian energy company Gazprom said it cut natural gas supplies to Dutch trader GasTerra on Tuesday. The move was announced before EU leaders agreed to the embargo. Russia already cut supplies to Bulgaria, Poland and Finland. It is considering doing the same to Denmark.

GasTerra said homes would not be affected; it had bought gas from other countries because it expected a possible shutoff.

Talks on Tuesday at EU headquarters in Brussels centered on ways to end the EU's dependence on Russian energy. Leaders also expected to discuss how to help Ukraine export millions of tons of grain trapped inside the country as a worldwide food crisis grows.

Leaders are calling on Russia to halt its attacks on transport infrastructure in Ukraine and lift its blockade of Black Sea ports so that food can be shipped. Ukrainian President Volodymyr Zelenskyy has said Russia has prevented the export of 22 million tons of grain, much of it meant for people across the Middle East and Africa. He accused Russia of "deliberately creating this problem".

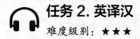

任务 2. 英译汉
难度级别：★★★

> 训练要点：本文介绍了关税的由来以及其对经济贸易发展产生的影响。本文专业术语较少，前半部分用历史故事的形式介绍了关税的由来，并过渡到特朗普政府为何加征关税以及加征后对经济和国际贸易产生的影响。在源语记忆时，学生背景知识的压力减少了，脑中存储的相关知识被激活，这会大大缩短源语信息的处理时间，从而更快速地进行语言转换。但本文篇幅较长，涉及不同类型文本的听辨和记忆，比如叙述性（前半截文章）和说理性（后半截文章）行文。因此在听解过程中，学生要注意逻辑记忆，抓住经济的总体走势，通过第二和第三层次信息进行辅助记忆，从而实现记忆与文本逻辑的有机结合。本文文风轻松，但口语色彩较重，因此输出的译文也要尽量保持与原文一致的语体风格，尽量避免翻译腔。

The History of Tariff and Triumph's Tariff Policy

We get into tariffs—the heart of the Donald Trump economic plan.

We should talk about the Chicken War. The Chicken War is a clucking good story. In post-World War II, West Germany, people started eating a lot of chicken, specifically American chicken. Midway through 1962, US farmers were on track to sell more than $50 million worth, half a billion in today's money. This made European farmers mad. So, the organization that later became the European Union put a tariff on chicken. A 5-pound chicken that started as $1.60 became 2.25. Imports quickly dropped. US chicken farmers and politicians were furious.

And we thought, Germans are big market for chicken, and so if we hurt the Germans, this may well get them to change their mind on chicken.

So, the US put a 25% tariff on trucks like Germany's Volkswagen, and it worked. Their truck sales in the US fell by half, and they never really recovered. Meanwhile, Germans paid more for their chicken, and Americans had fewer truck options. It's kind of a perfect example of what tariffs do: hurt consumers while protecting very specific industries, or attempt to get countries to change their behavior, while they haven't been a large part of trade policy in decades.

President Donald Trump wants to change that: "Some might say it's economic nationalism. I call it common sense. I call it America first."

President Trump is really serve; brought a lot of people out to think that tariff might be something that's useful in America's economic arsenal, in a way that hasn't been used in the past.

Here's how tariffs work, and what Trump's proposals would do. Let's start in 2018, when President Trump put tariffs on "washing machines going to benefit our consumers, and we're going to create a lot of jobs". Since then, whenever a washing machine is imported to the US, the company on the US side doing the importing pays a tariff to the US government.

Their margins are pretty low. They've got to pass that price on to consumers who ultimately pay it. That's the whole point, in some sense, to reduce demand for those goods and create space for domestic producers.

After the tariffs, not only did the price of imported washing machines go up, so did the ones made in the US.

There's this myth out there, that if we tax imports, domestic producers won't change their prices, and that's not the case. You're creating more demand for them.

So naturally, the price goes up. And it wasn't just washers. Dryers went up in price too, even though they weren't part of the tariffs.

Usually, it's the case if you buy a wash or you buy a dryer. So even though driers weren't directly affected by the tariff, they're indirectly affected by the shifting demand.

Now, it wasn't all bad. These tariffs did "create a lot of jobs", about 1,800, mostly from those foreign companies like Samsung and LG, opening plants in the US. And the study found the US collected $82 million annually. But because of those price increases, it cost consumers 1.5 billion more. So they basically paid $815,000 per job.

This is a very expensive job creation program.

 任务 3. 汉译英
难度级别：★★★★

> 训练要点：本文是演讲类文本，内容逻辑性较强，从各个角度对进博会的成果、举办意义以及中国外贸未来发展趋势进行了介绍。学生要学会对源语信息进行整理、类化和组织。但本文篇幅较长，提到了较多与中国外贸有关的政策与文件，学生在翻译时应注意两国文化的差异。学生在听解过程中要注意逻辑结构与要点结合记忆。

第五届中国国际进口博览会开幕式上的致辞

尊敬的各位国家元首、政府首脑，尊敬的各位国际组织负责人，尊敬的各代表团团长；各位来宾、女士们、先生们、朋友们：

大家好！我谨代表中国政府和中国人民，并以我个人名义，向出席第五届中国国际进口博览会的各位嘉宾，表示热烈的欢迎和诚挚的问候！

五年前，我宣布举办进博会，就是要扩大开放，让中国大市场成为世界大机遇。现在，进博会已经成为中国构建新发展格局的窗口、推动高水平开放的平台、全球共享的国际公共产品。

开放是人类文明进步的重要动力，是世界繁荣发展的必由之路。当前，世界百年未有之大变局加速演进，世界经济复苏动力不足。我们要以开放纾发展之困、以开放汇合作之力、以开放聚创新之势、以开放谋共享之福，推动经济全球化不断向前，增强各国发展动能，让发展成果更多更公平惠及各国人民。

女士们、先生们、朋友们！

中国共产党第二十次全国代表大会强调，中国坚持对外开放的基本国策，坚定奉行互利共赢的开放战略，坚持经济全球化正确方向，增强国内国际两个市场两种资源联动效应，不断以中国新发展为世界提供新机遇，推动建设开放型世界经济。

——中国将推动各国各方共享中国大市场机遇，加快建设强大国内市场，推动货物贸易优化升级，创新服务贸易发展机制，扩大优质产品进口，创建"丝路电商"合作先行区，建设国家服务贸易创新发展示范区，推动贸易创新发展，推进高质量共建"一带一路"。

——中国将推动各国各方共享制度型开放机遇，稳步扩大规则、规制、管理、标准等制度型开放，实施好新版《鼓励外商投资产业目录》，深化国家服务业扩大开放综合示范区建设；实施自由贸易试验区提升战略，加快建设海南自由贸易港，发挥好改革开放综合试验平台作用。

——中国将推动各国各方共享深化国际合作机遇，全面深入参与世界贸易组织改革谈判，推动贸易和投资自由化便利化，促进国际宏观经济政策协调，共同培育全球发展新动能，积极推进加入《全面与进步跨太平洋伙伴关系协定》和《数字经济伙伴关系协定》，扩大面向全球的高标准自由贸易区网络，坚定支持和帮助广大发展中国家加快发展，推动构建人类命运共同体。

女士们、先生们、朋友们！

"山重水复疑无路，柳暗花明又一村。"路就在脚下，光明就在前方。中国愿同各国一道，践行真正的多边主义，凝聚更多开放共识，共同克服全球经济发展面临的困难和挑战，让开放为全球发展带来新的光明前程！

谢谢大家！

模块四

技巧点拨：翻译记忆

任务1. 英译汉

>> 例一
难度级别：★★★★

According to Reuters, trade tension and tariffs between the US and China resulted in billions of dollars being lost over 2018. The industries hit hardest by the ongoing trade war are the automotive industry, the tech industry, and agriculture.

Wally Tyner, an agricultural economist at Purdue University said that the US and Chinese economies could lose about $3 billion annually due to tariffs on soybeans, corn, wheat and sorghum alone. US agricultural exports to China decreased by 42 percent during the first 10 months of 2018, dropping to $8.3 billion in value.

译文

据路透社报道，中美两国之间的贸易紧张和关税导致它们在2018年损失了数十亿美元。受持续贸易战打击最为严重的行业是汽车行业、科技行业和农业。

普渡大学的农业经济学家沃里·泰纳表示，单单对大豆、玉米、小麦和高粱征收关税，中美两国每年可能会损失大约30亿美元。2018年的头10个月里，美国对中国的农产品出口下降了42%，跌至83亿美元。

记忆点拨

1. 抓住文章主要信息，如中美两国、贸易紧张、关税、损失、汽车、科技和农业、农产品、美国对中国出口下降。根据主要信息搭建起框架后，增补次要信息。
2. 梳理信息逻辑。

第一层次：中美两国贸易紧张和关税导致两国经济受损。

第二层次：受贸易战打击最为严重的是汽车行业、科技行业和农业。

第三层次：对大豆、玉米、小麦和高粱等农产品征收关税，造成中美两国损失，美国对中国的农产品出口下降。

逻辑记忆图：

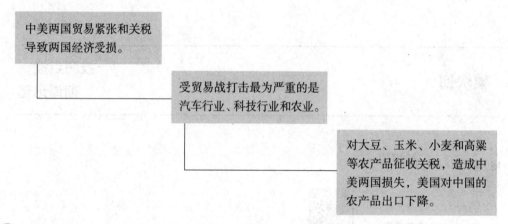

策略分析

本段内容层层递进，首先提出中美贸易紧张，之后进一步阐释受贸易战影响最大的产业，再举出具体例子阐述在农业这一具体产业中两国的实际损失。在口译时主要抓住重点信息，有利于学生对文本建立起全面的了解，减少记忆负担。尤其是在无笔记口译时，可以舍去一些次要信息，重点关注文章的大意。翻译有数字的口译语篇时，学生着急把数字信息记全，结果损失了文字信息，这是错误的做法。比如，本段的"2018年损失了数十亿美元""30亿美元""2018年的头10个月""下降了42%，跌至

83亿美元"都可以被弱化成"损失很多",否则的话,人的记忆容量无法精确融入所有信息。

>> **例二**
难度级别:★★★

The World Trade Organization says international trade is forecast to fall between 13 and 32 percent due to the coronavirus pandemic. The WTO says in the report that the drop would be worse than 2008 global financial crisis. And the wide range in its forecast is due to the pandemic's unpredictable nature. And it remains uncertain when business will be able to resume work. And the WTO also says that the scale of any recovery next year is equally uncertain.

译文

世界贸易组织称,由于新冠肺炎病毒大流行,国际贸易预计将下降13%~32%。世贸组织在报告中说,这一降幅将超过2008年全球金融危机。其预测范围之广是由于疫情的不可预测性。目前仍不确定企业何时能恢复工作。世贸组织还表示,明年复苏的规模同样不确定。

记忆点拨

1. 本段关键信息:世贸组织、新冠肺炎、国际贸易下降、复苏情况不定。
2. 本段逻辑结构:

    第一层次:国际贸易预计将下降,复苏规模不确定。

    第二层次:国际贸易下降的原因是新冠肺炎病毒,降幅超过2008年全球金融危机,预测范围广是因为疫情不可预测。

逻辑记忆图:

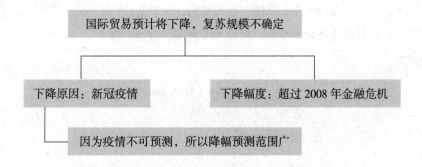

策略分析

翻译本段内容时，首先要把握住主旨内容，即国际贸易预计下降，复苏规模不确定。之后根据主旨，进一步增补次要信息，即贸易下降的原因、下降幅度、预测范围广的原因。在交传中，学生不必拘泥于原文顺序，可按照梳理过后的逻辑逐一翻译原文内容。

任务 2. 汉译英

>> 例一
难度级别：★★★★

今天最新公布的数据显示，2021年我国对外贸易总额达到39.1万亿元。同比逆势暴涨21.4%，进出口贸易额再次创下新高。其中，中国对外出口同比上涨了21.2%，进口额也增长了21.5%。值得一提的是，在疫情仍在冲击全球经济之际，我国不论是在贸易规模方面还是在国际市场份额方面都取得进展。

译文

The latest data released today shows that China's total foreign trade reached 39.1 trillion Yuan in 2021. Against the trend, the import and export volume surged by 21.4% year on year. Among them, China's export increased by 21.2% year on year and its import increased by 21.5%. It is worth mentioning that while the epidemic is still impacting the global economy, China has made progress both in terms of trade scale and international market share.

记忆点拨

1. 本段关键信息：对外贸易增长、疫情、贸易规模、国际市场规模。
2. 本段逻辑结构：

第一层次：尽管有疫情冲击，我国对外贸易仍保持增长。

第二层次：增长体现在两个方面：贸易规模和国际市场份额。

逻辑记忆图：

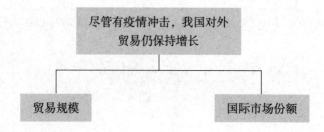

策略分析

汉语相较于英语来说，更为注重意合，不太注重形式的变化。因此在汉译英的口译过程中，首先要抓住主要信息进行强化记忆，不必过于注重细枝末节的内容，否则因小失大。尤其是在翻译有数字的段落时，学生可以借助笔记下数字，但需在脑海中对段落整体结构和逻辑有一个整体的把握。例如在本段中，我国对外贸易保持增长是主要信息，理解到了这一点，对全篇的基调也就有了一个大致的了解。

>> **例二**
难度级别：★★★

RCEP15 个成员国的人口和经济总量以及贸易总额均占全球总量的 30%，是世界上最大的自贸区。随着 RCEP 的正式生效实施，中国与东盟、新西兰等成员国之间零关税产品比例大幅提高，并朝着 90% 以上的货物贸易最终实现零关税的目标前进。这将释放区域内巨大的贸易增长潜力，是推进全球贸易与投资自由化便利化的重大步骤。

译文

The population, total economic output and total trade volume of the 15 member countries of RCEP account for 30% of the global total, making it the largest free trade zone in the world. With the official implementation of RCEP, the proportion of zero tariff products between China and ASEAN, New Zealand and other member countries has increased significantly, moving towards the goal of achieving zero tariff for more than 90% of goods trade. This will unleash the huge potential for trade growth in the region and is a major step in promoting global trade and investment liberalization and facilitation.

记忆点拨

1. 本段关键信息：RCEP、自贸区、成员国零关税产品、全球贸易、投资自由化。
2. 本段逻辑结构：

　第一层：RCEP 正式实施；

　第二层：RCEP 总体介绍，RCEP 正式实施将带来许多积极影响；

　第三层：影响一、影响二、影响三。

逻辑记忆图：

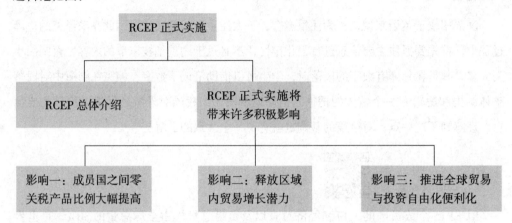

策略分析

本段内容结构较为清晰。首先对RCEP进行总体介绍，之后阐述RCEP实施带来的三个积极影响。原文中没有明确地说明影响一、影响二、影响三，因此需要学生在记忆过程中首先梳理出逻辑结构，强化记忆，否则信息杂糅易导致漏译的问题发生。

模块五　　　　　　　　　　　　　　　　　　　　　　拓展练习

任务1:
口译记忆练习

请对下列句子进行记忆练习。

1. The trade war initiated by the US government on China, which now includes the possibility of tariffs on all $500 billion worth of goods the US imports from China, hurts everyone involved. The collateral damage of these unilateral protectionist moves includes China, the US and the world economy. What the US has done jeopardizes China's interests. But it also brings unexpected harm to the global supply chain, undermines free trade, and places great uncertainty on the world economy.

2. The present US trade deficit with China does not mean the US is suffering a loss. Huge imports from China help keep the US inflation rate relatively low by providing

inexpensive high-quality products. On the other hand, the US has a surplus in services trade with China, which reached $55.7 billion in 2016. As a strategic market, China is a place where American companies profit greatly. US companies operating in China sell a great amount of their products to the Chinese market with a total value of $600 billion.

3. "贸易战"一旦爆发,将严重冲击全球多边贸易体制,使正回升的世界经济蒙上阴影。在经历了 20 世纪 30 年代"大萧条"和第二次世界大战的惨痛教训后,国际社会就全球贸易秩序安排达成共识,签署关税与贸易总协定,成立世界贸易组织,为全球贸易及经济增长做出了重大贡献。

4. 中国将坚定不移全面深化改革开放,敞开国门与各国深化经贸合作,这一基本国策不会改变。未来 15 年,中国将进口 24 万亿美元商品。今年 11 月,中国将举办首届国际进口博览会,与世界各国分享中国发展机遇、共享中国市场红利。

任务 2:
对外贸易口译练习

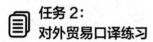

语篇 1
难度级别:★★★

Down but Not out

○ 词汇

COVID-related products including computing equipment for home-working have accounted for the majority of China's year-on-year export growth in each month since June. Eytan Buchman of Freightos, an online marketplace, reports that ocean-freight prices are surging for routes between America and South-East Asia, partly because of "near-**frantic**" e-commerce offerings by small businesses.

frantic
疯狂的

Policymakers have played a **pivotal** role in the trade revival. Monetary and fiscal firepower was bigger and faster than trade experts had expected. Central-bank **liquidity** measures kept trade finance flowing better than it did during the financial crisis, says Jennifer McKeown of Capital Economics, a **research outfit**. "Although the trade performance is cause for relief, no one should declare victory yet."

pivotal
关键的

liquidity
流动性

research outfit
科研机构

A second wave of lockdowns, or overhasty efforts to curtail economic stimulus, could **derail** the recovery. The value of exports from South Korea dipped in August relative to July, as did those of China after adjusting for an artificially depressed base in 2019. Robert Koopman, chief economist of the World Trade Organization, which oversees global trade, doubts there will be a **sustained** V-shaped recovery. Overlaying this is a concern about the lingering unevenness of trade. Brad Setser of the Council on Foreign Relations, an American think-tank, says that the trade slump has shrunk the gap between most countries' imports and exports, reducing imbalances. Yet there have been two standout exceptions. The first is China, whose rapid reopening has sent its exports of goods surging to a level last seen before the Sino-American trade war—almost $60 billion higher than imports in August. The second is America, whose policies to stoke demand have had the side-effect of causing its trade deficit to increase further—to around $80 billion in July.

This imbalance is **ominous**. Although the so-called Phase One trade deal between America and China was meant to **prop up** American exports to China, so far it has disappointed. Meanwhile, President Donald Trump is **haranguing** China ahead of elections in November. Trade may not have performed as badly as many feared. But it still has an alarming ability to pack a Thurmanesque punch.

> 词汇
>
> derail
> 脱轨
>
> sustained
> 持久的；坚定的
>
> ominous
> 不祥的
>
> prop up
> 支撑
>
> harangue
> 长篇大论，高谈阔论

语篇 2
难度级别：★★★

大家好，今年是中国加入世贸组织20周年，入世20年来，中国对世贸组织做出了哪些贡献呢？我们说，自从中国入世以来，中国已经成为世贸组织多边体制的最大贡献者。第一，我们说中国发展成为世界第二大经济体、全球第一大货物

> 词汇

贸易国、全球第一大外资吸收国，经济总量增长了近11倍，中国已经成为**多边贸易体制**最大的经济贡献者。那么对全球经济增长的年均贡献率接近30%，是拉动世界经济复苏和增长的重要引擎。但新冠疫情袭来的2020年，中国更是全球唯一实现经济正增长的主要经济体。第二，中国加入世贸组织以来，还改变了世界贸易的整体格局。以中美关系为例，中国大量物美价廉的商品源源不断地卖到了美国市场，让美国的普通民众也得到了极大的福利和生活上的改善，这样不仅抑制了美国的通货膨胀，也降低了普通民众的生活成本。第三，中国加入世贸组织以来，不仅在维护世贸组织的自由公平方面作出贡献，也在维护**多边主义**体制方面发挥了重要作用。近年来，一些国家的**逆全球化**浪潮和**单边主义**危机威胁着世贸组织的秩序，多边主义贸易体制的权威性和有效性遭到了质疑。作为多边主义体制的受益者和贡献者，中国在维护多边主义体制和坚持全球化方面做出了重要贡献。比如说中国一直坚持支持全球化，与支持多边主义的国家一起反对**制裁**、反对政治化、反对单边主义和贸易保护主义，这些斗争都维护了世界组织的自由公平。

> **词汇**
>
> 多边贸易体制
> multilateral trading system
>
> 多边主义
> multilateralism
>
> 逆全球化
> deglobalization
>
> 单边主义
> unilateralism
>
> 制裁
> sanction

模块六

译海拾贝：达沃斯论坛中的口译错误

世界经济论坛（World Economic Forum，WEF），又被称为"达沃斯论坛"，是以研究和探讨世界经济领域存在的问题、促进国际经济合作与交流为宗旨的非官方国际组织。作为最有影响力的国际会议，来参加的国家、企业代表数不胜数，因此口译员对于该论坛的重要性不言而喻。

然而在这么重要的场合，也出现过很多次口译失误现象。有些听众并未注意到，或是当场一笑了之，并未造成严重后果，但也有一些引发了各界的激烈讨论，甚至造成了较为严重的后果。这里举两个达沃斯论坛中的口译失误案例，让大家从其中了解译员在正式会议场合应具备的素养。

第一个案例是2008年的天津夏季达沃斯论坛中的数字口译错误。在高端经济论坛中，数字在讲话中的出现频率无疑会非常高，其重要性也不言而喻，然而由于论坛公开会议的即席性、对话内容的高专业性等原因，译员在数字口译中往往会出现漏译、误译。在2008年的这次世界经济论坛长达11小时的9场公开会议中，共出现了939组数字，有17名职业译员负责这次工作，他们的口译中出现了148次错误，其中大部分错误为漏译，主要失误原因是讲话人语速过快、讲话内容过于复杂，而译员的自身因素也是原因之一，译前准备不充分、临场紧张都是导致出现数字口译错误的原因。这些失误并没有引发致命的误会，一些地方听众甚至都没有注意到，但难免会给现场听众带来一些信息获取和理解上的困难。

第二个案例是在2019年大连夏季达沃斯中，蒙牛集团总裁发言遭到误译，这件事在当时引起了国内媒体和民众的轩然大波，甚至让蒙牛集团的企业声誉一度降到谷底。当天蒙牛集团总裁到底说了什么、译员又出现了什么失误才导致了这场舆论风波？

就像上述所说，达沃斯论坛会议具有很强的即席性，在极大的压力下，译员出现漏译、误译非常普遍，译员自身素质不够也是原因之一。当时的现场对话如下：

主持人史蒂芬·恩格尔：Have you overcome the perception gap of the quality issues from 2008? When you go abroad, these issues do come up, right?（你们是否已经克服2008年质量危机对中国乳制品造成的偏见？在开拓海外市场的时候，就会面临这些问题的挑战，对吧？）

蒙牛总裁卢敏放：The main reason is that we always want to go there with the best product, the premium product, high quality innovation, so that changes the perspective.（我们总是希望向当地展示最好的、最高端的和高水平创新的产品，由此来改变他们对中国产品的偏见。）

当时的同传译员错把best这个词当作关键词，将这句话翻译成了"我们希望把更好的产品卖到国外"，这样的话传到现场的那些记者耳朵里，信息被扭曲成了"我们希望把好产品卖到国外，把差产品留在国内销售"，这样一经报道便引起了针对蒙牛集团的一场舆论风波，在网上引发"蒙牛集团对国内与国外市场区别对待"的争论。对此，蒙牛集团多次公开澄清，在品牌全球化发展中，达到全球化标准品质的同时，该公司也一直坚持着"三同"原则，即"同线、同标、同质"，内外销产品在同一生产线、按相同的标准生产，从而保证达到相同的质量水平。而译员的翻译失误经过媒体的渲染发酵，险些对一家致力于走向世界、向全球讲述中国乳业故事的企业造成了严重打击。

以上两个案例都表明，译员的职业素养是十分重要的，提高个人能力、做好译前准备、心态放平放稳等，都是口译实践成功不可或缺的因素。译员在日常练习时，多了解和掌握实战策略,记忆负荷中要"挑大放小",关键信息不要出错;注意专业词汇和背景知识积累;培养过硬的心理素质,在应对各种场合时都要保持冷静,发挥出自己的翻译水平,确保在正式口译工作中不出现致命的错误。

模块七　译员风采：崔天凯从译员到外交官的历程

外交家崔天凯的外交生涯可以用"破冰融冰、辗转奔波、任重道远、心诚志坚"来概括,他也代表了我国外交战线队伍中部分成员的职业路径的一个缩影:大学期间学习外语专业,以译员身份进入外交战线,长期磨砺,形成了语言素质之外的高度政治敏感性和外交才能,从而走上了外交家的道路。

1952年,崔天凯出生在上海,就读于培养了多位外交家的上海外国语大学附属外国语学校,从1969年到1974年他都在黑龙江农村插队。1974年,他进入华东师范大学外语系英语专业学习,后又进修于北京外国语大学联合国译员培训班。在中国恢复了联合国合法席位后,急需中英译员,经过"联合国译员培训班"培训的崔天凯就顺其自然地以译员身份进入了联合国总部秘书处会议服务司中文处。

20世纪80年代初,联合国翻译司中文处占据了纽约联合国总部大楼的整个23楼,也为后来中国的外交事业培养出了一批中流砥柱。崔天凯、何亚非、郎胜铄和刘军是其中的四位年轻译员。何亚非（后曾担任国侨办副主任）翻译速度快,被称为"快手",崔天凯（后为中国驻美大使）则擅长于对词句的推敲。

1986年,担任外交部国际司三等秘书的崔天凯再次回到校园,在美国约翰·霍普金斯大学国际问题高级研究院学习,并取得硕士学位。2007年,该校公共交流和市场部部长克鲁伯斯在接受《中国新闻周刊》采访时介绍,至少有9年公共事务管理和工作经验的优秀人才才能读这个专业。

出色的能力使得崔天凯很快从基层岗位中走出,先后担任国际司参赞、外交部发言人、新闻司副司长、常驻联合国代表团参赞、外交部政策研究室主任等。这些工作锻炼出其儒雅却利落的处事风格,为后期的大使工作奠定了重要基础。在六方会谈中,日本媒体共同社评价他"谈判桌上的他,思维缜密,出言无懈可击;在短时间内,多次精准地修改了声明草案,为最终达成共识做出贡献"。

崔天凯的外交生涯中有两次担任大使的经历。第一次是在2007年9月,55岁的崔天凯被任命为驻日大使。在他履任期间,日本发生了消费者食物中毒事件,疑为食用了被农药甲胺磷污染的中国出口速冻水饺,崔天凯作为驻日大使到访了西日本地区最大的华侨聚居地神户,在神户中华街上的老字号东荣酒家和当地华侨代表一边吃饺子一边交谈,而且这些饺子都是在中国手工制作的速冻饺子。日本《关西华文时报》的报道称:崔天凯大使边吃边称赞"好吃极了",以自己的实际行动缓解了日本国民对于中国食品不信任的危机。

2013年4月2日,61岁的崔天凯从美国纽约乘坐火车抵达华盛顿,履新第十任中国驻美国大使。这是他第二次担任驻外大使。

同年6月7日,《纽约时报》发表题为《崔天凯,沟通中美的外交能人》的文章,称崔天凯是最了解美国的中国外交官。文章认为,作为中国外交部的高级官员,崔天凯参加过许多国际会议,他曾在这些会议上与美国外交人员展开较量,而且总能消除分歧。

驻美八年,崔天凯大使始终致力于维护健康互利的中美关系,谴责不实言论,重塑中国的对外形象。2021年6月22日,崔天凯卸任驻美大使,并发表致全美侨胞的辞别信。信中提到,当前中美关系正处在关键十字路口,美国对华政策正经历新一轮重构,面临在对话合作和对抗冲突之间做出选择。

回顾其外交生涯,崔天凯通过重重磨炼,形成专业的精神和高超的智慧,睿智与宽容并举,柔韧与坚定共存,有力地捍卫了国家利益与尊严!

第五章

物流
Logistics

模块一　　　　　　　　　　技能概要：笔记的基本要素

记笔记是译员所需的一项基本技能。口译笔记是用简单的符号、文字、线条来记录源语信息的逻辑关系和重要信息点。学生在口译时使用的是短时记忆，记忆十分有限。而笔记作为辅助记忆的工具，能够补充学生的短时记忆，帮其减轻脑力负担，提高工作的耐久度，从而保证口译质量。原则上来说，发言者的讲话超过一分钟，学生就应求助于笔记，通过笔记辅助回忆所听到的信息，确保译文的完整性与准确性，从而进行流利的表达。然而，只有了解了如何正确记笔记、用什么记笔记，理解笔记的作用和特点，学生才能在口译中充分发挥其作用。本模块主要介绍了记笔记的工具和功能、听解、记忆与笔记的交互，以及记笔记的原则。

记笔记的工具一般是带有活页圈的笔记本、按压式的笔和 A4 纸。译员做会议口译时用线圈本，最好是一手能拿得了的大小，有活页圈才能来回翻页，方便操作；笔一般用按压笔，方便携带，并带两支笔以防墨水用尽；自己练习时可以用 A4 纸，对折使用。

口译笔记的功能如下：

第一，帮助整理逻辑，把握大意。口译笔记中的逻辑关系可大致分为以下五大类：①因果；②转折；③让步；④假设和条件；⑤目的。笔记必须体现说话人的整体思路框架、叙述逻辑。一个好的笔记呈现，句和句之间、意群和意群之间、段落之间的逻辑关系应一目了然。学生可以适当使用表示逻辑关系的符号，这样看到笔记，便能迅速抓住说话的逻辑层次，更好地完成口译任务。

第二，帮助记录重要信息点。口译笔记应记录的信息点通常包括数字、对象、概念、命题、专有名词、专业术语等。其中，数字极其容易出错，又常常是关键，所以学生更应该谨慎对待。而对于专有名词（如专业术语、人名、地名等），学生应加强平时的积累，以免进行口译时犯难。一般而言，一个句子的主干为主要信息，且要点信息通常多集中在名词或名词词组上，所以记笔记时要以名词为主。

第三，帮助延长记忆，缓解压力。在实际的交替传译工作中，要求学生有强大的短期记忆能力，但即使是经验丰富的译员，也会借助口译笔记来减轻记忆的压力。因为人的短时记忆有限，学生需要笔记来记录容易遗忘的信息，如数字和专有名词等，同时利用笔记也能刺激回忆记录的内容，从而将简洁的笔记符号与听到的大量内容联系起来。

同时，学习笔记也要注意处理听解、记忆与笔记之间的关系。首先，学生要意识到笔记只是记忆的辅助手段，不能代替记忆。记忆和笔记互为补充，但是就重要性而言，笔记是对记忆的延伸和补充，听辨和记忆应占首要地位。正如塞莱斯科维奇（Seleskovitch）所说："对于有经验的译员来说，笔记能够起到不可估量的帮助作用，但对于学习翻译的人，记笔记在开始时会成为一种障碍，记笔记会分散注意力。"学生往往出现笔记太多、主次不分，难以快速回忆原文，反而成了负担的情况，这正是由于他们过分依赖笔记和忽视记忆的首要作用。无论是记忆还是笔记都应以理解为基础，在精力有限的情况下，学生应将重点放在对原文的理解和逻辑分析上。所以对于信息的正确听解和记忆应是笔记的前提和基础。

理解笔记的功能和内容只是第一步，如何将听辨和理解到的内容记录到笔记本上，才是笔记的重中之重，建议学生按照以下原则，循序渐进地练习笔记的方法。

第一，少字多画：少写文字、多画线条，用简单的符号代替文字，用缩写或者不完整拼写来代替完整的书写，缩短书写时间，自己能看懂即可。若记录太多笔记，学生很难准确定位并翻译出原文关键信息，影响听辨，从而导致语言转换难度增大，造成输出语卡顿、犹豫等现象。

第二，纵写缩进，宽松留白：竖着写，采取从上往下的阶梯结构记录，更加能体现上下文的逻辑结构。不要怕浪费纸，尽量记录得清楚，多行书写。

第三，逻辑划分：帮助断句、区分意群。有时候记录的信息太多会阻碍记忆，要分清意群，分清主次信息。可以借助"/""——"或箭头来作为句或段的划分线，这样在读解笔记的时候会一目了然，迅速解码。

在做笔记练习时，学生应先树立对笔记要素的正确认识，准备好练习工具，从题材比较熟悉、信息点不太密集、语速较慢、语篇较短的材料开始练习，平衡好听解与记录笔记之间的关系，准确判断该记下什么信息，放弃什么信息，逐渐培养听辨源语和写笔记同时进行、互不干扰的能力，熟能生巧，时间长了自然能掌握自如。

模块二　　　　　　　　　　　　　　　　　　　　　　　　　　　译前准备

◎ **1. 背景知识**

物流是指为了满足客户的需要，通过运输、保管、配送等方式，将标的物由商品的产地到商品的消费地所进行的计划、实施和管理的全过程。

本模块涉及的概念主要有刘易斯与克拉克远征、路易斯安那领地、德国邮政和敦豪等。

刘易斯与克拉克远征（Lewis and Clark Expedition）：发生时间为1804—1806年，是美国国内首次横越大陆西抵太平洋沿岸的往返考察活动。该活动由托马斯·杰斐逊总统发起，领队为美国陆军的梅里韦瑟·刘易斯上尉（Meriwether Lewis）和威廉·克拉克少尉（William Clark）。

路易斯安那领地（Louisiana Territory）：1699年，法属路易斯安那领地正式建立，1803年，拿破仑将整个法属路易斯安那领地以总价1 500万美元、每英亩4美分的低价卖给美国，这次购买使美国领土第一次得到扩大。今天的美国路易斯安那州仅为路易斯安那领地的一小部分，美国政府从路易斯安那领地中先后划分出了路易斯安那、密苏里、阿肯色、得克萨斯等州。

德国邮政（Deutsche Post of Germany）和**敦豪**（DHL）：德国邮政是德国联邦邮政于1995年成立的私有制邮政公司，当前主要业务包括邮件、快递、物流和金融四个方面。德国邮政通过企业收购（DHL等）构建起德国邮政国际网。敦豪是中国第一家国际航空快递公司，由全球快递、物流业的领导者DHL与中国对外贸易运输集团总公司各注资50%，于1986年成立，是中国成立最早、经验最丰富的国际航空快递公司。DHL的服务网络覆盖全球220多个国家和地区，在全球拥有约285 000名员工。

美国联合包裹运送服务公司（UPS, United Parcel Service, Inc.）：成立于1907年，总部设于美国佐治亚州亚特兰大市，是全球领先的物流企业，提供包裹和货物运输、国际贸易便利化、先进技术部署等多种旨在提高全球业务管理效率的解决方案。

联邦快递（FedEx）：成立于1971年，是一家国际性速递集团，提供涵盖运输、电子商务和商业运作等一系列的全面服务，总部设于美国田纳西州孟菲斯，隶属于美国联邦快递集团（FedEx Corp）。

贸易壁垒（trade barrier）：正常贸易受到阻碍、市场竞争机制作用受到干扰的各种人为措施，均属贸易壁垒的范畴，如进口税或起同等作用的其他关税，商品流通的各种数量限制等在生产者之间、购买者之间或使用者之间实行的各种歧视措施或做法（特别是关于价格或交易条件和运费方面），国家给予的各种补贴或强加的各种特殊负担，以及为划分市场范围或谋取额外利润而实行的各种限制性做法等。

Parcel Hero：英国最大的在线快递公司之一，通过全球最大的UPS、FedEx和DHL向英国和超过220个国家或地区提供快速、便捷和低成本的包裹递送服务。

◎ 2. 核心词汇

logistics firm	物流企业	international express delivery	国际快递
protectionist	保护主义者	free-trade area	自由贸易区
doldrum	萧条	tailwind	顺风
cross-border e-commerce	跨境电子商务	customs exemption	关税豁免
trade barrier	贸易壁垒	State Post Bureau	国家邮政局

模块三　　　　　　　　　　　　　　　　　　　　　语料实训

 任务1. 英译汉
难度级别：★★★

> 训练要点：本文介绍了物流的历史起源以及相关故事，进一步探寻了英文单词logistics的根源。文章没有很多生僻晦涩词汇，但是缺乏历史背景知识也会产生理解障碍。另外，本文的信息点比较琐碎，容易被细节绊住，所以在记笔记时要把握好文章的大致脉络和主要信息，有的放矢，次要信息少记或不记。

The Lewis and Clark Expedition

In 1803, the United States purchased a large part of North America from France. The area was called the Louisiana Territory. After the deal was made, President Thomas Jefferson proposed a fact-finding trip, or expedition, to the Louisiana Territory. He chose Meriwether Lewis to lead the expedition team. Lewis, in turn, asked a friend, William Clark to join the team in its trip across what is now the northwestern part of the US mainland. There are many things that must be done to organize a complex activity, like an expedition. These things are called logistics. The word logistics has military roots. It comes from a late 19th century French word, "logistique", meaning sheltering and supplying troops. Now, let's consider two words that sound almost alike. They are "compliment", spelled with the letter "i", and "complement", spelled with an "e". To learn more about both words, we turn to Kelly Jean Kelly. She went on her own expedition, of sorts, to find out more about Lewis and Clark.

KJK: Anybody who has ever traveled knows how important logistics are. You have to make your plane reservations if you're flying. You have to make your hotel reservations. You have to figure out how far you're going every day. You have to figure out how to get where you need to go on time and what you need to bring and what you need to have. I am very bad at logistics. It is not my strength.

AM: It is not your strong suit.

KJK: It is not my strong suit. But fortunately, I have an absolutely wonderful travel partner, one of our other colleagues here in Learning English, named Roger Hsu. And Roger is the videographer and the producer of the history videos. And he's very good at telling a story with pictures. I usually think about telling a story with words. But Roger uses images to tell a story. So, that is one of his great strengths. Luckily for me, his other great strength is logistics. So, he made sure that we were always where we needed to be at the right time and with the right equipment. And that was incredibly, incredibly valuable. I'm very thankful for Roger.

AM: So it was important that you two were together as a team and someone was able to pick up the slack, meaning to do perhaps what the other person doesn't do very well.

KJK: Correct, correct. And this is one of the things that historians talk about with Lewis and Clark that those two men had what they call complementary skills. So complementary spelled with an "e" and not with an "i". A compliment is when you say something nice about somebody. So, Roger is a very nice man and a good travel partner. So, that's a compliment. But he and I are complementary in that we have different skills but they go together very well. Some historians say that Lewis was very good at logistics. He organized everything before the trip and he bought the supplies that they needed. And he made arrangements with the government to get the money and have everything organized. And William Clark, his partner, was very good with the people on the ground. He organized the other soldiers and other people on the expedition and he helped make friendly relationships with the people that they met. So Lewis and Clark were an excellent team because they had complementary skills.

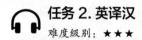

> 训练要点：本文介绍了在贸易壁垒回归和跨境电子商务兴起的背景下，迅猛发展的快递业迎来了机遇与挑战，对比了过去与如今快递业的发展现状，并对未来的形势做出了预测。文章中包含了许多物流的基本知识，如一些著名的快递公司。本文的信息点较为密集，做笔记时一定要记住"脑记大于笔记"的原则，将重心放在听辨上，把握文章脉络，厘清主要信息点，不可埋没于冗杂的笔记中。

Logistics Firms: Boxed in

The return of borders poses a challenge to the soaring parcel-delivery business. During the day, Leipzig's airport is quiet. It is at night that the airfield comes to life. Next to the runway, a yellow warehouse serves as the global sorting hub for DHL, a delivery firm owned by Deutsche Post of Germany. A huge extension, which opened in October, means it can sort 150, 000 parcels each hour, says Ken Allen, DHL's CEO. It was built as business soared. But the express-delivery industry faces a new challenge: the return of trade barriers due to the protectionist bent of Donald Trump and because of Brexit. The slower-moving shipping and air-cargo business has long been in the doldrums as a result of slow overall growth in trade in recent years. Yet the rise of cross-border e-commerce has still meant booming business for express-delivery firms.

On January 31st UPS revealed record revenues for the fourth quarter of 2016; FedEx and DHL are expected to report similarly buoyant results next month. Since 2008, half of the increase in express-delivery volumes has come from shoppers buying items online from another country. Falling trade barriers have greatly helped them. When DHL and FedEx were getting going in the 1970s, there was little demand for international express deliveries. Packages often got stuck in customs for weeks and were heavily taxed. The expansion of free-trade areas, lower tariffs and the Internet brought years of growth. But after Mr. Trump's threats to raise tariffs on goods from China and Mexico, together with the indication last month from Theresa May, that the country will leave the EU's customs union, there are widespread fears that the favorable tailwinds enjoyed by the industry for decades are gone. "It's all a real nightmare," groans David Jinks of Parcel Hero, a British parcel broker which works with DHL, FedEx and UPS. Start with Brexit. More physical border checks between Britain and Europe would do little direct damage. Most packages arriving in Britain have already been checked for drugs and dangerous items. Goods from outside the EU go through customs 95% of the time without any inspection or delay. Instead, post-Brexit costs will probably come from long wrangles over which of 19,000 customs codes should be applied to a consignment.

As an example of what could happen, Halloween costumes from China often get stuck at Britain's border while customs officials work out whether they are toys or children's clothes, which attract different duties. Such complexity would force delivery firms to put up their prices to customers, Mr. Jinks says. Sending an item from Britain to Switzerland (outside the EU) costs 150% more than it does to Italy (inside the EU). The most severe impact on business would come from higher tariffs, which would hurt demand for cross-border imports and deliveries in favor of local goods. This is where Mr. Trump's threats come into focus. A trade war would hit the massive volume of consignments that DHL's, FedEx's and UPS' planes carry every day in and out of America. For the moment, a customs exemption exists for packages worth under $800. This means that higher tariffs on a Chinese watch imported in bulk into the United States, for instance, could be avoided by an American ordering direct from Alibaba, a Chinese retailer, for delivery direct to their home. But if Mr. Trump is serious about cutting imports, he could get rid of this exemption. It was only last March that Barack Obama increased it to $800 from the previous $200. If it were lowered or eliminated by executive order, logistics-industry people would really panic.

They are putting a brave face on things. DHL's Mr. Allen has emphasized that "globalization is here to stay", whatever Mr. Trump does. UPS' boss, David Abney, hopes the president is not really against trade agreements. Even more telling are the actions of Fred Smith, FedEx's founder and CEO. Last week, he quietly gave up running the firm day-to-day to spend more time campaigning for free trade.

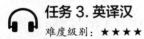

> 训练要点：本文介绍了中国几大物流巨头之间的激烈竞争；以京东物流为主要例子，对比分析了其物流业务情况、收入情况、运营模式以及未来发展趋势。本文逻辑脉络较为清晰，笔记难点在于大量的数字，容易出错。所以记笔记时要学会在各个任务间进行合理的调配，听到难点和主要信息点，可以放慢记录的节奏，把更多的精力放在听辨上，记录时下手要快。

Formula Races

When it comes to delivery, Chinese tech titans take divergent routes. In 2019, Richard Liu told couriers working for JD.com that the Chinese e-commerce giant he founded would cancel their base pay after a 2.8-billion-yuan ($438 million) loss the previous year, its 12th consecutive one in the red. Riders would make only a commission on deliveries. If the company did not cut back on spending, Mr. Liu warned, it would go bust in two years.

Far from collapsing, two years on JD Logistics, JD. com's delivery division, is on a roll, fueled by a boom in Chinese e-commerce. Its parent company's revenues jumped by 39%, year on year, in the first quarter, to 203 billion yuan. On May 26th, Pinduoduo, an upstart rival that also offers customers delivery by JD Logistics couriers, reported quarterly sales of 22 billion yuan, 239% higher than a year ago.

The State Post Bureau expects logistics companies to deliver more than 100 billion parcels this year, twice as many as in 2018. Overall spending on logistics in China is projected to hit 16 trillion yuan in 2021 and surpass 19 trillion yuan by 2025. That would make it the world's largest market.

Domestic and foreign investors have been pouring money into the industry, say lawyers working on deals involving such businesses. JD Logistics has attracted investments from big private-equity groups such as Sequoia China and Hillhouse Capital. The market buzz around the firm is as frenetic as the pace at which its 190,000 workers fulfill and ferry orders. On May 21st it raised $3.2 billion in Hong Kong's second-largest initial public offering this year. Its shares are scheduled to begin trading on May 28th. The company's backers are betting that its Amazon-like approach of creating a fully integrated delivery network has more mileage than a similar offering from SF Express, a stodgier incumbent similar to FedEx, or a rival model championed by Alibaba, which has plumped for a more distributed system.

JD Logistics is the only large Chinese delivery service to grow out of an e-commerce parent. It became a separate entity from JD.com in 2017, in part so that it could take orders from other online retailers. It still delivers the bulk of JD.com's packages but a large chunk of its revenues now comes from orders outside the group. By owning much of its technology, lorries and warehouses, and directly employing staff, the firm has been able to ensure faster delivery time while monitoring quality. It operates China's largest integrated logistics system, covering a good's entire journey and including a fully autonomous fulfilment center in Shanghai and driverless vehicles. The system can also flip into reverse, sending customer feedback to product designers that JD Logistics claims, helps it produce better products and bolster brands.

Contrast that with Cainiao, in which Alibaba has a controlling stake. It does not own many of the logistics assets in its network. Instead, it allows around 3, 000 logistics companies employing some 3 million couriers to plug into its platform. Its aim is to integrate and streamline the vast delivery resources that already exist across China, rather than build its own. The company has teamed up with most large logistics services—and taken investments from them as well. Alibaba, for its part, has bought minority stakes in several large operators as a means of exerting more influence over the industry. Cainiao is not publicly listed and does not disclose many operational details or, for that matter, how exactly it makes money.

In terms of revenues, both JD Logistics and Cainiao trail SF Express. Similar to JD Logistics, that firm operates its own network. It still leads the market in "time-definite" delivery, a service that requires couriers to pick up and drop off parcels on a rapid, predetermined timetable. Like FedEx in America, but unlike JD and Cainiao, it did not emerge from the tech industry, so lacks its rivals' technological chops. Which model emerges victorious will ultimately depend on which best controls costs, thinks Eric Lin of UBS, a bank. JD Logistics may have to lower prices further as it tries to get more business beyond JD.com. Analysts predict it could lose a combined 12 billion yuan over the next three years, and turn a profit only in 2024.

 任务 4. 汉译英
难度级别：★★

> 训练要点：本文介绍了年底迎新春时物流业繁忙的景象以及企业和快递人员是如何应对的。全文用词简单，对于学生是比较适宜的。同时值得注意的是，本文存在多个并列句，在记笔记时，学会如何处理好细碎的并列信息也是十分重要的。

你的年货在路上

年底物流忙，配送小哥化身"包裹侠"。又到了年货占满后备厢的季节，橘橙、腊肉、干果等年货随着物流线路输往各地。1月6日，记者联系上物流从业人员杨女士。得知目前日均收发量已经明显上升，较平常上涨了大概50%，她告诉记者："越往后

可能件量涨幅会更大，年货物资寄递需求上涨，配送小哥有的回家过年，有的阳而未康。"这个年底，我们的包裹由谁来守护？

企业从一个月前就开始筹备。杨女士告诉记者，这已经是他们公司度过的第16个不打烊春节。从一个月前开始，公司就筹备了专门的项目小组，根据大数据的预判来筹备人员、运力、场地等资源。她还介绍，目前主要运输的包裹大致有三种：第一种是橘橙销售旺季背景下，永兴等地的橘橙输送；第二种是年底电商平台开始举办促销活动，有比较多的电商件；第三种则是大家的年货、家乡特产的寄递。人手不足如何解决？杨女士介绍，他们主要有两种解决方式：一种是招聘临时用工人员、同城小哥加入快递员队伍；另一种是跨区域调拨支援，充分结合弹性资源调配补充。其余则是在节假日期间，通过减少商业区、学校等区域人员整合网点。既能让小哥们安心回乡，又能保障正常寄递需求。

配送小哥每天都在为大家的包裹全力以赴。每天早上六点过一刻，大家还在床上享受美梦时，长龙街道星工场营业点的黄波就要起床为接下来的一天做准备。初次联系黄波时，其正因交接班忙得脚不沾地。忙碌中他抽空告诉记者，目前连收带派，自己每天经手的包裹有四五百个。现在正是年底高峰，加上前段时间很多同事都阳了。他们压力巨大，每天都像绷紧的弦。所幸生病的同事都在康复的第一时间迅速返岗，站点得以正常运转。

黄波还向记者介绍，自己是长沙本地人，就住在站点附近。过年会留在站点继续上班，把轮休机会让给外地的同事，让每一个人都能享受到团圆的滋味。他说："今年情况特殊，可能配送的速度稍有放缓，希望大家没有收到快递时不要着急，多一点耐心、多一点包涵。我们知道身在外地的游子不能回家，所以每天都在全力以赴，力求把家乡味、家乡菜送到这些游子手上。"

模块四　　　　　　　　　　　　　　技巧点拨：如何平衡听辨与笔记记录

🎧 任务1. 英译汉

 例一
难度级别：★★★

FedEx, or Federal Express, is an international logistics company. It began operations in 1973 and has grown to serve and

○ 词汇

reach every corner of the world. The company website gives an overview: "FedEx provides customers and businesses worldwide with a broad portfolio of transportation, e-commerce and business services. Consistently ranked among the world's most admired and trusted employers, FedEx inspires its more than 275,000 employees and contractors to remain absolutely, positively focused on safety, the highest ethical and professional standards and the needs of their customers and communities."

○ 词汇

contractor
承包商

注：画线内容为笔记应记录的重点。

译文

联邦快递是一家国际性的物流公司。它始创于 1973 年，通过发展，公司的服务范围遍布全球。其企业官网的概述如下："联邦快递为全球顾客和企业提供涵盖运输、电子商务和商业运作等一系列的全面服务。联邦快递一直被评为世界上最受尊敬和最值得信赖的雇主之一，激励其 27.5 多万名员工和承包商高度关注安全问题，并恪守道德规范和职业操守，最大程度地满足客户和社会的需求。"

策略分析

口译笔记的第一步是听辨。口译笔记应该在听辨的基础上记意思而不是记字词，对中心词、转折词、数字、专有名词等进行记录。笔记能够帮助学生把握讲话内容，快速地转换成译文，可以说笔记就是翻译的"半成品"了。口译笔记在精不在多。

本段落行文逻辑比较简单，主要介绍了国际性物流公司联邦快递的基本信息，包括创始时间、服务范围、主要业务等。第一句中 Federal Express 这类专有名词可以取字母缩写记为"Fx"，international 可以用"∅"来表示，这个符号还可以用来表示与"全球，国际"相关的单词短语（如 universal、across the world、worldwide、global、the earth 等），而 globalization 可在其右上角加一个"n"来表示。第二句中的 began 可以用"⊕"表示，类似的词还有 start、initiate、open、originate、launch、pioneer、commence、inaugurate 等，这个符号还可以表示"形成，产生，出现"（如 establish、found、create、appear、emerge、occur、come out、break out、come into being/existence 等）或"医疗卫生"（如 Red Cross、hospital、medical care 等）。has grown to 可以用"↑"，同时这个箭头也可以表示"发展，加强，推进"（如 develop、strengthen、promote、boost、improve、enhance）或"上升"（如 up、upward、rise、increase 等）。第三句话的 overview 可以记录为"○k"，其中"○"可以表示"整体，全部，总共"（如 whole、all、total、 entire、complete、overall、general、universal、integral、gross、intact、on the whole、all in all 等）或"团结，统一，团聚"（如 united、unification、gather、get together 等），而"k"取自 know，可以表示"想法，观点，看法，认为"。对于 customers and businesses 和 transportation, e-commerce and business services 并列结构的处理，逻辑上可以采取用"{"或是"("将它们包括起来，内容上可以记录为英文的缩写或是中文的偏旁部首。最高级 most admired and trusted 可以用"^"写在信息点上方，另外"^"除表示"顶点，最高级"（如 peak、top、supreme、utmost、maximum、climax 等）外，还可以表示"领导，监督"（如 lead、supervise、head 等）。

笔记要点

1. 做好听辨是记好口译笔记的第一步。
2. 学会用缩略语，如本文笔记中的"Fx"。
3. 学会用字母、图像、符号，如圆圈、箭头、加号等。
4. 学会使用并列关系、与最高级相关的口译笔记表达方法。

笔记示范

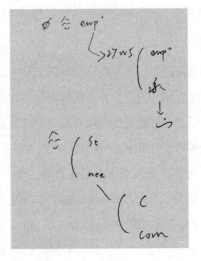

》 例二
难度级别：★★★★

The online store Amazon is testing a new method of delivering parcels. It wants to start using drones to get packages to customers, in just 30 minutes. The drones are small, remote-controlled helicopters called "octocopters". They look like toys. Amazon's CEO Jeff Bezos talked about them on the American TV show "60

○ 词汇

drone
无人机

remote-controlled
遥控的

Minutes". He said: "I know this looks like science fiction. It's not." He added: "We can do half-hour delivery and we can carry objects, we think, up to 2.3 kg, which covers 86 percent of the items that we deliver." He joked that Amazon would not be able to deliver some things. He said: "It won't work for everything. We're not going to deliver **kayaks**, or table saws this way."

词汇

kayak
皮船

译文

网上商城亚马逊正在对全新配送方式进行检测。亚马逊希望利用无人机仅用30分钟向客户运送货物。这种无人机比较小，需要远程控制，看起来就像是玩具。亚马逊首席执行官美国电视节目《60分钟》里谈论了此事。他说："我知道这看起来有点科幻，但是这是真实的。"他还说："我们将会在30分钟内送达，我们可以运输物品，最大重量能够达到2.3公斤，覆盖了所有货物的86%。"他开玩笑地说我们不是什么都能送达的。他说："无人机不能运输所有的物品，例如皮船或桌锯。"

策略分析

如何平衡听辨与笔记记录是初学笔记时的主要问题之一。学生在初步掌握了记笔记的要领后，记笔记时恨不得每个字每句话都记录下来，无法判断哪里是重点，这样做的结果往往是把听到的内容密密麻麻记了一堆，最后要么辨认不出来笔记内容，要么没有厘清译文逻辑，要么没有做好译文转换。还有些人会走向另一个极端，什么都用脑记，记忆负担太重，非常影响最后的输出。笔记是对记忆的延伸和补充，听辨和记忆应占首要地位，但同时也要善用笔记这个记忆辅助工具，记录些专有词汇、数字、长句或比较复杂的内容。

本段落主要介绍了亚马逊对利用无人机配送货物的方式。本段第一句中的 online store Amazon 可以记为"ol Az"或"囧 Az/冂 Az"，delivering parcels 可以记为"→p"。学会基础的口译笔记后，可以根据自己的习惯，自己再设定，比如箭头加字母，如"→g"表示"到达；传达"。第二句中的 just 可以记为"#"，谐音中文的"仅"。remote-controlled 可以记为"扌"，作为"控"的偏旁，"扌"还可以表示"挑战"。"We can do half-hour delivery and we can carry objects, we think, up to 2.3 kg, which covers 86 percent of the items that we deliver."这句话虽然看起来长，但所要讲的信息很清楚，所以记笔记时需要简化一下，只用记下"W/{30 →辶 /2.3kg ^/86%"。not be able to 和下文的 won't work 可以记为"×"，这个符号还可以表示"错误，失误"（如 wrong、incorrect、something bad、negative 等）。

笔记要点

1. 学会如何平衡听辨与笔记记录，听辨为主，笔记为辅助。
2. 学会基础的口译笔记符号后，再根据自己的习惯进行拓展。
3. 将所听到的内容简化为信息点；不要全盘记录，而要简化加工后再记录。

笔记示范

» 例三
难度级别：★★★★

Internet shopping not only makes buying things easier, but also has led to the rise of a new kind of thief: the porch pirate. Porch pirates **scour** door steps for deliveries that have been made when a householder was out, and **nab** them. Sometimes, they will stalk delivery vans to do so. Residents of New York City, for example, lose an astonishing 90,000 parcels every day to porch pirates, according to a report in the *New York Times*. Porch piracy is a problem that may be solved by the spread of parcel-delivering drones. Because each drone delivery involves a separate journey, rather than having to be fitted into a round, it will be easier for courier and customer to agree on when a drone should arrive than on the arrival time of a van.

○ 词汇

scour
翻找

nab
捉住

译文

网络让购物变得更加容易，但也导致了一种新型的门廊窃贼的兴起。包裹窃贼会在住户外出时，在门口的台阶上搜寻投送的快递，然后把快递偷走。有时他们会跟踪送货车进行偷窃。例如，根据《纽约时报》的报道，纽约市的居民每天因包裹窃贼而丢失多达9万个包裹。无人送货机的普及或许可以解决包裹窃贼的问题。因为每一架无人机都只送一家货物，而不是来回运送多家，所以快递员和客户更容易就送货时间达成一致，而不是货车何时到达。

策略分析

口译笔记需要有逻辑性。口译笔记建立在听取、理解和分析的基础之上，因此记笔记时要做到条理清晰，反映出发言内容的逻辑关系。具有逻辑性的笔记能够帮助学生更快地在脑子里重现源语信息，同时也可以反映学生的理解程度。在记笔记的过程中，比较推荐的做法是将笔记本的右侧三分之一的部分留白，用于做逻辑标识。

本段落是很好的训练逻辑材料，主要描述了随着网购的兴起，包裹窃贼也增多了，并介绍了解决这一问题的措施。本段第一句话中存在转折逻辑，转折逻辑（but、however）可以用"b"，取自 but 或是反转箭头来表示，easier 这种积极正面的词可以用"笑脸"表示，负面贬义的词可以用"哭脸"表示，"-"可以表示"少，减去，除去"（little、few、lack、minus），new 可以用"x"表示，这个符号也可以表示"创新，发明"，所以第一句话的笔记可以记为"冂 $/•⌣•, b/↑x thf"。遇到 when 引导的时间状语从句，英译中时，往往会将其放到前面来翻译。在口译中，遇到时间状语从句可以用"[ ]"标记一下，而介词状语结构可以用"( )"标记起来，或者通过换行来提醒自己。所以遇到 when a householder was out、according to a report in the *New York Times* 这样明显的时间状语从句和状语结构，可以用括号标记，或者换行处理，方便翻译时调整顺序。文中的第五句话是一个逻辑难点，首先遇到因果逻辑，可以采用数学符号"∵"和"∴"来标记，rather than 相当于 not，可以用"×"表示，it will be easier 前可以加一个"∴"，或在上面的原因后加一个"→"。与英文不同，中文的关联词往往成对出现，在英译汉的时候要注意这一点。表示目的可以直接加一个"→"；表示让步可以记为"al"，取自 although；表示假设可以记为 if。

笔记要点

1. 注意笔记的逻辑性，把握文章大致脉络。
2. 注意常见逻辑符号的笔记表达。

笔记示范

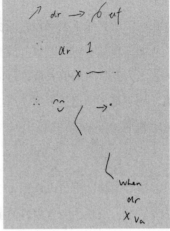

任务2. 汉译英

例一
难度级别：★★★★

根据国务院物流保通保畅工作领导小组办公室监测汇总数据显示，1月5日，国家铁路货运继续保持高位运行，运输货物1 096.4万吨，环比增长2.44%；全国高速公路货车通行753.1万辆，环比增长2.3%；监测港口完成货物吞吐量3 280.8万吨，环比下降5.8%，完成集装箱吞吐量73.9万标箱，环比下降11.3%；民航保障航班9 787班，环比下降0.4%；邮政快递揽收量约4.02亿件，环比基本持平；投递量约3.9亿件，环比增长4.6%。

译文

According to data from the Office of the Leading Group of the State Council for ensuring smooth logistics, on January 5, the national railway freight continued to maintain a high level of operation, with the transport of 10.964 million tons of goods, a month-on-month increase of 2.44%. There were 7.531 million trucks on expressways, up 2.3% from the previous month. The cargo throughput of the ports was 32.808 million tons, down 5.8% from the previous month, and the container throughput was 739,000 TEU, down 11.3% from the previous month. The number of civil aviation flights was 9,787, down 0.4% from the previous month. The volume of postal express delivery was about 402 million, basically unchanged from the previous month. About 390 million items were delivered, up 4.6 percent from the previous month.

策略分析

数字笔记的难点是由于中英计量单位不同而造成的。学生需要熟悉不同的记录方法，完成双语间数字的转换。在中文里，数字是以个、十、百、千、万、十万、百万、千万、亿来计量，而在英文体系中，数字则是每三位数为一计量单位，即 thousand（1,000）、million（1,000,000）、billion（1,000,000,000）。因此，在中英数字转换的过程中就会出现因不对应而引起数字不准确的问题。

本段落的数字密集，在练习的时候若是把握不准，可以多听几遍。由于中英的记数差异，遇到数字时，记笔记最好以目标语为主，如数字"1 096.4 万吨"推荐的写法为"10.964 m tn"，而不是"1 096.4 万"，因为如果笔记以中文为主，回头翻译时，便会增加单位转换的负担。另外值得注意的是，听辨时的数字单位也很重要，不然会出现记下了数字，却不知道它所表达的含义的情况。文中的"增长""下降"可以用箭头"↑""↓"表示。文中的"环比"可以翻译为：① month on month；② from + 时间：from the month before / from last quarter；③ compared with/to+ 时间，所以笔记可以记为"m/m"或是"时间 + ↓"。同理，"同比"可以翻译为：① year on year / year over year；② from + 时间：from a year earlier；③ compared with + 时间：compared with a year ago；④其他翻译方法：against the previous year / on similar comparison / like-for-like growth / in the year to，所以笔记可以记为"y/y"或是"时间 + ↓"。

笔记要点

1. 注意中英数字笔记转换。
2. 注意与环比和同比相关的笔记表达。

笔记示范

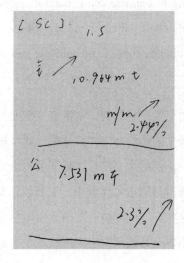
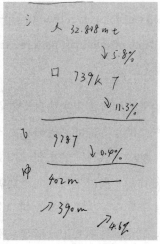

例二
难度级别：★★★★

从去年到今年，已经传言六次要上市的**京东物流**终于尘埃落定。2月16日晚间消息，京东物流宣布正式向**港交所**提交招股申请，而京东物流业务构成、营收概况以及募资用途等核心信息也首次全面披露。**招股文件**显示，2020年京东物流**前三季度的收入**达到**495**亿元，同比增长43.2%。这一数字在2018年和2019年全年分别为379亿元和498亿元，保持**稳定增长**。同时，京东物流拟将全球发售募集资金，用于升级和扩展物流网络，开发与**供应链解决方案**和物流服务相关的先进**技术及扩展解决方案的广度与深度**，**深耕**现有客户和**吸引**潜在客户等。

词汇
京东物流
JD Logistics

港交所
Hong Kong Exchanges and Clearing Limited（HKEX）

招股文件
prospectuses

译文

From last year to this year, JD Logistics has been rumored to go public for six times. The news of going public is finally confirmed. On the evening of February 16th, JD Logistics announced that it had formally submitted an application to the Hong Kong Exchanges and Clearing Limited for a share offering. Moreover, the core information of JD Logistics, such as its business composition, revenue and purpose of raising funds, was also fully disclosed for the first time. According to prospectuses, JD Logistics' revenue in the first three quarters of 2020 reached 49.5 billion yuan, up 43.2 percent year on year. The figure stood at 37.9 billion yuan in 2018 and 49.8 billion yuan in 2019, maintaining steady growth. Meanwhile, JD Logistics plans to use the funds raised from the global offering to upgrade and expand its logistics network, develop advanced technologies related to supply chain solutions and logistics services, expand the breadth and depth of solutions, nurture existing customers and cultivate new accounts.

策略分析

听辨时要有意识地分清主次信息，进而形成逻辑框架。学生容易犯的一个错误就是不知道要根据信息的重要程度来搭建英文译文的结构框架，具体来说就是把主要信息放到了修饰成分，如"定状补"的次要结构中，而把次要信息放到了主句里面。这是不符合英文的语言规律的，所以学习如何平衡听辨与笔记尤为重要。主要信息要放到"主谓宾"构成的"主干"中，次要信息放到"定状补"的"枝叶"中，所以学会构建笔记的结构尤为重要。笔记的结构要记录清楚，不要只是按照文字顺序从左往右从上往下随意记关键词。并列结构可以上下并列记，用大括号连接并列成分。主从关系可以通过换行或者箭头提示。

本段主要介绍了京东物流的上市。关于时间的口译笔记记法，通常采用的方式是字母缩写法，如 y（year）、m（month）、d（day）、w（week）、h（hour）、m（minute），这个点"."（dot）的位置不同，表示的概念也不一样。".d"表示 yesterday，".y"表示 last year，".2m"表示 two month ago，"y"可以表示 this year，所以段落中的"从去年到今年"，则可以记为".y — y"。做口译时，还要学会对原文进行脱壳，而不是局限于语言的形式，如本文中的"终于尘埃落定"意思就是完成了，笔记可以直接记为"√"。本文还存在一些专有名词，如"港交所"可以记为"HKEX"，平时要多积累。本段落最后一句话存在一个很长的并列句，"用于升级和扩展物流网络，开发与供应链解决方案和物流服务相关的先进技术及扩展解决方案的广度与深度，深耕现有客户和吸引潜在客户等"，都表示募捐资金的用途。若遇上修饰成分过多的信息点，一定要学会抓主要信息，记下本句话中的核心点，如物流网络、技术、解决方案、客户，其谓语部分笔记都可记为"↑"，这也要求学生平时多积累相应的表达，且要追求多样化。

笔记要点

1. 要有意识地分清主次信息，进而形成逻辑框架。
2. 学会时间相关的笔记写法。
3. 学会语言脱壳，不是记下个别单词，而是要记下信息点。
4. 平时要多积累专有名词和相关表达。

笔记示范

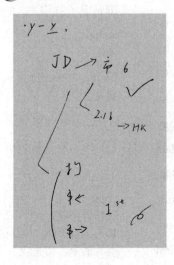
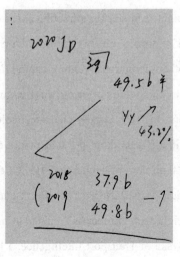

模块五　拓展练习

任务：物流口译练习

语篇 1
难度级别：★★★★★

Logistics: Digital Decongestants

A **flotilla** of startups promises to **streamline** the world supply chains. **Forto** seems an unlikely **tech-darling**. It does not make gadgets, build the **metaverse**, forge **cryptocurrencies** or launch rockets. The six-year-old startup from Berlin, whose main business is arranging the transport of cargo from one place to another, has nevertheless managed to raise nearly $600 million from venture capitalists. Its backers reckon the firm can shake up the **archaic freight-forwarding** industry. It has tripled its business in each of the past four years, boasts Michael Wax, its boss, and is now one of the top ten forwarders in the busy trade lane between China and Germany. In Marchs, it announced $250 million in new funding at a valuation of $2.1 million.

Forto is not the only freight tech startup attracting investors' attention. With the world's supply chains gummed up by bottlenecks, lockdowns and other disruptions, venture-capital (VC) firms are pouring billions into companies offering ways to make freight transport more efficient. In 2021, supply-chain-technology firms raised more than $62 billion, according to PitchBook, a data provider, more than twice the figure in pre-pandemic 2019. Of that, nearly $9 billion went to freight-tech startups. Pitch Book counts more than a dozen private freight-tech "**unicorns**", valued at more than $1 billion. Viki Keckarovska of Transport Intelligence, a firm

词汇

decongestant
解决拥堵；解充血药

flotilla
船队

streamline
简化

Forto
国际著名数字化物流服务商

tech-darling
科技新宠

metaverse
虚拟实境，虚拟世界

cryptocurrency
加密电子货币

archaic
古老的

freight-forwarding
货运代理

unicorn
独角兽企业（成立不足10年且估值超过10亿美元的未上市企业）

of consultants, expects more funding rounds this year.

Part of the appeal lies in the industry's size and potential for disruption. The freight-forwarding business alone is worth $475 billion in annual revenues, reckons Armstrong & Associates, a supply-chain research and consulting firm. The broader "third-party logistics" market, which includes transport management and warehousing, generates sales of $1.4 trillion. At the same time, freight remains technologically backward, especially the cross-border sort. "This industry is completely offline," marvels Zvi Schreiber, boss of Freightos, a digital-freight marketplace. "You would expect that shipping a container would be just as digital as booking a flight," he says, "but it is not at all." Just getting a quote can be a headache. "For 90% of the freight-forwarders today, it still takes one or two days to come back with a price," says Mr. Wax.

This is starting to change thanks in part to **whizzy** new software platforms designed to streamline the process of shipping freight overseas. Flexport, a digital freight-forwarder based in San Francisco, automates many of the supply-chain processes that were traditionally done manually, including getting **quotes**, filling out documents and coordinating with **shippers** and **carriers** along the supply chain. The nine-year-old startup, which earned $3.2 billion in revenues in 2021, was recently valued at more than $8 billion. Project 44, a supply-chain visibility platform from Chicago, lets retailers and brands monitor milestones in their cargo's journey, such as when it is loaded onto a ship, leaves the port or arrives at its final destination—all in real time. They can also make adjustments or reroute shipments if needed.

One common feature of such platforms is the ability to **glean** insights from data. Big shippers and logistics providers typically manage their shipments in software known as a transport-management system (TMS), which tracks shipments as they make their way along logistics networks, from the factory to the port and

词汇

whizzy
技术先进的

quote
报价

shipper
托运人

carrier
承运人

glean
收集（资料）

finally to the customer. Such systems, which have been around since the late 1980s, are useful databases of information, says Evan Armstrong, president of Armstrong & Associates. But they are not clever. "The first step was getting everything onto a TMS. Now the next step is taking those TMSs and making them intelligent."

Although recent supply-chain **snarl-ups** have played a part in boosting demand for logistics software, they are not the main force behind the boom. That, industry-watchers agree, would be Amazon. The E-**emporium** "is the absolute No.1 **catalyst** for supply-chain transformation, no question", says Julian Counihan of Schematic Ventures, a VC firm. Whereas the supply chain has historically been seen as a cost center, Amazon has turned it into a money-maker. With the rise of next-day and same-day delivery, consumers' expectations have changed dramatically. "As shipping times **plummet**, logistics requires more supply-chain technology," says Mr. Counihan.

Some skepticism is in order. Many of the startups look little different from the **incumbents** they are seeking to disrupt. Kuehne & Nagel, a big Swiss freight-forwarder, has invested heavily in digitization even if it doesn't "sing and dance that they are a 'digital' freight forwarder", as Mr. Schreiber of Freightos freely admits. C.H. Robinson, a big American logistics firm, is "really a digital freight broker", says Mr. Armstrong. And although some of the big incumbents rely on antiquated technology, he adds, they have much more scale than any of the newcomers. That lets them secure lower prices from ocean liners, air freighters and other carriers.

Still, as Ms. Keckarovska points out, the upstarts have a shot. The freight-forwarding market remains highly fragmented, so they need not take on a huge incumbent. DHL and Kuehne & Nagel, the two biggest brokers, have a combined global market share of just 6%. And despite their digital aspirations, the incumbents' technology leaves plenty of room for improvement. Of the 20

○ 词汇

snarl-up
阻塞

emporium
大百货商店

catalyst
催化剂

plummet
大跌

incumbent
现任者

biggest established freight-forwarders, 15 apparently use the same off-the-shelf TMS to manage their shipments.

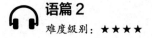

The Bots Taking over the Warehouse

A decade ago Amazon started to introduce robots into its "fulfilment centers", as online retailers call their giant distribution **warehouses**. Instead of having people wandering up and down rows of shelves picking goods to complete orders, the machines would lift and then carry the shelves to the pickers. That saved time and money. Amazon's sites now have more than 350,000 robots of various sorts deployed worldwide. But even that is not enough to secure its future.

Advances in warehouse robotics, **coupled with** increasing labor costs and difficulty in finding workers, have created a **watershed** moment in the logistics industry. With COVID-19 lockdowns causing supply-chain disruptions and a boom in home deliveries that is likely to endure, fulfilment centers have been working at full tilt.

Despite the robots, many firms have to bring in temporary workers to cope with increased demand during busy periods. Competition for staff is fierce. In the run-up to the holiday shopping season in December, Amazon brought in some 150,000 extra workers in America alone, offering sign-on bonuses of up to $3,000.

The long-term implications of such a high reliance on increasingly hard-to-find labour in distribution are clear, according to a new study by McKinsey, a consultancy: "Automation in warehousing is no longer just nice to have, but imperative for sustainable growth."

This means more robots are needed, including newer, more

词汇

warehouse
仓库

coupled with
加上，此外

watershed
分水岭

efficient versions to replace those already at work and advanced machines to take over most of the remaining jobs done by humans. As a result, McKinsey forecasts the warehouse-automation market will grow at a compound annual rate of 23% to be worth more than $50 billion by 2030.

The new robots are coming. One of them is the **prototype** 600 Series bot. This machine changes everything according to Tim Steiner, chief executive of Ocado Group, which began in 2002 as an online British grocer and has evolved over the years into one of the leading providers of warehouse robotics.

The 600 Series is a strange-looking beast, much like a box on wheels made out of **skeletal** parts. That is because more than half its components are 3D-printed. As 3D-printing builds things up layer by layer, it allows the shapes to be optimized, thus using the least amount of material. As a result, the 600 Series is five times lighter than the company's present generation of bots, which makes it more agile and less demanding on battery power.

Ocado's bots work in what is known as the "**Hive**", a giant **metallic grid** at the center of its fulfilment centers. Some of these hives are bigger than a **football pitch.** Each cell on the grid contains products stored in plastic **crates**, **stacked** 21 deep. As orders arrive, a bot is dispatched to extract a crate and transport it to a picking station, where a human worker takes all the items they need, scans each one and puts them into a bag, much as happens at a supermarket checkout.

It could take an hour or so walking around a warehouse to collect each item manually for a large order. But as hundreds of bots operate on the grid simultaneously, they are much faster. The bots are **choreographed** by an artificially intelligent computer system, which communicates with each machine over a wireless network. The system allows Ocado's current bot, the 500 Series, to

○ 词汇

prototype
原型

skeletal
骨骼的

hive
蜂巢

metallic grid
金属网格

football pitch
足球场

crate
板条箱

stack
堆栈

choreograph
编排

gather all the goods required for a 50-item order in less than five minutes.

The new 600 Series will match or better its predecessor's performance and use less energy. It also "unlocks a **cascade** of benefits", says Mr. Steiner, allowing Hives to be smaller and lighter. This means they can be installed in weeks rather than months and at a lower cost. That will make "micro" fulfilment centers viable. Most fulfilment centers are housed in large buildings on out-of-town trading estates, but smaller units could be sited in urban areas closer to customers. This would speed up deliveries, in some cases to within hours.

Amazon is also developing more efficient robots. Its original machines were known as Kivas, after Kiva Systems, the Massachusetts-based firm that manufactured them. The Kiva is a squat device which can slip under a stack of head-height shelves in which goods are stored. The robot then lifts and carries the shelves to a picking station. In 2012, Amazon bought Kiva Systems for $775 million, and later changed its name to Amazon Robotics. Amazon Robotics has since developed a family of bots, including a smaller version of a Kiva called Pegasus. These will allow it to pack more goods into its fulfilment centres and also use bots in smaller inner-city distribution sites.

词汇

cascade
小瀑布，一连串事情

模块六　　　译海拾贝：口译员的隐身与现身

译员的"隐身"与"现身"是译员实践中重要的职业准则。译员的"隐身"是指尽量减少译员对于翻译和翻译活动的痕迹，追求译文的通顺自然；译者的"现身"是指发挥译者的主观能动性和翻译的创造性。下文将带大家具体了解一下译员的"隐身"和"现身"。

译员的"隐身"

诺曼·夏皮罗（Norman Shapiro）曾说过："我认为，翻译的目标就在于生产出透明的译文，最好就像没有翻译过的译语原文一样。好的翻译就像一块玻璃，只有在玻璃上出现一些小小的瑕疵——擦痕和气泡的时候你才会注意到它的存在。""隐身"就是要让译者"不可见"，不能自作主张。在这样的观念下，一个好的译者要尽可能做到"隐身"。

一个合格的译员始终要记得，口译工作服务于会议，不能喧宾夺主；会议的主角是谈判双方。口译员的核心任务就是要清晰流畅、准确无误地传递信息。若是会场没有人注意到口译员的存在，这个口译员就是完全隐身，一定程度上说明译员工作到位了。译者的礼仪规范可以很好地体现译者的"隐身"。译员要"戴着镣铐跳舞"，不能随意发挥。在不影响工作的情况下，译员要与发言人保持一定距离，站在一个合适的位置，译员能听到发言人讲话，发言人也能够听到译员翻译。在一些有摄影、摄像记者在场的活动的场合，译员要进行"隐身"，主动避开镜头。

但是同样值得注意的是，在翻译实践中，双方文化的差异往往会使两种语言完全对等的情况无法存在。若是一味地追求译者的"隐身"，将这些差异化作矛盾的激化点，那双方的合作往往有破裂之势。例如，在谈判会议中，中国企业家们对于对方提出的要求通常会满口答应，以表示合作的诚意。而英国人的思维里，这被视作不牢靠的体现，他们倾向于用谈细节的方式表达诚意，先把双方的矛盾亮到明面上，但有的中国企业家会认为对方不愿合作。这些因为盲区的存在而导致的不理解，会影响到合作。考虑到这一风险，译员往往需要减少差异在口译活动中的影响，不一定要逐字翻译，脱离文本的形式，以传递重要信息为主，适当解释文化差异。

译员的"现身"

译者作为翻译实践的主体，发挥着极其重要的作用，贯穿于翻译活动的全过程。在口译的实践活动中，译员往往要根据实际情况，发挥主观能动性，对于译文进行有意识地简化，或增加一些文化背景知识。

有一则外交轶事很好地体现了译者的"现身"。1956年4月，赫鲁晓夫访问英国，首相安东尼·艾登亲自前往迎接，双方宾主之间其乐融融。然而，赫鲁晓夫本人十分喜爱喝酒，会见了英国实业精英后，在宴会上喝了不少伏特加，以至于在后来的演讲场合中，赫鲁晓夫有些醉得忘乎所以。他在演讲中丢掉了原本的演讲稿，开始随性发挥，痛快淋漓，大肆抨击西方的资本主义。而这却苦了当时的翻译，好在他急中生智，决定还是按照原来的演讲稿翻译，不翻译赫鲁晓夫酒后失言的部分，选择发挥译者的"现身"作用。当时在台下的大部分英国人也都不懂俄语，而译员所翻译的原稿内容基本是对英国以及苏英之间的友谊的赞美和两国共同发展的蓝图，于是演讲结束后，全场响起了轰鸣般的掌声，译员通过"现身"挽回了局面。

应该"隐身"还是"现身"？

译者的"隐身"与"现身"实际上是翻译的两种策略，并没有明确的优劣之分。译员一方面具有独立性，在翻译过程中必须发挥主观能动性和创造性；另一方面，译者受制于服务对象、服务场合等各种因素，必须在尊重这些因素的基础上进行翻译实践。译者应该"隐身"还是发挥"主体性"作用，往往要根据现场实际情况灵活调整，这对口译员的能力提出了更高的要求。初学者在学习中要积累职业素养，树立良好的职业道德，打好基础，扎实双语功底以及广博的文化知识，培养语言感悟力和审美素养。

模块七　译员风采：林超伦与他的 KL Communications

林超伦是英国外交部的首席中文翻译官。自 20 世纪 90 年代中期以来，他负责英国女王、多任英国首相及其主要内阁成员的口译任务，参与接待多位中国领导人，并担任英中贸易协会以及著名跨国企业的口译员，成为首位来自中国、获得女王勋章的英籍华人。然而，这些闪亮的履历背后，其实一切都是从零开始的。从福建莆田的青年成长为当代传奇翻译官，他做过老师、卖过保险、当过记者。我们一同来探寻林超伦求学经历和职业生涯。

人若有志，万事可为。1977 年，高考恢复，林超伦在几乎零基础的情况下开始学习英语，复习其他文化课，虽不知道未来路在何方，但他抓紧最后的时间冲刺，成功考入北京对外贸易学院（现对外经济贸易大学）的英语专业。由于基础差底子薄，一开始他连学校的课程都跟不上，但他刻苦钻研，最终以成绩优异留校任教并获取硕士学位。1986 年，林超伦迎来人生的另一次转机，获得了英国兰卡斯特大学攻读语言学博士的机会。他曾这样感叹道："刚来英国时，每天都会有新发现——原来世界还可以这样运转，感觉整个生命被拓宽了。"

潜心研究，持之以恒。读博期间，适应新环境并不容易，但林超伦像一块海绵一样吸收新知识。他经常去酒吧，不是为了娱乐，而是和不同的人聊天学习地道表达，融入英国人的生活，他通常一待就是两小时，回家后还要复盘，温习在聊天过程中学到的语言。另外，林超伦还做过保险销售。他拜访了 300 多户英国家庭，跟他们聊家庭、人生乃至夫妻关系。这些经历，让他对真实的英国家庭生活和英国语言文化都有了进一步了解。博士毕业后，林超伦到英国广播公司国际广播部工作。

日积月累，厚积薄发。一天，林超伦在工作时，遇见英中贸易协会接见中国一个贸易代表团打电话来英国广播公司中文部，急需翻译，于是邀请他担任那次会议的临时翻译。由于表现出色，他又被推荐给英国贸易工业部等政府部门。1995 年，他首次为时任英国首相约翰·梅杰会见中国政府代表团做翻译。此后他担任了更多重要外事活动的译员角色。

目光敏锐、远见深刻。随着中国的崛起，在英国的中文服务需求也日益旺盛，林超伦顺势成立了自己的翻译公司 KL Communications。从自己做口译跨度到创立口译公司并非易事，公司业务量增长很快，但同时也面临挑战。面对公司培养高质量员工的效率不足的问题，林超伦结合自己多年口译经验，提出并实践了高级口译大规模培训计划，口译员培训过程得到优化。他积极营造企业文化，为了让员工对公司产生更深刻的认同感和归属感，公司向员工派发股权，让员工的个人成长和公司发展相结合。之后林超伦为了适应市场的变化，开始着手研发线上英语课程和付费知识内容。

冯道曾在《天道》一诗中感叹道："但知行好事，莫要问前程。"林超伦曾向媒体分享了一个口译学习的秘诀，每次做完口译，他都会反思，问自己三个问题：自己哪些方面做得好？哪些方面没有做好？哪些方面本来可以做得好？长此以往，才能不断进步，在口译道路上走得越来越远。

第六章
经济发展
Economic Development

模块一　　　　　　　　　　　　　　　　　　　技能概要：
　　　　　　　　　　　　　　　　　　　　　　　　笔记符号

　　我们在第五章的口译笔记训练中提到，口译笔记是辅助学生完成口译工作的工具，是帮助学生记忆的手段。在口译中，学生要采取正确的口译笔记方法，不能因为笔记不当分散精力，导致漏听或误听，否则就是本末倒置了。因此，在口译中，学生往往会使用大量的笔记符号来代替原本复杂的语义，这样不仅大大提高了效率，也保证了其口译的准确性。不同的学生使用的口译笔记符号各不相同，一部分借鉴于已经约定俗成的符号，另一部分则由学生根据自己的需要进行创造。在口译过程中，学生根据符号的提示回忆讲话内容，降低记忆方面所耗费的精力，将更多的精力投入到输出译语方面，这样的精力分配模式能够帮助学生更好地完成口译工作。当进行口译时，记笔记是非常重要的一项技能，因为学生需要在同时听和口译的情况下，记录要点，以便更好地传达信息。以下是一些常见的口译笔记符号：

"-" 表示"连接，相关"

"√" 表示"正确；同意"

"×" 表示"错误；不同意"

"○" 表示"人或与人有关"

"△" 表示"重要或强调的信息"

"：" 表示"某人的讲话或意见"

"？" 表示"不确定或疑问句"

"！" 表示"突出或强烈的感情"

"∵" 表示"因为"

"∴" 表示"所以"

"↑" 表示"向上；增加；提升；恶化"

"↓" 表示"向下；减少；降低；改善"

"←" 表示"向内；来；因此"

"→"表示"离开；向外；导致"

"$"表示"与钱有关；金融"

"<"表示"不足；少于；优于"

">"表示"超过；超出；劣于"

  这些符号可以帮助学生在口译中更快速、更准确地记录信息。但是，不同的学生可能会使用不同的符号或方法来记笔记，这取决于个人的偏好和经验。有的口译书推荐了大量的口译符号，除了这些符号外，学生也可使用英文首字母或者其他缩写形式来替代完整书写，如 y、m、d 分别表示"年""月""日"；e 表示"经济"；cc 表示"气候变化"；inf 表示"通货膨胀"等。但是要注意缩写的统一和规范，以免造成混淆。

  除了符号，标点符号也能够帮助提高笔记效率。口译笔记中使用的标点符号要清晰、简明，以便于理解。常用的标点符号包括逗号、句号、感叹号、问号、冒号、分号、括号等。记录笔记的过程中要注意分段，每段只记录几个关键词，上下行和上下段之间的口译笔记中用因果或者箭头符号表明上下文之间的逻辑关系（如箭头、星号、横线、圆圈等，用于标注重要内容、强调、连接），也就是在实现"少些多画"的笔记策略基础上，尽量明示上下文之间的逻辑关系，以便解读笔记时候迅速理解。

  口译笔记是一把"双刃剑"，掌握了良好的笔记方法能够帮助学生更好地完成口译工作，但如果在笔记中投入过多的精力，忽略了听辨等要素，学生的目标语输出也会受到影响。因此，要通过学习和大量练习才能掌握适合自己的口译笔记方式，让自己的口译能力更上一层楼。

模块二　　译前准备

◎ 1. 背景知识

  经济发展类话题是学生在口译中经常会接触到的热门话题之一。在全球化进程如火如荼的今天，经济发展是各国各组织关注的核心问题，因此学生在平时需要储备大量相关知识，来面对口译工作中涉及该方面的话题。本模块中涉及的相关概念主要有：

  美联储加息（the interest-rate rise by the Federal Reserve）：指的是由于美国国内的高通货膨胀率，美国联邦储备系统在召开议息会议后，决定上调联邦基金利率。这是一种紧缩性货币政策，美联储希望通过这种强制干预手段，回收市场上流通的货币。

通货膨胀（inflation）：指的是在一国范围之内，该国的货币贬值所导致的物价上涨现象，一般来说发生在货币供给大于货币需求、现实购买力大于产出供给的情况之下。2020年后，美国的通货膨胀率达到了40年来的最高水平，这不仅影响了本国国民的正常生活，也波及世界经济的恢复和发展。

俄乌冲突（the conflict between Russia and Ukraine）：指的是自2014年克里米亚危机爆发后，北约持续东扩，俄罗斯和乌克兰在双方边界不断摩擦，最终于2022年2月爆发的俄乌军事冲突。该事件不仅影响了区域的和平与稳定，也对世界范围内的经济形势造成了严重冲击。

国际金融组织（International Finance Organization）：国际金融组织是由多个国家共同创建的金融机构，旨在促进全球金融稳定和经济增长。这些组织提供贷款、技术援助、投资和其他支持，以帮助发展中国家和其他经济体发展经济、减轻贫困和促进可持续发展。

超发（overissue）：金融学是指国家发行的货币面值总额大于经济价值总量，经济正常运行的货币发行量应该是小于或等于经济价值总量的70%，否则会引起通货膨胀等一系列问题。

SWIFT（Society for Worldwide Interbank Financial Telecomm）：环球同业银行金融电讯协会是国际银行间非营利性国际合作组织，支持几乎所有货币的支付。它成立于1973年，为银行的结算提供了安全、可靠、快捷、标准化、自动化的通信业务，大大提高了银行的结算速度。美国对SWIFT支付系统的控制，是与美元在全球货币体系中的地位密切相关的。

◎ 2. 核心词汇

Federal Reserve	美联储	nascent	新生的，初期的
strip out	剥离，拆除	spike	猛增
volatile	动荡不安的，易挥发的	defy	违抗，不服从
year-on-year	与上年同期数字相比的	bloc	集团，阵营
monetary tightening	货币紧缩	contraction	收缩，萎缩
S&P 500 Index	标准普尔500指数	hawkish tone	鹰牌腔调
dodge	躲开，施计回避	bond pricing	证券定价
clogged	堵塞的	Zimbabwe	津巴布韦
resilient	有弹性的	Venezuela	委内瑞拉
doom-monger	末世论者；散布恐怖威胁论的人		

模块三　　　　　　　　　　　　　　　　　　　　语料实训

任务 1. 英译汉
难度级别：★★★★

> 训练要点：本文介绍了通货膨胀对美国经济的影响。专业术语较少，数字信息丰富，全文按时间顺序行进。学生在记笔记过程中应避免误记漏记数字信息，使用笔记符号（如"%"表示"百分比"，"↑"表示"增长"，"↓"表示"下降"，"!"表示"令人惊讶"，缩写"m"表示"月"，"Fed"表示"美联储"等）进行记录，同时使用竖向记录厘清逻辑脉络。注意平衡书写笔记和听辨之间的矛盾，笔记记下的是重点，而不是全部。

The US Economy: Fed Res

America's inflation fever may be breaking at last.

"We will stay the course until the job is done, " said Jerome Powell, the Federal Reserve's chairman, on December 14th, shortly after the central bank's latest interest-rate rise. As a statement of intent, his words were both straightforward and utterly sensible. But what it means for the job to be done is becoming a matter of controversy.

Inflation remains uncomfortably high. Meanwhile, the aggressive monetary tightening of the past year is only now filtering through to the economy, complicating assessments of whether the Fed has in fact done enough to rein in prices. Promisingly, after a difficult two years, inflation does appear to be easing its grip on the American economy.

Overall prices increased by a mere 0.1% month-on-month in November, according to data published on December 13th, making for that rarest of recent occurrences: a downside surprise. Most encouraging was a breakdown showing that core inflation, which strips out volatile food and energy costs, had decelerated for a second consecutive month. Investors and analysts, scarred by America's relentless run of inflation, have learned to restrain their hopes after a single month of rosy data.

Year-on-year rates of inflation remain elevated at 7.1% for headline inflation. But the disinflation in November follows a similarly cheerful batch of data for October. Optimism is on the rise, albeit still mostly of the cautious rather than the unbridled kind. Since mid-October the S&P 500 Index of leading American firms has recovered some of the ground it lost earlier this year. Concerns are shifting to the prospect of weaker growth. Many economists forecast a recession early next year.

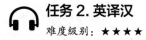

任务 2. 英译汉
难度级别：★★★★

> 训练要点：本文介绍了俄乌冲突对欧元区经济发展状况的影响，含有少量数字信息和专有名词。学生在记笔记过程中要善于运用笔记符号（如"×"表示"否定"，"%"表示"百分比"，"↑"表示"上升"，"↓"表示"下降"等）加快速度；同时也要厘清框架和逻辑，用逻辑符号指代上下文关系，便于解读笔记并迅速输出译文。听辨与记笔记的精力匹配矛盾是学生遇到的常见问题，需要大量的训练才能有效协调两者的精力匹配。

Wartime Economics

Europe dodges recession, but the continent's new normal looks grim. After three years of pandemic shutdowns, reopening booms, war, clogged supply chains and nascent inflation, European policymakers thought that 2023 would be the year the old continent returned to a new normal of decent growth and sub-2% inflation. Europe's economy is indeed settling down. Unfortunately, though, the new normal is considerably uglier than economists had expected.

Start with the positives. The Eurozone has proved remarkably resilient, considering the shock of Russia's conflict with Ukraine and the energy crisis. Gas is now cheaper than it was on the eve of the conflict, after prices spiked last summer. Governments were not forced to ration energy as had been feared at first, in part thanks to unseasonably warm weather. Headline inflation, having reached a record 10.6% in October, is falling. Nor, as doom-mongers predicted, has industry collapsed because of the cost of fuel.

In Germany, energy-intensive factories have seen output drop by a fifth since the war started, as imports replaced domestic production. But production overall had fallen just 3% by the end of the year, in line with the pre-pandemic trend. The latest IFO survey shows manufacturers as optimistic as they were before COVID-19. Although Germany's economy shrank slightly in the fourth quarter of 2022, the Eurozone defied expectations of recession.

According to the European Commission's latest forecast, the bloc will avoid a contraction this quarter, too. Recent sentiment surveys support this projection.

The widely watched purchasing-managers' index (PMI) has risen in recent months, suggesting a rosier picture is emerging in manufacturing and, especially, services.

Economic stability keeps people in jobs. The number in work across the bloc rose again in the fourth quarter of 2022. The unemployment rate is at its lowest since the euro came into existence in 1999; in surveys, firms indicate appetite for new workers. And jobs keep people spending. Despite high energy prices, consumption contributed half a percentage point to quarterly growth in the second and third quarters of 2022.

In many countries, "The energy shock takes time to affect consumers because high prices are only passed on with a lag," says Jens Eisenschmidt of Morgan Stanley, a bank, "In the meantime, financial help from governments has helped households spend."

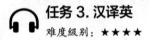

任务 3. 汉译英
难度级别：★★★★

> 训练要点：本文介绍了通货膨胀的概念，文字通俗易懂，文体简明扼要娓娓道来，逻辑脉络十分清楚。学生在记笔记过程中要根据文章脉络记录，分清主次，不要在笔记中记录过多的非重点信息，以免误听漏听。同时可以使用符号"?"表示"问题"，"-"表示"相关"，"$"表示"货币"等。

什么是通货膨胀？

这几年，我们经常听到津巴布韦人民上街买菜，需要拉一车的钞票出门、委内瑞拉纸币面额再创新高等新闻。而这些信息的背后，都有一个共同点，那就是通货膨胀。

通货膨胀是指在纸币流通条件下，因为货币供给大于货币实际需求，导致货币贬值，从而引起的一段时间内物价持续而普遍的上涨现象。其实对这种现象的简单理解就是东西贵了，钱变得不值钱了。

例如委内瑞拉，这个国家的通胀严重到什么地步呢？几乎人人都是百万富翁，但工资只买得起一公斤的肉。货币的严重贬值使得人们宁愿以物换物。也许有的人会说，这已经比去年好了吧？但委内瑞拉通胀形成是多种因素衍生的结果，除了货币超发，还有政策因素、国际大宗商品价格因素等。

所以通胀都是那么可怕的吗？其实不是，上面的例子是关于恶性通胀的，而并非全部通胀都是恶性的。通胀也分恶性通胀、低通胀等。事实上，适当的通胀能刺激经济增长，适度的通胀、产品价格上涨会刺激厂商生产，同时也会逐步改变人们的消费模式，因为价格总是涨的，人们就有消费或者生产的冲动，就有利于发展经济。

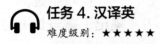

> 训练要点：本文介绍了俄乌冲突以来，美国、欧盟等对俄罗斯实施多方面制裁，全球经济和俄罗斯经济受到了影响。文章内含较多专业术语，学生在记笔记时要注意专业术语的记录，可选取单词首字母（如"R"表示"俄罗斯"，"We"表示"世界经济"，"m"表示"月"，符号"↓"表示"冲击"，"$"表示"金融相关"等）进行记录，以提高效率。文章的专业背景强，语速较快，都增加了记笔记的难度。要结合前几个章节的听辨要点，将听辨知识与笔记结合，记录关键信息。

俄乌冲突下全球经济秩序面临调整

自 2022 年 2 月俄乌冲突爆发，至今已过去一年，这是冷战结束以来最重大的地缘政治事件。美国对俄罗斯实施了九轮制裁，给俄罗斯经济带来一系列挑战，制裁引发的反噬效应和溢出效应对欧洲经济、全球产业链和世界经济稳定也造成严重冲击。制裁压力下，俄罗斯经济表现超出预期，显现较强韧性，欧洲经济受制裁反噬陷入困境，中俄经贸合作不断深化。

从世界经济发展大趋势看，全球经济秩序面临深度调整。制裁下，俄罗斯经济表现超出预期。美国对俄罗斯实施大规模极限制裁，其强度、范围和系统性不同以往。制裁由美国发起，欧盟跟进。参与制裁的国家和地区达 48 个，制裁措施密集。

2014 年至 2022 年 2 月 22 日，美国对俄罗斯实施了 2 695 项制裁，而从 2022 年 2 月 23 日到 4 月 21 日，美国新增对俄罗斯制裁措施 9 138 项，截至 2023 年 1 月 8 日共 12 695 项。制裁内容严厉，包括冻结俄罗斯央行外汇储备，把俄罗斯 11 家最重要的银行踢出 SWIFT 系统、禁止使用美元、欧元、英镑、日元交易等金融制裁，还包括对俄罗斯军工和民用实体经济部门实施全面出口管制、对石油天然气及其制品限价制裁、对俄罗斯企业组织和个人制裁。

在大规模制裁冲击下，俄罗斯金融市场 2022 年 3 月上旬出现严重混乱，卢布汇率贬值 50% 以上，国际结算和物流受阻。出口管制和禁运导致依赖国际供应链的企业生产停顿。

而进口品匮乏和国内企业生产停顿引发商品市场剧烈波动，物价快速上涨。在此背景下，4月11日世界银行预测，2022年俄罗斯经济将出现11.2%的负增长。

模块四　　　　　　　　　　　　　　　技巧点拨：笔记示范与分析

🎧 任务1. 英译汉

>> 例一
难度级别：★★★

The US economy added nearly half a million jobs in March. **The Dow Jones Industrial Average** is within 6% of its record high. And US households accumulated roughly $2.5 trillion in excess savings throughout the pandemic. Still, despite all the good news, predictions of an impending recession are widespread on **Wall Street**.

词汇

the Dow Jones Industrial Average
道琼斯工业平均指数

Wall Street
华尔街

译文

3月，美国增加了近50万个就业岗位，道琼斯工业平均指数涨幅创下6%的新高，美国家庭在疫情间的储蓄总额累计达到近2.5万亿美元。尽管这些都是好消息，但是华尔街却普遍认为美国经济即将陷入衰退。

笔记策略分析

本段落先是列出了美国经济中的三个好消息，然后在最后一句中得出与之相反的结论，逻辑结构清晰。听辨中的核心信息，分别是三个现象（added jobs、Dow Jones Industrial Average、households excess savings）和结论（recession），同时也要注意前后两者的转折关系，在本段中这种转折关系通过still和despite两词体现出来。在笔记学习中，学生要训练用适当的逻辑所指线条体现上下文之间的逻辑。如果数字信息无法准确地记录下来，学生要进行大致描述，比如"新增了很多就业岗位"。

笔记要点

1. 把握段落框架，把握三个现象和结论之间的转折关系。

2. 注意"数字+修饰信息",如 50,000 em、6% DJ 和 saving 250m。如果只是记下数字,不知道数字所修饰的信息,记录数字是无意义的。

>> **例二**
难度级别:★★★★

Former **Treasury Secretary**, Lawrence Summers, emphasized in a recent *Washington Post* **op-ed** that current economic conditions are undeniably reminiscent of previous pre-recession periods in US history. "Over the past five years, every time inflation has exceeded 4% and unemployment has gone below 5%, the US economy is gone into a recession within two years," Summers wrote. Today, the US inflation rate is nearing 8%, and the unemployment rate fell to just 3.6% in March. As a result, Summers now sees an 80% chance of a US recession by next year.

○ **词汇**

Treasury Secretary
(美国)财政部部长

Washington Post op-ed
《华盛顿邮报》专栏文章

译文

美国财政部前部长劳伦斯·萨默斯在近期发表在《华盛顿邮报》上的一篇专栏文章中强调,当前的经济状况无疑让人联想起美国历史上几次衰退前的情形。萨默斯写道:"在过去 75 年间,每次通胀率超过 4%,失业率降到 5% 以下,美国经济就会在两年内陷入衰退。"如今,美国通胀率接近 8%,失业率在 3 月降至 3.6%。因此萨默斯认为美国有 80% 的概率将在明年陷入经济衰退。

笔记策略分析

本段主要有两个信息点:第一个是美国财政部前部长的专栏文章主旨,第二个是阐述经济衰退。在信息量较大、数字密集的情况下,记笔记时不需要把所有内容都记录下来,只要记下主要逻辑框架和关键信息点即可,比如:

current → e↓（注意符号含义）

   infl 4
   unem 5 }reces
now: infla 8
   umemploy 3.6

→明年 recess

以上笔记将笔记层次、符号等都收入其中。学生始终记住笔记是短时记忆的辅助,避免精力分配不当造成口译失误。

笔记要点

1. 掌握本段逻辑框架，在笔记中标注清楚。
2. 如果不能将数字和修饰的文字信息一起记下，只记录数字是无效的。

🎧 任务 2. 汉译英

》**例一**
难度级别：★★★★

世界经济论坛 16 日发布《首席经济学家展望报告》指出，大多数经济学家认为，受**地缘政治**局势紧张、美欧可能进一步收紧货币政策等因素影响，今年世界经济预计陷入衰退，欧盟国家经济增长前景尤为黯淡。报告显示，近三分之二的受访首席经济学家预测，2023 年，世界经济预计出现衰退。世界经济论坛执行董事萨迪亚扎西迪指出，世界经济正处于不稳定状态，当前的高通胀、低增长、高债务、高碎片化环境，使得为恢复经济增长和改善世界最脆弱群体生活水平而进行所需投资的动力减少。

词汇

世界经济论坛
World Economic Forum

《首席经济学家展望报告》
the *Chief Economist Outlook Report*

地缘政治
geopolitical

译文

According to the *Chief Economist Outlook Report* released by the World Economic Forum on the 16th, most economists believe that affected by geopolitical tensions, the United States and Europe may further tighten monetary policy and other factors, the world economy is expected to fall into recession this year. The economic growth prospects of EU countries are particularly bleak. The report shows that nearly 2/3 of the chief housing economists predict. In 2023, the world economy is expected to decline, said Sadiazazidi, Executive Director of the World Economic Forum. The world economy is in an unstable state. The current environment is characterized by high inflation, low growth, high debt and high fragmentation. This will reduce the impetus for investment needed to restore economic growth and improve the living standards of the world's most vulnerable groups.

笔记策略分析

本段逻辑脉络清晰，主要可分为两部分内容：第一部分是报告中的详细情况介绍，第二部分是执行董事的观点，数字信息较少，但并列信息较多，在笔记时要特别注意。在笔记中遇到 2~4 个或者更多并列成分时，要注意记录的效率，通常情况下学生会采用脑记一半、笔记一半的方法进行记录，但一定要在笔记中标示出并列成分的数量，以避免漏译。

笔记要点

1. 注意信息分层记录，梳理文章脉络，使译文更加清晰。
2. 要格外注意并列信息的笔记，避免漏记。

例二
难度级别：★★★

2022 年 12 月，美国**消费者价格指数**虽然**环比**下降 0.1%，但与前年同期相比，却增长 6.5%。由于通胀水平仍处高位，美国民众对美国经济的预期继续持悲观态度。根据**芝加哥商品交易所集团**的一项跟踪数据，去年美国 12 月消费者价格指数发布后，市场预计美联储将在 1 月底会议上加息 25 个基点的可能性飙升至 93.2%。

词汇

消费者价格指数
consumer price index

环比
month-on-month

芝加哥商品交易所集团
Chicago Mercantile Exchange Group

译文

In December 2022, although the US consumer price index fell by 0.1% month-on-month, it increased by 6.5% compared with the same period of the previous year. As inflation is still at a high level, the American people continue to be pessimistic about the expectations of the US economy. According to a tracking data of the Chicago Mercantile Exchange Group, after the consumer price index of the United States was released in December last year, the probability that the Federal Reserve will raise interest rates by 25 basis points at its meeting at the end of January is expected to soar to 93.2%.

笔记策略分析

本段主要含有两个信息点：一个是美国消费者价格指数较高，另一个是芝加哥商品交易所提供的一项数据信息。在笔记时要注意分层记录，梳理清楚，便于输出。同时也要注意本段中的两个日期和四个百分比数字，在记录中要避免误记。学生还要注意使用笔记策略，如省略重复信息等，加快笔记效率。本段信息中，日期是次要信息，如果兼顾不了，可以放弃部分信息。

> **笔记要点**

1. 注意信息分层记录，把握逻辑框架。
2. 正确记录数字信息，避免出错。

>> **例三**
难度级别：★★★

当地时间 7 日，**欧盟委员会**发表声明称，俄乌冲突持续，能源成本高企，欧盟经济遇到严重干扰。根据**国家援助临时危机框架**，欧盟委员会批准了价值 1 亿欧元的**斯洛文尼亚援助计划**，补贴因能源账单升高而裁员或减少工时的公司，该计划旨在保持斯洛文尼亚就业水平并避免裁员。欧盟委员会批准了瑞典在俄乌冲突背景下减少电力消耗的计划，该计划将采取财政措施以支持能源削减目标。此外，委员会还批准了价值 1 500 万欧元的**芬兰担保援助计划**，以支持**奥兰地区**的电力公司正常运营。

词汇

欧盟委员会
the European Commission

国家援助临时危机框架
the temporary crisis framework for state aid

斯洛文尼亚援助计划
the Slovenian Aid Plan

芬兰担保援助计划
the Finnish Guaranteed Aid Plan

奥兰地区
the Oran region

> **译文**

On the 7th local time, the European Commission issued a statement saying that the Russian-Ukrainian conflict continued, energy costs were high, and the EU economy was seriously disrupted. According to the temporary crisis framework for state aid, the European Commission approved the Slovenian Aid Plan worth 100 million euros to subsidize companies that cut jobs or reduce working hours due to the rise of energy bills. The plan aims to maintain the employment level in Slovenia and avoid layoffs. The European Commission approved Sweden's plan to reduce electricity consumption in the context of the Russian-Ukrainian conflict, which will take financial measures to support the energy reduction target. In addition, the Committee also approved the Finnish Guaranteed Aid Plan worth 15 million euros to support the normal operation of the power companies in the Oran region.

笔记策略分析

本段主要有两大信息点，逻辑框架为并列关系。

第一层：Ru-Uran → EU eco ×

第二层：斯 + 电力↓ + 芬

具体分析，第一层是介绍俄乌冲突对欧洲经济的影响；第二层则是介绍欧盟委员会的应对措施。其中第二层应对措施包含三个信息：斯洛文尼亚援助计划、瑞典减少电力消耗计划和芬兰担保援助计划。在笔记中要注意分层记录，这种逻辑再现对笔记记录的缩进要求比较高。本段中有一个日期和两个数字信息，要格外注意中英文大额数字信息的转化，一般可采用"点三杠四"法（具体方法详见下章的数字讲解部分）进行记录，但本段中的数字信息是整数，平时记好对应的整数英文直接译出即可，建议记录时用目标语进行记录。

笔记要点

1. 注意信息分层记录，梳理文章脉络。
2. 注意大额数字信息的中英文转化，熟记整数的对应中英文，多加练习非整数的记录和转换。

模块五   **拓展练习**

任务：经济发展口译练习

语篇 1
难度级别：★★★★

The Euro Area: Danger Zone

Europe's economy **grapples with** an acute energy shock. For the best part of a decade, rock-bottom interest rates seemed like a fact of life in the Eurozone—as did low inflation. Now consumer prices are rising at an annual rate exceeding 8%, well above the **European Central Bank's** target of 2%. Members of the bank's

词汇

grapple with
努力应对

European Central Bank
（ECB）
欧洲央行

governing council have signaled their intent to raise rates soon, a message they were expected to reaffirm at a monetary-policy meeting on June 9th, as we went to press. But the ECB finds itself in a tricky position of contending not only with surging prices, which might warrant rapid rate rises, but also gloomier growth prospects, which might warrant patience. The root cause of both developments is a severe energy-price crunch.

Prices of oil and natural gas had already been rising before Russia's conflict with Ukraine; the conflict sent them soaring higher still. These price rises have played a much bigger role in pushing up consumer-price inflation in Europe than in America, where stimulus has also been a **culprit**. Energy prices in the Eurozone—which rose at a whopping annual rate of 39% in May—are contributing about four percentage points to headline inflation, compared with two in America.

The effects are starting to spill over to other prices. "Core" inflation, which excludes food and energy prices, was higher in the Eurozone in May than economists had expected. German producer prices rose at a record clip of 33.5% in April, compared with last year, driven by not only energy, but also energy-intensive goods such as concrete and chemicals. The result is a big hit to firms' costs and households' purchasing power.

In how much danger does it put the Eurozone's economy? One consequence of the energy shock is lower household incomes in real terms. Wage growth has been picking up modestly across the zone, but still trails behind inflation. Some employers have made one-off payments to workers, to compensate them for surging prices without incurring higher recurring wage costs. Even then, however, annual pay growth in the Netherlands, where the labour market is tight, stood at just 2.8% in May. In one sense, this is good news for the ECB, because it reduces the risk of a wage-price spiral. But it may feed into lower consumption, weakening the

○ 词汇

culprit
罪魁祸首

rest of the economy in turn. A moderation in demand only adds to a heap of woes for the manufacturing sector, where confidence is already in steep decline.

Supply disruptions as a result of China's recent lockdowns and high energy prices are hurting businesses, with Germany and Eastern Europe looking most vulnerable to an industrial slowdown. New orders for the zone's manufacturers in May fell for the first time since June 2020, indicating weaker demand. Export orders declined at their fastest pace in two years. Economists are therefore penciling in slower growth over the rest of the year. But few expect an outright recession just yet. That is because some parts of the economy confront the energy shock from a position of strength, rather than weakness.

Many services firms are still reaping the rewards from the end of Omicron-related lockdowns. Southern countries are benefiting the most, given their reliance on tourism. In Spain, arrivals of sun-seeking northerners almost reached pre-pandemic levels in April. Overall, business sentiment in services remains strong, with many firms reporting a growing backlog of work.

Jobs are still plentiful, too. Across the bloc, there were three vacancies for every 100 jobs in the first quarter of 2022, a high level by historical standards. Firms' hiring expectations are solid, albeit slightly weaker since the start of the conflict with Ukraine. More than one in four businesses in Europe say that a lack of staff is preventing them from producing more.

A **hoard** of savings built up during lockdowns should also provide consumers with some **cushion** against the energy shock. According to our calculations, such "excess" savings in France and Germany amounted to a tenth of disposable incomes in the first quarter of 2022. These buffers will blunt the impact to the energy shock. But they will not offset it altogether.

Excess savings, for a start, are not evenly distributed.

词汇

hoard
囤积

cushion
缓冲

Poorer people in rich countries, and most households in poorer countries, have precious little left. In Slovakia, for example, the savings rate never rose much during the pandemic. "Consumption weakness will come from lower-income households," says Jens Eisenschmidt of Morgan Stanley. Retail sales, in real terms, have moved sideways for months. Many governments have put together spending programs to shield households from high energy prices. According to Bruegel, a think-tank in Brussels, Germany, France and others are spending between 1% and 2% of GDP. Not all of that is well-targeted, however. Much of it is going on relief for better-off households that do not need it; other measures have involved meddling with prices, with some of the benefit going to energy suppliers.

Even if the Eurozone is spared a recession, then, the energy shock will be a drag on growth. The ECB faces an **unenviable** dilemma. With every increase in inflation on the back of food and energy prices, the European economy is getting weaker.

unenviable
不值得羡慕的

Can the Economy Grow Forever?

Let's say you discover a magical gold coin that doubles every 25 years. 75 years later, you'd only have eight coins, but a thousand years later, you'd have over a trillion. And in just 4,600 years, your gold coins would outweigh the observable universe. This periodic doubling is an example of **exponential** growth, and while we're not in any danger of discovering a real-life **golden goose** coin, something almost as consequential has been growing like this for the past 200 or so years, the global economy.

Many economists think that an eternally growing economy is necessary to keep improving people's lives, and that if the global economy stops growing, people would fight more over the fixed

exponential
越来越快的；指数的

golden goose
能够产生巨大利润或带来巨大优势的事物

amount of value that exists, rather than working to generate new value. That raises the question: is infinite growth possible on a finite planet?

We measure economic growth by tracking the total financial value of everything a country or the world produces and sells on the market. These products can help us meet basic needs or improve our individual and collective quality of life. But they also crucially take resources to invent, build or maintain.

For example, this smartphone. It's valuable in part because it contains **aluminum**, **gallium** and **silicon**, all of which took energy and resources to mine, purify, and turn into a phone. It's also valuable because of all the effort that went into designing the hardware and writing the software. And it's also valuable because a guy in a black **turtleneck** got up on stage and told you it was.

So how do we grow the total financial value of all things? One way is to make more things. Another way is to invent new things. However you do it, growing the economy requires resources and energy. And eventually, won't we just run out? To answer this question, let's consider what goes into the economy and what comes out of it. Its inputs are labor, capital, which you can think of, and money and natural resources, water or energy. Its output is value.

Over the past 200 years, economies have gotten exponentially more efficient at producing value. If we, as a species, are able to keep upgrading our economies so that they get ever more efficient, we could theoretically **pump out** more and more value using the same or, let's be really ambitious here, fewer resources.

So how do we do that? How do we increase efficiency with new technologies? This is where we **hit a snag**. New tech, in addition to making things more efficient, can also generate new demand, which ends up using more resources. We're actually not in **imminent** danger of running out of most resources, but we have a much bigger and more immediate problem. A global economy, and in particular those of rich countries, are driving climate change and destroying valuable natural environments on which all of us depend, soil, forests, fisheries and countless other resources that help keep our civilization running. So what should we do?

This is where economists disagree. Most economists think that new ideas will be able to fix most of these problems. They argue that in the same way that exponentially increasing resource and energy use have fueled exponential economic growth, human ingenuity has also increased exponentially and will rise to meet these challenges in ways that we simply can't predict. For example, between 2000 and 2014, Germany grew their GDP by 16 %, while cutting CO_2 emissions by 12 %. That's impressive, but it's not cutting emissions fast enough to limit warming to 1.5 degrees Celsius.

For this reason and others, some economists think the solution is to re-engineer our economies completely. They make the case that what we should really be doing is **weaning** ourselves from the addiction to growth and shifting to a post-growth economy. What would that look like? A post-growth economy wouldn't assume that the economy should grow. Instead, it would require us to focus on improving what we really need, things like renewable energy, health care and public transportation. To do that, post-growth economists suggest that rich countries should do things like guarantee living wages, reduce wealth and income inequality and ensure universal access to public services like health care. In such an economy, people would be theoretically less dependent on their jobs to earn their living or get healthcare. So it might be more feasible to scale down production of things deemed less necessary.

But this raises other questions: Who gets to define what's necessary? How would we resolve the inevitable disagreements? Could we really do away with entire industries? The "we'll come up with new ideas to solve these problems" approach can

○ 词汇

wean
断奶；断了念头

seem as realistic as well a magical gold coin. And the "we have to fundamentally change our economies" approach can seem politically **daunting**, particularly in rich countries. One way or another, we have to find a way to benefit everyone while also taking care of our planet.

○ 词汇

daunting
使人畏惧的，使人气馁的

模块六

译海拾贝：口译中听不懂的对策

口译员在执业过程中遇到最大的问题集中在两点：听不懂、翻错了。除了基本功因素之外，其他多种原因也会导致口译中听不懂话。

听不懂的原因

原因一：源语的专业性较强。口译工作常见的工作领域包括政治、经济、文化、贸易、商务、技术、医学、法律等。除了政治、经济、文化、贸易和商务领域的词汇和背景知识相对简单，诸如技术领域（如化工、机械、设备器械）、医学和法律等行业的口译工作，具有专业词汇密集、背景知识复杂等特点，如果不经过大量的译前准备，熟悉词汇和了解行业知识背景，即使口译基本功再高都无法胜任这些工作。

原因二：语速较快。母语英语的操持者正常语速是 140~180 单词/分钟，如果每分钟的讲话速度在 120 单词以下属于慢语速，高于 180 单词/分钟属于较快的。常见的外媒中，VOA 的语速为 140 单词/分钟，VOA 慢速英语的速度是 90 单词/分钟，BBC 在 150~180 单词/分钟。快语速的情况下，无论是陪同、交传还是同传，译员的转换和记忆压力都会增大，从而影响口译效果。译员可以在平时训练中多加入快语速的音频视频资料来适应快语速的翻译场景。

原因三：发言人口音较重。国际交往中除了英语母语操持者外，译员经常会遇到非母语的发言人，一场国际会议只有英美国家或者澳大利亚、加拿大的发言人，这只能是理想状态；实际情况是，既然是国际会议，必然会有来自世界各地的发言人操持着南腔北调的英语，译员需要听得懂印度英语、日本英语、非洲英语等各种口音的英语才能胜任国际会议译员的角色。平时学习中，可以通过联合国官网、世界经济论坛官网等途径多练习非母语演讲者的视频和音频，熟悉不同英语的发音特征，才能在实战中得心应手。

解决方案

会前做大量深入的准备工作是有效防止口译中听不懂的最有效手段,熟练掌握相关词汇,适度了解所处行业的背景知识,能够帮助现场联想,并通过掌握的知识串联没有掌握的知识,形成有效的上下文信息提示。

会前尽量与讲者沟通,熟悉其口音。特别是在联络口译、陪同口译和交替传译的场合,事前与讲者沟通,约定讲话时长,因为有的讲者喜欢滔滔不绝讲很久才停下来让译员翻译,这会明显增加翻译难度。如果讲的时间过长,可以通过手势等提醒讲者,及时中停,给译员翻译时间。

即使是一个身经百战的译员,也会偶尔在口译中出现听不懂的情况。如果听不懂,特别是在陪同口译和交替传译中,译员可以和讲者沟通,请求对方再说一遍,或者用通俗的话语将术语较多信息复杂的内容解释一下。有的译员碍于情面,觉得这样做会降低翻译效果,导致观众不信任,但是这比起翻译不准要更有性价比。

需要说明的是,没有一个翻译是完美的,没有一个翻译是不犯错误的。哪怕是一场评价极高的翻译现场,也都会有小瑕疵。比如在1972年尼克松访华时,尼克松说:"《中美联合公报》发布后,中美两国之间的距离就更近一步了,况且本来就不是太远,也就是1.7万英里左右……"结果外交部译员的四朵金花之一的章含之翻译成了1700英里。精通英语的周总理笑着说:"含之,太近了点儿吧。"章含之纠正后,尼克松却幽默地说道:"那样更好,中美两国的距离岂不是更近了!"章含之随之纠正了其译文。翻译发现错误,需要视情形进行纠正。比如同传现场,当时纠正会影响下文的正常翻译,可以简单记录,全文翻译结束时再补充说明。如果错误不严重,并不影响实质性内容的交流,翻译可以选择不修正。

模块七

**译员风采:
四代领导人译员施燕华**

我国外交部译员队伍中,走出很多优秀的外交官,施燕华就是其中一员。她出生于普通劳动人民家庭,为新中国的四代领导人做翻译,职业生涯在翻译和外交官两个角色之间交替转换并多有建树,与同是学外语出身的外交官丈夫吴建民为中国的外交事业做出不可磨灭的贡献。前外交部长杨洁篪这样评价道:"她是公认的外交翻译佼佼者。她长期担任中国领导人的口译,有大量的一线翻译实践经验。1991—1994年,她担任外交部翻译室主任，领导过外交部的翻译班子，在翻译理论上也颇有造诣。"

1939年12月，位于上海东台路的普通家庭里迎来了一个未来会影响新中国外交事业的新生命。身为家中的第六个孩子，她目睹了父母哺育他们兄弟姐妹九人的辛苦过程。贫寒的家境、艰难的成长过程让这九个孩子只能依靠自身的努力。正如施燕华和弟弟施良驹共著的《也同风雨也同晴：我们姐妹兄弟》一书中所提到过的："生长在我们这样经济条件、生活环境都不好的家庭的孩子，何以能成长为驻外大使、光通信专家、作家、高级工程师、科学家、艺术家、高级教师等，并在各自的工作岗位上焕发出自己的光彩？"正是这种艰苦又有爱的家庭环境铸就了施燕华吃苦耐劳、坚毅果敢的性格。

1958年，19岁的施燕华考入北京外国语学院，大学毕业后又考取了本校的研究生，并于1965年成为外交部实习生，从此开启了自己的翻译外交生涯。彼时正值新中国百废待兴之际，外交方面也是如此，因此刚加入外交部的施燕华成为第一批被派往美国的外交官，于1971—1975年作为中国常驻联合国代表团其中的一员，负责口译及笔译工作，成为这一重大历史事件的见证人之一。1971年10月25日是无数中国人难以忘怀的一天，全球目光汇聚在美国纽约的联合国大厦，一场历时20余年的申请即将落下帷幕。128个国家的代表团齐聚联合国大厦，为联合国第2758决议投票，这个决议关乎是否恢复中国在联合国的合法席位、是否将台湾当局驱逐出联合国。当电子计票牌显示出最终结果的那一刻，全场响起了热烈的掌声。中华人民共和国在联合国的合法席位最终以76票赞成、35票反对、17票弃权的压倒性多数得以通过。

1975年，施燕华回国后到外交部翻译室工作，担任各位中央领导人的翻译，此后十年，在中美建交谈判、中美联合公报谈判等重大场合，施燕华始终跟随在周恩来、邓小平等领导人的身边。身为四代领导人译员的翻译生涯为其日后担任外交官工作奠定了扎实的基础。

1985年后，施燕华陆续被派往联合国、比利时、卢森堡、法国担任参赞、大使等职位。2003年她卸任回国后担任外交部外语专家。在此段工作期间，施燕华陆续出版了很多译作，并于2022年4月获得中国翻译协会"翻译文化终身成就奖"。作为资深的外交家和翻译家，施燕华对翻译工作提出了很多重要的指导原则，认为"高层会谈政治性很强，要求准确完整，有时甚至要牺牲语言的美"。

首先，译者要保持政治敏感度。这和杨洁篪主张的"首先要有一颗拳拳报国之心，要有过硬的政治素质和很高的政策水平，同时要刻苦、勤奋、细致、认真"的外交翻译精神是互相映射的。譬如"缓和"一词的翻译，今天我们会用relaxation，而非detente，后者是用来形容冷战时期美苏之间关系的"虚假缓和"，滥用词汇会给政治关系蒙上一层不友好的烙印。

其次，翻译要精准通顺。受到周总理"完整准确、通顺易懂"所指示的翻译精神的深深影响，施燕华主张翻译要以准确为目标。施燕华以《中美联合建交公报》为例，介绍了短短270个字英文单词中所含的政治复杂性和严谨性。比如我国提出在台湾问题上要"断交、废约、撤军"。我方的译文是："The United States must sever its diplomatic relations with Taiwan"，而美方措辞为"On that same day, January 1, 1979, the United States of America will notify Taiwan that it is terminating diplomatic relations..."。双方用词焦点在于 sever 和 terminate。不同措辞表现出双方在建交过程中的高度政治敏感度和复杂性。我方的立场是"一刀两断"，考虑到美方的措辞"表示有一个过程，语气比较缓和"，经过审议，我方接受了美方的用词。

作为历史风云变幻的亲历者，施燕华无比感慨，她感叹道："我能感受到我所做的事情真的是实实在在为国家，这让我感到骄傲。""现在如果再让我选择，我还会选择外交。"如今，年近90岁的施燕华仍在为推进中外交流做出自己的贡献。

第七章

银行
Bank

模块一

技能概要：数字

数字信息是商务交往的重要组成部分。数字翻译能力不过关会影响翻译准确性、降低翻译信度；数字口译不准确会给商务交往带来困扰，甚至导致生意失败。因此准确翻译数字信息是学生绕不开的一个话题。中英数字信息的翻译难度主要是中英语言数位不对应所造成的。在进行复杂数字翻译时，学生需要进行数位转换。在数字口译中，学生要准确转换数字，但是如果学生纠结于具体数字而忽略数字所修饰的具体内容，会造成输出卡顿、信息丢失、语速明显慢于讲者，导致翻译质量下降。

本模块将按照由简到难、循序渐进的原则，从以下两个方面分别训练数字翻译的技能：第一，数字记录与转换；第二，数字相关搭配与表达法。

1. 数字记录与转换

（1）基本数位对应

整数常常以数字加单位的形式出现，具有数字大、位数少的特点，同时也是学生在实际口译当中最常遇见的数字形式之一。因此在口译时，数字记录的难度不大，学生应多将注意力放在数字转换上，甚至在听到数字时同步进行数字转换，并记录转换好的数字。要实现这一点，学生要做到：

①牢记常见中英数字单位换算。

下表为常见的中英数字对照表：

一百（100）	one hundred
一千（1,000）	one thousand
一万（10,000）	ten thousand
十万（100,000）	one hundred thousand

续表

百万（1,000,000）	one million
千万（10,000,000）	ten million
一亿（100,000,000）	one hundred million
十亿（1,000,000,000）	one billion
百亿（10,000,000,000）	ten billion
千亿（100,000,000,000）	one hundred billion
万亿（1,000,000,000,000）	one trillion

由上表可知，中英文的"百""千""百万""十亿""万亿"是相互对应的，而"万""十万""千万""亿""百亿""千亿"等则需通过借位转化。学生要牢记"万""十万""千万""亿"等常见单位的换算，通过记忆机制形成自动加工转换能力，就可以加快口译输出速度、提升准确性。在记录时，汉语中每四个数为一个单位，只需在听到"万"和"亿"时，将其缩写为"w"和"y"；英语中每三个数为一个单位，只需在听到 thousand、million、billion、trillion 时，将其缩写为"t""m""b""tr"。其中 thousand 也可用"k"来记录。

例如：

原文	记录方式1	记录方式2	翻译
90万	90w	900k	nine hundred thousand
10亿	10y	1b	one billion
800 million	800m	8y	八亿
70 thousand	70k	7w	七万

②巧妙运用小数点

该技巧的具体操作方法如下：在翻译较大数字时，先确定最大的单位，后面加小数点，之后的数字顺次读出即可。在熟练掌握了第一种方法之后，可以巧妙运用添加小数点的方法，使翻译出来的数字更加简洁，进一步提高口译速度，减轻记忆负荷。数字的读法经常有多种，尽量选择简易版本的读法，缩短输出时间。

例如：

原文	笔记1	笔记2	简约译文	复杂译文
65亿	65y	6.5b	six point five billion	six billion, five hundred million
568万	568w	5.68m	five point six eight million	five million, six hundred and eighty thousand
54 thousand	54k	5.4w	5.4万	五万四千
78 million	78m	7800w	7800万	

（2）多位数对应

在听辨和记录多位数时，通常是按照"听到什么写什么"的规律。而在翻译多位数时，普遍采用的是"点三杠四"的方法。即英译汉时，按照中文的数字规律，从右往左数，每四个数字为一组，用斜杠隔开，每个斜杠从右往左分别代表万、亿、万亿；汉译英时，按照英文的数字规律，从右往左数，每三个数字为一组，用逗号分隔开，每个逗号从右往左分别代表thousand、million、billion、trillion。

例如：

原文	记录	转换	翻译
五十六亿七千八百九十六万三千四百零九	56y7896w3409	5, 6y78, 96w3, 409	five billion, six hundred and seventy-eight million, nine hundred and sixty-three thousand, four hundred and nine
seventy-eight million, six hundred and seventy-seven thousand, eight hundred and nighty	78m677t890	78m67/7t890	七千八百六十七万七千八百九十

由于汉语中每四个数字为一个单位，英语中每三个数字为一个单位，汉语中读数不会读出两个连续的0，英语中如果0处于一个单位内的最前面，也不会读出。因此，如果一个单位中不满三个或四个数字时，需要进行补零，补齐之后再进行"点三杠四"的操作，方能确保数字的准确性。

例如：

原文	记录	转换	翻译
seven hundred and eighty million, thirteen thousand, five hundred and sixty	780m013k560	7/80m01/3k560	七亿八千零一万三千五百六十

续表

原文	记录	转换	翻译
五千亿零一十三万零四百二十	5000y0013w0420	500, 0y00, 13w0, 420	five hundred billion, one hundred and thirty thousand, four hundred (and) twenty

2. 数字相关搭配与表达法

在口译中，准确地记录并翻译数字只是数字口译的第一步；将数字与上下文语境结合起来，输出符合规范的译语则是第二步。本小节将介绍数字相关的常见搭配及表达法，包括：（1）总数达到/超过/小于；（2）上升/增加；（3）下降/减少；（4）倍数表达法。

（1）总数达到/超过/小于

①在英语中，表示"总数达到"可用 add up to、total、reach to、amount to、come to、stand at、remain 等词语直接加数字表达，也可直接用"be + 数字"表达。

②表示"总数超过"，可用 exceed、more than、surpass、top、outnumber 等词表达。

③表示"总数小于"，可用 less than、under 等词表达。

（2）上升/增加

"上升了……"可表达为 increase by、raise by、grow by；如要表示"激增"，则可用 rocket to，或者在 increase、raise、grow 后面加上 exponentially、rapidly 等副词。

（3）下降/减少

"下降了……"可表达为 decrease by、drop by、fall by、decline by、reduce by；如要表示"急剧下降"，则可用 collapse、plunge、slump 等词。

（4）倍数表达法

倍数表达的是两个数字之间的对比。英汉双语在倍数表达上不尽相同，需注意二者之间的差异，切忌望文生义，造成翻译错误。

①倍数增加

中文表达	英文表达
A 增加到原来的 N 倍 = A 增加了 N-1 倍	A increases N times/fold.
A 是 B 的 N 倍 = A 比 B 多 N-1 倍	1. A is N times larger/bigger than B.
	2. A is N times as large/ big as B.
	3. A is N times the size/length/width of B.

②倍数减少

中文表达	英文表达
A 减少到原来的 1/N = A 减少了原来的（N−1）/N	A decreases by N times/fold.
A 是 B 的 1/N = B 是 A 的 N 倍	A is one Nth（相应数字的序数形式）of B.

需注意，若倍数是减少的，在汉语中不可表述为"A 比 B 减少了 N 倍"。中文中的翻一番指的是变成原来的两倍；翻两番则是变成原来的四倍；翻三番是变成原来的八倍，不可将其与英语中的 triple 等同。类似的数字表达在英语中数不胜数，学生应熟练掌握每一项最为常用的几种方法，而不是单一地只记一种，方能在口译中做到游刃有余。

数字是口译的难点和重点，数字翻译的准确性常常具有重大影响。学生的数字口译转换的瓶颈期会略长，但只要注意循序渐进、不断练习，就能做到迅速反应，准确输出。

模块二　译前准备

◎ 1. 背景知识

银行是支撑经济发展和现代社会正常运行的金融机构之一，按照功能，银行可以分为央行、政策性银行、商业银行、投资银行等。

本模块涉及的概念包括：

汇丰银行（HSBC）：全称香港和上海汇丰银行有限公司（The Hong Kong and Shanghai Banking Corporation Limited），简称"汇丰"，是中国香港最大的注册银行以及中国香港三大发钞银行之一，其他两个是中国银行（香港）和渣打银行。

证券公司（securities company）：从事有价证券买卖的法人企业，包括证券经营公司和证券登记公司。不同国家中对证券公司称呼不一样。美国的证券公司叫作投资银行（Investment Bank）或证券经纪商（Broker-Dealer）；英国证券公司被称作商业银行（Merchant Bank）；欧洲大陆（以德国为代表）的投资银行是作为全能银行（Universal

Bank）的一个下属部门；在东亚被称为证券公司（Securities Company）。

不良贷款（non-performing loan）：不良贷款是指借款人违约导致未能支付的贷款，分为逾期贷款（overdue loan）、呆滞贷款（idle/dead loan）和呆账贷款（bad loan）。逾期贷款指的是到合同期限，仍未能按时归还的贷款。呆滞贷款是指超过规定年限但仍未归还的贷款，或虽未逾期或逾期不满规定年限但生产经营已终止，借款人无法偿还的贷款。不良贷款会给银行带来损失风险。

风险加权资产（risk-weighted asset）：风险加权资产是指对银行的资产加以分类，根据不同类别资产的风险性质确定不同的风险系数，以这种风险系数为权重求得的资产。一般来说，风险权重与资产收益成正比。

首次公开募股（initial public offering）：也叫首股招募，是企业第一次将它的股份向公众出售，以此向公众筹集资金。首次公开上市完成后，公司即可以申请到证券交易所或报价系统挂牌交易。

投资银行（investment bank）：简称投行，具有中介功能，服务于资本市场，其金融服务包括：证券发行、承销、交易、企业重组、兼并与收购、投资分析、风险投资、项目融资等。知名的投行包括高盛（Goldman Sachs）、摩根士丹利（Morgan Stanley）、汇丰集团（HSBC Group）、瑞银集团（United Bank of Switzerland，UBS）、中国中金（China International Capital Corporation，CICC）等。

商业银行（commercial bank）：商业银行与投资银行相对。商业银行业务范围包括吸收公众存款、发放贷款以及办理票据贴现等。商业银行通常没有货币发行权。知名的商业银行包括美国银行（Bank of America）、中国工商银行（Industrial and Commercial Bank of China，ICBC）、富国银行（Wells Fargo）、中国建设银行（China Construction Bank，CCB）等。

信贷损失准备金（loan loss reserve）：信贷损失准备金又称贷款损失准备金，是银行预留的用于应付坏账的款项。如果借款人拖欠贷款，银行可以使用贷款损失准备金来降低这部分的损失。贷款损失分为预期损失和非预期损失，贷款损失准备金是与预期损失相对应的概念，其大小是由预期损失的大小决定的。

量化紧缩（quantitative tightening，QT）：量化紧缩与量化宽松（quantitative easing，QE）相对，是央行使用的一种紧缩性的货币政策工具，用于降低一个经济体中的货币供应水平、货币流动性，是应对通货膨胀的手段之一。

利空因素（negative factor）：利空因素是指使股价下跌的信息，利空常导致股市大盘整体下跌，不断的利空消息会造成股市价格不断下跌，形成"熊市"。下列因素都可以造成利空，如上市公司经营业绩恶化、银行利率调高、经济衰退、通货膨胀、天灾人祸，以及其他政治、经济军事、外交等方面促使股价下跌的不利消息。

标普 500 指数（S&P 500 Index）：标普 500 指数由标准普尔公司提出，该指数覆盖的公司均为在美国主要交易所（如纽约证券交易所、纳斯达克交易所）的上市公司。目前，这些公司的总市值超过 25 万亿美元，覆盖了美股市场约 80% 的市值。因此，该指数被认为是美国大盘股的最佳单一指标，比道·琼斯指数（Dow Jones Indexes）更具权威性。

抵押支持证券（mortgage-backed securities）：一种金融工具，由一组抵押贷款组成，这些贷款被打包成证券并出售给投资者。

◎ 2. 核心词汇

interim chief executive	临时首席执行官	Goldman Sachs	高盛集团
net profit	净利润	JPMorgan Chase	摩根大通集团
return on tangible equity (ROTE)		Bank of America	美国银行
	有形资产收益率	Citigroup	花旗集团
risk-weighted asset	风险加权资产	Wells Fargo	富国银行
Brexit	英国脱欧	mortgage-backed securities	
entwine	缠住；盘绕		抵押担保证券
lull	间歇，暂时平静；低谷期	monetary easing	放松货币政策
bonanza	富矿带；带来好运之事	chief financial officer	首席财务官
whipsaw	锯开；使受双重损失		
bumper trading revenues	丰厚的交易收入		

模块三　　　　　　　　　　　　　　　　　　　　　　　　语料实训

 任务 1. 英译汉
难度级别：★★★★★

> **训练要点**：本文介绍了汇丰银行最近面临的困境及其相应对策。本文数字和专业术语较多，数字大多是整数，具有一定难度。学生在听文本的过程中，需同时兼顾数字和语境，避免陷入盲目记下数字、忽略上下文的误

> 区，否则即使数字再准确，也没有意义。数字是笔记记录的重点内容，但数字服务于核心信息，如果没有记下核心信息，只有数字是没有意义的。学生需要平衡听辨、笔记和数字之间的关系，听辨为主、笔记为辅，数字记录辅助主要信息。

The Latest Plan of the HSBC

When Noel Quinn took over as interim chief executive of HSBC from John Flint, ousted by the board in August, analysts expected a change in style. Whereas Mr. Flint was seen as a cerebral introvert, Mr. Quinn is forthcoming, verging on blunt.

On that front, at least, HSBC's first quarterly-results announcement on his watch did not disappoint. Although its Asian business "held up well in a challenging environment", performance in other areas was "not acceptable", Mr. Quinn said on October 28th. Third-quarter net profits, down by 24% on the same period last year, to $3 billion, undershot pundits' forecasts by 14%. Revenues fell by 3.2%, to $13.4 billion, missing expectations by 3%. Return on tangible equity (ROTE), its chief measure of profitability, reached 6.4%, compared with analysts' forecast of 9.5%. Investors agreed with Mr. Quinn: the bank's shares dropped by 4.3% on the news in London. They have fallen by about 11% in the past six months.

HSBC's woes can be blamed in part on broader conditions: low interest rates, a slowing global economy, business uncertainty in Brexit-hit Britain and trade tensions (HSBC is the world's largest provider of trade finance).

Yet that is hardly likely to reassure investors. Tom Rayner of Numis Securities, a broker, points out that although some of these trends may be reversed; others, such as Brexit and the trade wars, may linger. Interest rates may well fall further. Investors are not yet pricing in any impact from protests in Hong Kong, where HSBC is the largest lender. That is too optimistic, says Fahed Kunwar, at Redburn, another broker.

Mr. Quinn does not deny the scale of the challenge. HSBC is ditching its ROTE target of 11% for 2020, and there are hints of a radical overhaul. Mr. Quinn spoke of accelerating plans to "remodel" poorly performing businesses. In August, the bank announced a plan to complete 4,700 redundancies by the end of this year. Reports suggest HSBC could seek to cut additional 8,000–10,000 jobs from its headcount of 238,000. A spokesperson declined to confirm the number of jobs to go.

Yet after years of cost-cutting, analysts are divided as to whether much more fat can be trimmed. Daniel Tabbush of Tabbush Report, an Asia-based research firm, says HSBC "is not particularly bloated". The bank may also partially exit some share-trading activities in Western markets, and wants to sell its French retail operations.

But a hasty disposal of badly performing units, which also include its American wholesale arm, may force it to write down part of their value. So hopes must be placed in the second prong of HSBC's grand reform—to move capital away from the dreariest businesses and towards "higher growth and return opportunities".

HSBC's cost-to-income ratio is 104% in Europe, compared with 43% in Asia, where it generates nearly 90% of its profits. It makes only a quarter of its lending in Britain, yet the country generates 35% of its non-performing loans, says Mr. Tabbush. Its $98 billion of risk-weighted assets allocated to America produce only $527 million in annual profit.

The bank's management has so far declined to provide any guidance as to where newly released capital might be sent. HSBC is already the largest corporate lender in Asia by market penetration, according to Greenwich Associates, a research firm. And getting more deeply into China may prove tricky. Other dynamic markets, like Vietnam and Indonesia, are tiny by comparison.

There are also limits to how much HSBC can re-jig its various lines of business. Its strength in trade finance has so far failed to translate into clout in investment banking. Global capital markets are more lucrative, but volatile. In 2018, HSBC launched a new motto, "Together We Thrive". Its difficulties may have more to do with this grand ambition than with external forces. By trying to do too much for too many people in too many places, it has seen its returns diluted. Yet even for its candid interim boss, that conclusion may be rather too blunt.

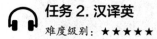

任务 2. 汉译英

难度级别：★★★★★

> **训练要点**：本文主要介绍了美国经济衰退对银行所产生的影响。本文数字数量适中，但专有名词较多，例如各大银行的名称以及经济术语，译者需做好充分的译前准备。学生在多重任务（如听辨、笔记、调动背景知识的认知加工、记录数字）中，始终要把听辨逻辑和关键词放在第一位。口译不是像复读机一样要面面俱到，而是将重点信息表达清楚流畅。本文专业术语集中、语速偏快，如果只抓细小信息，比如数字，则会导致顾此失彼。

主要银行业绩预期

当地时间13日，美国多家主要银行公布了2022年第四季度业绩。数据显示，受美国经济将陷入衰退预期的影响，各大银行普遍增加信贷损失准备金，导致其业绩受到明显的拖累。

数据显示，摩根大通银行、美国银行、花旗集团、富国银行等美国主要银行，2022年第四季度都增加了信贷损失准备金。

对此，摩根大通集团首席财务官吉里米·巴达姆13日表示，美国经济衰退预计将在2023年第四季度出现，失业率预计将升至4.9%。

美国银行首席执行官布莱恩·莫伊尼汉表示，美国经济将出现温和衰退，在悲观预测情形下，美国失业率将在2023年早些时候达到5.5%，并预计2024年年底仍维持在5%或更高水平。

花旗集团首席执行官简·弗雷泽表示，维持美国将在2023年第二季度出现温和经济衰退的预测。此前，美国经济在2022年第一季度和第二季度均出现萎缩，虽然当年第三季度按年率增长3.2%，失业率也在当年12月降至3.5%。

但专家普遍认为，当前业绩尚未充分反映出地缘政治紧张和空前量化紧缩等利空因素对相关经济数据的最终影响。瑞银集团财富管理全球首席投资官马克·黑菲尔表示，由于美联储激进加息、疫情形势变化、美元走势和劳动力成本增加等利空因素足够强大，预计标普500指数成分公司在2022年第四季度的合计盈利将不会有同比增长。

 任务3. 英译汉
难度级别：★★★★★

> 训练要点：本文介绍了银行现金激增对银行借贷所产生的影响，文中数字均为整数。学生在听文本时可直接在脑海中转化，并记录转化后的数字，将更多的精力放在听辨文本信息上，提高口译速度和准确度。

Have Banks Now Got Too Much Cash?

The fates of the economy and banks are normally closely entwined; when customers endure misfortune, loans go unpaid. The summer was marked by a lull in COVID-19 cases and recovering economic activity. Winter has brought with it more infections and shutdowns. Yet banks' profits were slender in the summer and, as fourth-quarter earnings released between January 15th and 20th revealed, fattened at the end of the year. What is going on?

One explanation is that the trading desks and investment banks housed in most big banks have fared well, thanks to a rush of initial public offerings and booming markets. Profits were sky-high at banks that earn most of their revenues from investment banking and trading. Goldman Sachs made $4.5 billion in the fourth quarter, half of its annual profits in 2020. JPMorgan Chase's investment-banking profits in the same quarter almost doubled on the year. The firm's total earnings were a record $12.1 billion in the fourth quarter.

The bread-and-butter business of commercial and consumer banking also did well. This is, in part, an accounting quirk. When expectations of repayment tumble, banks must write down the value of their assets, which they book as a loss. As a result, many reported slim profits (and in some cases, losses) in the second and third quarters, even though borrowers mostly repaid their loans. Though delinquencies inched up in the fourth quarter, it also contained hope—in the form of a vaccine.

Recovery equals repayment. So America's biggest lenders—Bank of America, Citigroup, JPMorgan and Wells Fargo—have favourably re-evaluated their loan books. In September, JPMorgan expected as much as $33.6 billion of its $1 trillion loan book to eventually go unpaid. By the end of December, a little under $1.1 billion was written off for good. But the bank also now thinks that around $1.8 billion that it had previously expected to be lost will be repaid. These averted hypothetical losses add to profits.

This bonanza is a victory for those who spent the past decade attempting to make banks safer. In the past, investment bank earnings were more tied to the economy, thanks to fat portfolios of assets like mortgage-backed securities. Now banks must hold so much capital against volatile assets that they do not bother. When markets whipsawed last year, they earned the upside (bumper trading revenues) without the downside (losses on volatile assets).

But this earnings season has also revealed how sensible rules can go awry in bizarre times. Banks are usually keen to amass customer deposits. They are cheap sources of funding; the more deposits a bank holds, the more it can lend. Over the past year, monetary easing by the Federal Reserve has injected vast amounts of cash into the banking system and led deposits to balloon. In 2020, an additional $580 billion or so piled up at JPMorgan, and $360 billion at Bank of America. On one earnings call, an analyst called these deposit mountains an "embarrassment of money for the industry".

Yet post-financial-crisis rules make this cash pile a problem, not a victory. Big banks face high capital requirements if they grow too large. The penalties would be worthwhile if there were enough profitable opportunities. But loan demand has been low. System-wide loan-to-deposit ratios have plummeted, from 94% in 2008 to 64% last year. The result is that some banks are attempting to shoo away deposits. Jamie Dimon, JPMorgan's boss, told investors that the bank had asked some of its big corporate customers to move their cash, reducing the deposit base by $200 billion. The firm may "shy away from taking new deposits", said Jennifer Piepszak, its chief financial officer. The COVID-19 crisis has shown the resilience of the financial system. But it has also revealed its oddities.

模块四　　技巧点拨：数字转换与记录

🎧 任务1. 英译汉

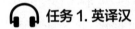

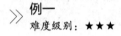

难度级别：★★★

On December 16, 2022, online food delivery giant Meituan started offering 20-yuan coupons ($2.90) to each user opening digital yuan wallets via **China Merchants Bank**. Meituan has granted coupons to more than 10 million users since it started accepting **E-CNY payments** in January. According to **PBOC's** digital currency research institute, more than 5.6 million shops and retailers have allowed E-CNY payments as of August 31, 2022. Up to 360 million digital yuan transactions have been made by the end of August, with the total amount exceeding 100 billion yuan.

词汇

China Merchants Bank
中国招商银行

E-CNY payment
数字人民币支付

PBOC
中国人民银行

译文

2022年12月16日，外卖巨头美团开始向通过在招商银行开通数字人民币钱包的每位用户提供20元优惠券，价值2.9美元。自1月开始接受数字人民币支付以来，美团已向1 000多万名用户发放优惠券。中国人民银行数字货币研究所数据显示，截至2022年8月31日，试点地区累计交易笔数3.6亿笔、金额超1 000亿元，支持数字人民币的商户门店数量超过560万个。

策略分析

本段中出现的数字较多,但有一定转换难度的数字只有 10 million、5.6 million、360 million 三个。因此,学生在听文本时应着重关注这些比较大的数字,至少确保数字量级与原文一致,不可将原文的"千万"翻译为"百万"。下面我们以表格的形式来讲述上述三个数字的记录方式与翻译。

原文	记录方式 1	记录方式 2	翻译
10 million	10m	1000w	一千万
5.6 million	5.6m	560w	五百六十万
360 million	360m	3.6y	三点六亿

本段中,较难转换的三个数字均出现在最后两句,出现的频率较为频繁,若学生一时无法转换,可先按照记录方式 1 记录,即听到什么写什么,翻译时再进行转换,尽可能地为自己争取一点时间。

此外,这三个数字均以 million 结尾,从一位数到三位数都有。在翻译时三个数字之间可以互相照应,在脑中转化出了第一个数字之后,后面的数字也会变得容易许多。

>> 例二
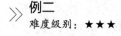

Europe's big banks followed the trend of their American counterparts with generally dismal first-quarter earnings. The share prices of UBS and **Commerzbank** fell sharply after each said net profit had fallen much more than had been expected compared with the same three months last year, to SFR707 million (712 million dollars) at UBS of Switzerland and 163 million euros (180 million dollars) at Commerzbank of Germany. HSBC's pre-tax income dropped by 14% to 6.1 billion dollars, but the bank pointed out it was on track in restructuring its business to focus more on Asia.

词汇

Commerzbank 德国商业银行

译文

欧洲大银行追随美国大银行走势,第一季度总体收益呈现低迷状态。瑞士联合银行和德国商业银行净利润同比出现明显跌势,分别跌至 7.07 亿瑞士法郎(折合 7.12 亿美元)和 1.63 亿欧元(折合 1.8 亿美元),远远超出了预想。随后,两家银行股价也出现了大幅度下跌。汇丰银行税前收入下跌 14% 至 61 亿美元，但汇丰指出，此次下跌是由于内部业务重组，以便将工作重心更多地集中于亚洲地区，一切都在掌控之中。

策略分析

本段中，转换难度较大的数字有 707 million、712 million、163 million、180 million、6.1 billion。其次，本段中出现了美元与瑞士法郎、美元与欧元之间的转换。根据常识可知，美元与欧元以及美元与瑞士法郎的汇率在 1 左右。因此，涉及二者转换的数字必然不会相差太大，至少在一个数量级之内。在翻译时明白这一点，虽然这些数字出现的时间间隔较短，学生也可以根据第一个数字的转换结果，依葫芦画瓢，迅速反应出第二个数字的转换结果。下面我们以表格的形式来讲述上述几个数字的记录方式与翻译。

原文	记录方式 1	记录方式 2	翻译
707 million	707m	7.07y	七点零七亿
712 million	712m	7.12y	七点一二亿
163 million	163m	1.63y	一点六三亿
180 million	180m	1.8y	一点八亿
6.1 billion	6.1b	61y	六十一亿

虽然本段落中数字出现的频率较高，但绝大部分都是以"三位数 + million"的形式出现。学生只要在脑海中快速反应出其中的任何一个，遇到类似的数字时，均可借鉴之前的转换方式，快速输出译语。

值得注意的是，在翻译时，输出的数字形式最好保持一致，以 707 million 为例，既可译为"七点零七亿"，也可译为"七亿零七百万"，选用哪种表达方式取决于译者的习惯，如果选择借用小数点的方式译为"七亿零七百万"，之后的数字最好采用同样的方式，反之亦然。

任务 2. 汉译英
难度级别：★★★

> 训练要点：本段音频中挑出两个实例来分析如何培养听辨能力。音频较长，听第一遍的时候，将全篇音频听完，尝试提炼全文主旨框架。第二遍复盘时，体会两处例子如何进行具体的框架提炼。

▶▶ 例一

当地时间 20 号，美国多家媒体引述银行业者提供给美国政府的机密文件称，在将近 20 年的时间里，美国多家大型跨国银行涉嫌转移大量非法资金，金额高达 2 万亿美元。根据**国际调查记者联盟**以及美国新闻网站巴斯菲德公布的文件，在这些事件中，汇丰银行、**渣打银行**、**德意志银行**和**纽约梅隆银行**等五家大型银行出现的频率最高。自 1999—2017 年，这几家银行进行了许多可疑交易，而这些非法转移的可疑资金总额超过 2 万亿美元。调查显示，这些银行提交给美国财政部防范金融犯罪部门的可疑交易报告超过 2 100 份。而在金融监管的过程中，金融机构在发现可疑交易或具有潜在可疑活动时，需向监管机构提交可疑活动报告。

词汇

国际调查记者联盟
the International Union of Investigative Journalists

渣打银行
Standard Chartered Bank

德意志银行
Deutsche Bank

纽约梅隆银行
New York Mellon Bank

译文

On the 20th local time, a number of US media quoted the confidential documents provided by the banking industry to the US government, saying that in the past 20 years, many large transnational banks in the US were suspected of transferring a large amount of illegal funds, amounting to $2 trillion. According to the documents released by the International Union of Investigative Journalists and the US news website Basfield, five major banks, including HSBC, Standard Chartered, Deutsche Bank and New York Mellon, have the highest occurrence in these events. From 1999 to 2017, these banks carried out many suspicious transactions, and the total amount of these illegally transferred suspicious funds exceeded $2 trillion. The survey showed that these banks submitted more than 2 100 suspicious transaction reports to the Financial Crime Prevention Department of the United States Treasury Department. In the process of financial supervision, financial institutions need to submit suspicious activity reports to the regulatory authorities when they find suspicious transactions or potential suspicious activities.

策略分析

本段中数字出现的频率不高，且数字"2 万亿"重复出现了两次，其记录方式与翻译如下表。

原文	记录方式 1	记录方式 2	翻译
两万亿	2wy	2tr	two trillion

值得注意的是，本段中"2万亿"虽然重复出现了两次，但第一个是"高达2万亿"，第二个是"超过2万亿"。前者可以采用 amount to / reach two trillion 进行翻译，后者则可采用 exceed / is over two trillion 进行翻译。笔记中用"="和">"来进行记录，切记不可只记数字，而忽略前面的信息，否则学生在极度紧张的情况下，很可能将二者混为一谈。

许多学生总是担心自己不能完整记下数字，将过多精力放在听记数字上面，而忽略上下文语境和数字前面的关键信息，导致记下了数字，但不知道该数字的含义。口译的首要目标并不是只翻译一个一个孤立的数字，而是整体的信息。在确保主要信息完整准确的情况下，某些数字可采用模糊化的方式进行处理，尤其是在遇到多位数时，在发言人语速非常快的情况下，可以只翻出一个概数，以确保整个信息的完整度。

》 例二

据悉，文件中还揭露了银行个人转移赃款的一些交易细节。据英国广播公司20号报道称，在2013—2014年间，中国汇丰银行在明知客户涉嫌**庞氏骗局**，存在欺诈行为的情况下，仍然允许其将8 000万美元的资金从其美国汇丰银行的账户转出。报道称，这8 000万美元涉及庞氏骗局，即欺诈者以层级式招揽会员或投资者，让他们参加所谓高息、高回报的投资计划。2012年，汇丰银行曾因洗钱指控被美国政府处以19亿美元（约合129亿元人民币）的罚款。在这几家银行的丑闻曝出后，截至当地时间21号收盘，汇丰银行和渣打银行在**伦敦证券交易所**的股价跌幅均超过5%。

○ 词汇

庞氏骗局
Ponzi scheme

伦敦证券交易所
the London Stock Exchange

译文

It is reported that the document also disclosed some transaction details of personal transfer of illicit money by banks. According to the BBC's report on the 20th, in 2013−2014, HSBC in China still allowed its customers to transfer $80 million of funds from its account with HSBC in America, even though it knew that those customers were suspected of Ponzi scheme. The report stated that the 80 million dollars involved the Ponzi scheme, and the fraudsters solicited members or investors in a hierarchical manner to participate in the so-called high interest and high return investment plan. In 2012, HSBC was fined US $1.9 billion (about 12.9 billion yuan) by the US government for money laundering. With bank scandals coming out, share prices of HSBC and Standard Chartered both fell by more than 5% on the London Stock Exchange as of the close of local time on the 21st.

策略分析

本段中，有"8 000万""19亿""129亿"三个较大的数字，并涉及货币的汇率问题。任务1的例二中涉及美元与瑞士法郎、美元与欧元之间的转换，本段中则涉及美元与人民币的转换。下面我们以表格的形式来讲述上述几个数字的记录方式与翻译。

原文	记录方式1	记录方式2	翻译
8000万	8kw	80m	eighty million
19亿	19y	1.9b	one point nine billion
129亿	129y	12.9b	twelve point nine billion

模块五　　　　　　　　　　　　　　　　　　　　　　　　　　拓展练习

任务1:
数字口译练习

熟练数字读法，看到数字时，迅速对数字进行翻译。

1. First-half net profit of the Industrial and Commercial Bank of China grew 12.5 percent on an annual basis to 123.2 billion Yuan (US$19.4 billion), the world's largest lender by market value said yesterday in a report prepared under international accounting rules.

2. Peer-to-Peer (P2P) lending, where retail investors are connected with borrowers via an online platform, has also started to make

 词汇

off with a significant chunk of capital from the formal banking system. The loan balance for P2P lending in May hit RMB 996 billion ($146 billion), up from only RMB 184 billion two years earlier, according to industry consultant WDZJ.

3. 目前,世界银行将2022年全球经济增长预测下调了近1个百分点。本周一,世界银行行长戴维·马尔帕斯宣布,将全球经济增长率预测值从4.1%下调至3.2%。今年1月,由于新冠疫情和供应瓶颈,世界银行已经将增长率预测值下调了0.2%。欧洲和中亚受到的冲击最为严重,经济预计将收缩4%以上。

4. 近日,**中国银联**和40余家商业银行宣布正式推出银联**云闪付二维码**支付系统。用户登录任意参与银行的应用即可实现二维码支付,类似流行的第三方支付服务支付宝和微信提供的支付方式。目前,支付宝和微信占据九成以上的二维码支付市场。

词汇

中国银联
CUP（China UnionPay）

云闪付
UnionPay

二维码
QR code

任务2:
银行口译练习

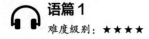

The Fear Factor: Preventing a Big European Bank Run

In continental capitals and bank boardrooms, there is a common fear. It is that the slow jog of deposits leaving banks in Greece and, more recently, Spain, may turn into a full-blown run that quickly spreads from bank to bank, and then from country to country. There have already been some warning signs, such as a sudden acceleration of deposit outflows from Greek banks in May.

A fierce debate is now taking place as to the best way to avert a run that, if it started, might be difficult to contain and could lead to massive **capital flight** from the **Eurozone's peripheral**

词汇

capital flight
资本流失

Eurozone's peripheral country
欧元区周边的国家

countries, which have 1.8 trillion euros (2.2 trillion dollars) in household deposits. Increasing numbers of people think the answer is greater **financial integration**. On May 30th, **the European Commission** said there ought to be "full economic and monetary union, including a banking union, integrated financial supervision and a single deposit guarantee scheme".

The first step is to shore up confidence in the region's banks by making sure they have enough capital to withstand a crisis. It is far cheaper to re-capitalise banks, after all, than to stand behind all of their deposits. Yet such efforts have been bungled time and again. Europe has twice over the past two years tried to reassure depositors and investors that its banks are sound by subjecting them to "stress tests" that were supposed to mimic an **economic downturn**. In each case, the tests were soon followed by revelations of deep **capital holes** in some banks (newly nationalised bank here among them). Since some national regulators have lost the confidence of markets, they are having to bring in outsiders to assess how much capital their banks need.

Actually, raising the capital is the next big problem for countries such as Spain or Italy, which are already struggling to convince markets that their public debt is sustainable. Ideally it should come from the **European Stability Mechanism** (ESM), Europe's new bail-out fund, as a direct capital injection into banks rather than as loans to governments, which then use the money to recapitalise their ailing lenders.

Injecting capital is politically difficult. Core countries such as Germany fret they will lose a lever of influence over government policies in peripheral countries by handing over equity. They also stand a greater risk of losing money, if the ESM takes on the risk of bank investing, not least because they know even less about the **balance-sheets** of individual lenders than those of national governments. Peripheral countries are less than keen on handing

---

词汇

financial integration
金融一体化

the European Commission
欧盟委员会

economic downturn
经济下行

capital hole
资金缺口

European Stability Mechanism
欧洲稳定机制

balance-sheet
资产负债表

ownership of important banks to bureaucrats in Brussels. And unless the capital is accompanied by supervisory reforms, local regulators may encourage banks to lend more freely at home since the risk of loss will have been exported.

Recapitalising banks would not put the catch on every trigger for a run, however. The worry among depositors is not just that their bank will go bust, it is also that their deposits in euros may overnight turn into a less valuable currency. So savers in the periphery would need some additional reassurance that their money is safe.

The job of providing this extra comfort usually falls to national deposit-insurance funds, ideally ones that are prefunded with assets worth about 1.5% of insured deposits, as is the case in America and Europe. If a medium-sized bank goes bust, prefunded schemes can usually pay depositors immediately; European countries insure qualifying deposits up to 100,000 euros. For big banks, or for **systemic crises**, funds are usually backed by their governments.

○ 词汇

systemic crisis
系统性风险

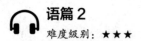

多家银行推出新措施　激发消费市场活力

工商银行提出：要围绕居民衣食住行，聚焦住房改善、**新能源汽车**等大宗消费和购物、美食、休闲、旅游等消费场景，加大资源投入，制定实施优惠利率、消费补贴等一揽子金融支持政策，促进消费潜力释放。工商银行还将对受疫情影响较为严重的零售、餐饮、文旅、物流等行业提供**贷款展期**、**延本延息**等**纾困服务**，帮助企业渡过难关，恢复活力。

农业银行提出：今年将围绕衣食住行、文化教育、健康养老等消费民生领域加大投入。加快支持一批县乡村电商快递物流配送等项目，对县域汽车家装等消费类贷款给予优惠费率支持。

○ 词汇

新能源汽车
new energy vehicle (NEV)

贷款展期
loan extension

延本延息
extension of paying back capital and interest

纾困服务
relief service

农业银行
Agricultural Bank of China (ABC)

邮储银行将联合多家汽车厂商在百城千县开展乡村"乡村加邮购车季"活动。配套给予零利息或低利息的优惠,助力县、乡居民汽车消费。

中国银行、**兴业银行**等多家银行也都明确了要加大对餐饮、住宿、文旅等领域的支持,激发消费潜力。江苏、福建、辽宁等地**银保监局**还出台多项措施,鼓励银行增加信贷投放,加大消费类金融服务减费让利力度。

> **词汇**
>
> 邮储银行
> Postal Savings Bank of China (PSBC)
>
> 中国银行
> Bank of China (BOC)
>
> 兴业银行
> China's Industrial Bank (CIB)
>
> 银保监局
> China Banking and Insurance Regulatory Commission

模块六　　译海拾贝:译前准备

一个优秀的口译员在口译过程中要深度了解所翻译对象的行业背景知识,严谨认真细致的译前准备是必不可少的一环。

广义的译前准备分为常识性背景和知识储备,以及短期的会议相关词汇和背景准备。前者需要译员通过持之以恒的训练实现目标;后者则需要译员在上场前的几天甚至几个小时之内,充分发挥快速学习能力,积累相关专业知识,包括以下内容:

熟悉会议主办方提供的资料

主办方提供的材料一般包括会议举办的时间与地点、参会人员(单位、头衔)、演讲嘉宾名单(顺序、单位、头衔、演讲题目及内容)、会议日程等,译员很多时候可以得到讲者的部分或全部发言稿件或幻灯片(PPT)。

这些讲稿或者 PPT 是译前准备中最为重要的内容。译员在接到任务之后,应主动与主办方联络,尽早拿到相关资料,为自己预留充分的准备时间,例如:查阅讲稿和 PPT 中的专业词汇和背景知识;在时间允许的情况下,可以提前翻译部分稿件,即使演讲者脱稿发言,译员也能从容不迫地进行翻译。如果能够多熟悉会议资料,译员对于口译任务也会多一份把握和从容。

查阅会议所涉及领域的行业专业知识

同声传译相对获取材料更容易，会议主办方一般都是主动将会议 PPT 讲稿等材料提供给译员。但是交替传译，比如谈判、会见，很难要到材料。

如果不能提前拿到讲者的发言稿或发言提纲等资料，译员需要从会议的主题、演讲（会见、谈判）主旨入手，充分发挥发散思维，广泛阅读相关背景资料，积累专业词汇。

以本章主题银行为例，我们可以预设讲者的演讲内容，如常见的各大银行、银行的作用、银行的功能、金融机构的盈利模式、银行面临的困境、借款贷款利率等。对于此部分内容而言，因为译员未能提前拿到讲者演讲稿，因此在背景知识的了解上，涉猎知识应尽可能地广泛，以便做到有备无患。

了解发言人

无论译员事先拿到的稿件是什么样子，最后都要根据发言人的现场发言进行翻译。即使译员提前拿到了发言稿，也不能只关注稿件或 PPT，以防发言人脱稿、改稿。译员需要通过会议议程所提供的讲者身份和演讲题目，上网搜索其背景资料和演讲的音频视频，熟悉其发言风格、语速和语音语调等。

其次，在口译活动开始前，译员应尽可能找机会与发言人进行沟通，熟悉发言人的讲话速度甚至口音，尤其是口音较重的发言人，译员应多与其交谈，尽快熟悉发言人的讲话模式。如果发言人讲话口音实在难以理解，译员可以事先与发言人沟通，请发言人控制语速以及停顿的时间。

提前到达会议场地

译员需要提前到达会议现场，理想状态下应提前 1~1.5 个小时。这么做的目的有：（1）防止交通堵塞，防止迟到。（2）再次向主办方确认是否有新材料并再次确认流程，若有新材料或者流程修改，应充分利用会议前的时间快速浏览材料，做好准备；经常有嘉宾临时调整演讲顺序或者缺席，不要照本宣科，译错嘉宾。（3）与双方发言人进行沟通，协调交替传译的讲与译的交替节奏。（4）熟悉场地和设备，在交替传译中沟通好译员所处位置，采取站立翻译或者翻译座位所处位置，调整麦克风；同声传译中要熟悉设备，特别是多语种接力的过程中同传设备使用略复杂，译员要确保及时切换按键与频道。

模块七

译员风采："银发铁娘子"傅莹

有一位女外交家曾斩获多个第一的名号,"中国外交史最年轻女大使""中国首位女性外交新闻发言人""首位少数民族外交大使""第一位出版职业女性时尚穿搭书籍的外交官"。这位出生于通辽、做过下乡知青、在北外主攻英语专业、35岁成为邓小平翻译的传奇女性,就是傅莹。在傅莹的外交生涯中,她坚决维护国家利益,以柔克刚、言辞犀利,多次怼得西方政要和记者哑口无言,包括美国议长佩罗西,被西方称为"最能清晰传递中国声音的使者"。《金融时报》报道如是评价她:"仪态优雅,笑容灿烂。她很有魅力,魅力也是可以作为武器的"。让我们一起走进傅莹的不平凡人生,感受其人生阅历。

奋发图强,夯实基础

1953年,傅莹出生在内蒙古通辽。她的父亲担任过当地军区宣传部的副部长一职。父亲渊博的学识给傅莹的人生带来了重要的影响,她从小就十分喜爱读书并形成批判性思维。她16岁的时候,响应知青下乡建设的号召到生产建设兵团中工作。虽然每天要承担繁重的体力劳动工作,但她依旧没有放弃学习,业余时间自学物理和数学知识。

"机会只青睐有准备的头脑"用来形容傅莹是再贴切不过了。1973年傅莹以工农兵学员的身份考入北京外国语学院,数学取得了满分的好成绩。大学期间,傅莹主修英语,并将法语作为自己的第二外语,在课余时间又学习了罗马尼亚语。在学习中,她不敢有一丝一毫的懈怠,总是一遍一遍地温习巩固,打下了良好的专业基础。

学海无涯,学无止境

1977年,大学毕业后的傅莹凭借出色的语言能力进入了外交部,开始了翻译生涯。曾为多个国家领导人担任高级翻译的她也不断积累自己的外交能力,为参与国际会议、外交谈判奠定了基础。

1985年,傅莹凭借着突出的业务能力,获得了公派到英国肯特大学深造的机会,并获得国际关系硕士学位。1988年,挪威首相布伦特兰夫人访华,傅莹成为邓小平同志的翻译。当邓小平同志说:"你们还年轻,我却已经到84岁该退休的年纪了"这句话时，傅莹误将"84岁"译成了"48岁"。错误并没有让傅莹消沉，反而成为学习的动力。此后，傅莹总是书不离手，利用一切可能的时间提升自己的能力，以防再出现这样的错误，这个习惯此后一直跟随着傅莹。

捍卫祖国，掷地有声

在2016年的慕尼黑安全会议上，一名记者向傅莹提出了一个十分刁钻的问题——中国是否失去了对朝鲜的控制？这个问题尖锐之处在于，无论直接回答"是"或"不是"，都是间接承认中国对他国主权的控制之心，难免给人落下话柄。多年的工作经验让傅莹一眼便识破了记者的别有用心，于是她微笑且坚定地回应："中国从来就没有想过要控制谁，当然同时也不会让别人有机会控制我们，这个问题问得很西方。"

2020年2月，美国众议院议长佩洛西在慕尼黑安全会议中称：世界各国建设5G网络应该远离中国的华为公司，因为他们正试图通过这家公司来实行数字专制，对那些还未采用中国技术的国家实行经济报复。如此说法背后的目的显而易见，因此，傅莹当场便站起来反驳道："民主制度是如此脆弱的吗？能够被华为一家高科技公司所威胁吗？"这样巧妙有力的回击得到了在场人士的一致掌声，这段话也在全世界范围内传播，让世界再次看到了傅莹这位"中国铁娘子"的风采。

内外兼修，光彩照人

傅莹的外交履历上被"中国外交部亚洲司司长""驻菲律宾大使""驻澳大利亚大使""驻英国大使""外交部副部长"等职位所写满，外国元首们称傅莹是"最能清晰传递中国声音的使者"。长期的外交经验和自身气质所驱动，她还被誉为"最美外交官"，其高雅气质与得体的衣服浑然一体，实现了外在美与内在美的高度和谐。她把自己多年从事外交工作的外交礼仪经验和自己的国事穿搭，写进了著作《大使衣橱——外交礼仪之旅》中，表达了"得体表达自己，从容面对世界"的外交家自信。

纵观傅莹大半的人生经历，我们不难看到她出色的能力，这份能力中天赋有之，更是她数十年中日复一日、年复一年的努力与勤奋。长年累月的积累造就了气质、学识、能力兼备的傅莹，才有了在国际交往中大放异彩的中国女外交大使。傅莹与我国许多的外交大使一样，用自己睿智的头脑、迅速的反应和坚定的爱国信念，为维护祖国的利益而坚毅果敢地站在了国际舞台上！

第八章

金融
Finance

模块一

技能概要：脱壳翻译

在口译学习的前期阶段，学生应该选取背景知识简单、语速较慢、语篇较短的语料，从而扎实地掌握听辨、记笔记等基本技能。但是随着源语内容变难、语速增快、篇幅变长，如学生完全被源语束缚，将影响口译的准确性和可持续性。因此，当基本功达到一定的能力层面的时候，学生需要了解如何通过脱壳翻译的方式来提高口译能力。脱壳翻译法是法国释意派理论的核心观点，是巴黎高等翻译学校的塞莱斯科维奇教授为代表的学者提出的。该观点认为，口译与笔译的加工机制不同，其现场性和不可回溯性使口译的认知负荷增加，如果完全对等地反映源语元素，不仅会增加翻译负担，也会带来冗余信息，还有可能影响整体准确性。因此学生需要打破源语语言外壳，口译只需做到意义对等，不应该受源语外壳表达形式的干扰。在口译实践中，学生如果能透彻地理解讲话人的意图和信息核心，就可以结合自己的背景知识和讲话主题，摒弃形式上的对等，完成意义对等的口语任务。

对于学生来说，由于接触口译的时间短，面临着口译精力匹配不足和商务背景知识缺乏的双重压力。如果在口译学习中，学生能够充分学习文化背景和常见商务场景的相关知识，强调语块核心信息和语流、逻辑框架特点，这将有助于他们把精力更多地分配到听译上，而非加工背景知识；在此基础上，平时训练的翻译场景将会通过自反式知识生成过程促进其信息加工和理解的正确性，从而大大提升口译质量。

脱壳能力建立在具有良好的听辨能力、掌握一定背景知识和灵活组建语块的基础上。学生可以尝试以下方法进行脱壳翻译训练：（1）概括翻译；（2）抓大放小；（3）意译；（4）去虚就实。

1. 概括翻译

概括翻译相当于主旨口译。当讲话人语速过快，特别是在英译汉的情况下，学生不得已采取这种对策。

例句：Each new scandal that erupts makes it more likely that genuine innovators will be frightened off and the industry will dwindle.

完整翻译：每一桩新丑闻的爆发都更有可能吓跑真正的创新者，从而使整个行业逐渐萎缩。

概括翻译：丑闻会吓跑创新者，导致行业萎缩。

2. 抓大放小

抓大放小是指在翻译过程中，由于学生的能力有限，无法重现所有信息，因此选择省略掉次要信息而保全主要信息。

例句：The Internet of Things offers great potential for sustainable development—from energy savings to remote medical procedures, from access to education to healthier nutrition. But digital technologies are also outpacing regulations and deepening inequalities.

完整翻译：物联网为可持续发展提供了巨大潜力——从节约能源到远程医疗程序，从获得教育到更健康的营养。但数字技术的发展速度也超过了监管，并加剧了不平等。

"抓大放小"翻译：物联网为可持续发展提供了巨大潜力，但是监管不力。

3. 意译

由于文化差异的存在，意译有时候比直译更能准确地表达出说话者的真实意图。

例句：IT 公司里总是阳盛阴衰。

直译：In the IT companies, men's power outweighs women's.

意译：In the IT companies, men outnumber women.

4. 去虚就实

这种翻译模式也是由于文化差异所造成的。如果按照字面的意译来翻译，话语的真实意图可能就被掩盖，导致听者闻其字而不明其意。好的译员能够一针见血地翻译，而不是被字面意思牵着鼻子走。

例句：长年以来，华为员工的高薪待遇可谓是"羡煞旁人"，总能让大家津津乐道。

完整翻译：For the past years, Huawei staff's high salary is envied by others, which is always mentioned by people.

"去虚就实"翻译：Huawei staff's high salary is, for long time, admired by people.

模块二　　　　　　　　　　　　　　　　　　　　　译前准备

◎ 1. 背景知识

金融是国家重要的核心竞争力。金融无处不在，并已形成一个庞大体系，涉及的范畴、分支和内容非常广，如货币、证券、资本市场、衍生证券、投资理财、各种基金（私募、公募）、国际收支、财政管理、贸易金融、地产金融、外汇管理、风险管理、投资等。中国金融市场正在走向国际化，对专业金融英语和金融口译的需求日益增多。

本模块涉及的概念包括股市、选股、股票期权、做空。

股市（stock market）：股市是股票市场的简称，股市是一个可以提供各种股票交易的平台或者场所。股票交易服务可以包括：股票的上市和发行、股票买卖等。股市可以分为一级市场、二级市场、三级市场和四级市场。

选股（picking）：选股是股民了解股市行情、明确投资方向的重要手段；股民通过选股了解资金流向，加强股票走向和趋势。股民可以通过个股评级、选股工具更轻松地选股，紧密地关注持股企业和行业的发展也非常重要。

股票期权（stock option）：股票期权是上市公司给予企业高级管理人员和技术骨干在一定期限内以一种事先约定的价格购买公司普通股的权利。期权是一种不同于职工股的崭新激励机制，属于长期激励的范畴，增加公司的所有者权益，是由持有者向公司购买未发行在外的流通股，直接从公司购买而非从二级市场购买。

做空（short sale）：做空是指预期未来某股票的价格会下跌，售出所持股票，等股价下降后再买进，获取利润差价。股票大涨（牛市）时投资者挣钱是人之常情，但股票大跌（熊市）时有人通过做空，能赚得盆满钵满，做空瑞幸的桥水基金（Bridge Water）就是个典型的例子。

◎ 2. 核心词汇

New York Stock Exchange	纽约股票交易所	broker	股票经纪人
listed	上市	overvalued/undervalued	估值过高 / 过低
stock option	股票期权	quantitative easing	量化宽松
short selling / go short	卖空 / 做空		

模块三　语料实训

任务 1. 英译汉
难度级别：★★★★

> 训练要点：本文介绍了股票投资者的投资依据，定义了股票、股价和选股因素。本文专业术语较多，是金融类常识性语篇，但是对于没有金融和股票背景知识的听者来说，具有一定难度。如果学生在听解过程中追求信息的完整对应输出，必然导致更多信息的遗漏，因此听译过程中需要通过切分语块、提取要点来打破原文复杂句子结构并实现脱壳翻译，最终实现意义等值而非语言外壳等值。

Musk Selling the Stock

Elon Musk, the founder of the electric car company Tesla, recently asked people on Twitter if he should sell billions of dollars in company stock. Musk is one of the world's richest people, so the request was unusual. He asked his millions of Twitter followers whether he should sell 10 percent of his stock in the company. That amount might be worth $20 billion or more. As of last summer, Musk owned about 170 million shares of Tesla.

On Saturday, Musk placed a poll on Twitter, asking if he should sell the stock. About 3.5 million people voted, and nearly 58 percent said he should. "I was prepared to accept either outcome," Musk said. On Monday, the shares of Tesla stock dropped a small amount. David Madden is a stock market expert in London. He said he did not believe the "dip" would last long. "Tesla has had such a phenomenal record of bouncing back from these sort of selloffs," he said. Musk said he understands people are concerned that very rich people avoid paying taxes. For example, many people who own millions of shares in a company like Musk does, do not sell their shares when they need money. Instead, they get loans from banks based on the value of the stock.

If they do sell shares of stock, they get taxed, so they get the loans to buy something like a new home. Stock is not money. It is an ownership share in a company. Investors exchange stock for money by selling it on a market. People who follow Musk's finances and company documents available to the public know that the businessman has a decision to make by next year. Until August 13, 2022, Musk will be able to buy more than 22 million shares of Tesla stock at a price of just over $6 each. Right now, Tesla stock sells for more than $1,000 per share. Musk says he is paid in what are known as stock options instead of money. An option is a financial agreement. It permits the owner of the option to trade stock at a set price for a set period of time. After that time period ends, the option is worth nothing.

任务 2. 汉译英

难度级别：★★★★

训练要点：本文介绍了做空的概念。数字信息较多，学生在听辨过程中要对重要信息和二级信息进行区别，在保全重要信息的基础上对数字进行精准翻译。本篇训练的脱壳技能是通过融合背景知识、简化冗余信息来实现的。这不仅有助于提高译文的准确性，也使目标语的表述简洁。

做 空

股票价格下跌时也能赚钱，其中一种方法就是做空。其实做空很简单，就是借入股票卖出去，然后买回股票还回去。做空者赌的是该股价会下跌。如果股票卖出后价格确实下跌，做空者会以较低的价格买回股票，将其返还。这一买一卖之间的差价就是赚的利润。

打个比方，如果一个投资者认为特斯拉（Tesla）的股票每股 625 美元，被高估了，觉得价格会下跌，那么投资者可以从经纪人那里"借" 10 股特斯拉股票，然后以 625 美元的价格卖出去。如果这只股票之后跌到 500 美元，投资者可以 500 美元买回这 10 只股票，还给经纪人。这样一买一卖就净赚了 1 250 美元（6 250-5 000 美元）。但是，如果特斯拉的价格涨至 700 美元，投资者会亏 750 美元（6 250-7 000 美元）。

任务 3. 英译汉

难度级别：★★★★★

训练要点：本文介绍了债务上限的概念。全文术语并不多，但是信息密集，上下文之间的逻辑关系层层递进，要求学生有较好的语块逻辑整理能力；听辨过程中，学生要对重要信息和二级信息进行区别，在保全重要信息的基础上对数字进行精准翻译。本文的脱壳翻译重点是概括与合并信息能力。

Why Can't Governments Print an Unlimited Amount of Money?

In March 2020, the COVID-19 pandemic rocked economies worldwide. Millions of people lost their jobs, and many businesses struggled to survive or shut down completely. Governments responded with some of the largest economic relief packages in history—the United States alone spent $2.2 trillion on a first round of relief. So where did all this money come from?

Most countries have a central bank that manages the money supply and is independent from the government to prevent political interference. The government can implement many types of economic policy, like decreasing people's taxes and creating jobs through public infrastructure projects, but it actually can't just increase the money supply. The central bank determines how much money is in circulation at a time. So why can't central banks authorize the printing of unlimited money to help an economy in crisis? They could, but that's a short-term solution that doesn't necessarily boost economic growth in the long term, and can actually hurt the economy. Why?

With more money in circulation, manufacturers of goods like food, clothing, and cars could respond to demand simply by raising prices, rather than manufacturing more of these goods and creating new jobs in the process. This would mean you could no longer buy as much with the same amount of money—a situation known as inflation. A little bit of inflation, about 2% a year, is considered a sign of economic health, but more can quickly derail an economy.

In recent decades, central banks have tried an approach called quantitative easing to infuse the economy with cash while maintaining a low risk of severe inflation. In this approach, a central bank increases cash flow by purchasing another entity's bonds. Anyone can buy bonds from corporations or governments. When you buy a bond, you're essentially loaning money to the company—or government—with the promise that they'll pay it back later with interest. This is why buying bonds is sometimes referred to as buying debt.

When an individual buys a bond, they're using money that's already in circulation. But when the central bank buys a bond, it essentially creates cash, supplying money that didn't exist before in exchange for bonds. Both during the 2008–2009 financial crisis and again in 2020, the United States' central bank, the Federal Reserve, bought bonds from the US government called treasury bonds.

Historically, many people have purchased these bonds as a safe form of investment, knowing the US government will pay them back with interest. In early 2020, the Federal Reserve pledged to buy unlimited treasury bonds, loaning the US government an unprecedented amount of money—cash that the government used to fund relief efforts like stimulus checks and unemployment benefits. This isn't equivalent to simply printing money, though it may sound similar. Because of the way bonds are priced, by buying so many, the Federal Reserve effectively lowered the return on them, which incentivizes other investors to lend to riskier entities—like small and midsize companies—in order to get a decent return. Encouraging lending this way should help companies of all sizes borrow money to funnel into projects and hires, boosting the economy over time, in addition to helping the government supply people with urgently needed cash in the short term.

The Federal Reserve's pledge to buy unlimited government debt has raised some questions—and eyebrows. In theory, this means the government could issue more bonds, which the central bank would purchase. The government could then use the money from the new bonds to pay off the old bonds, effectively meaning the government never pays back its debt to the central bank. Citing this and other theoretical scenarios, some economists have raised concerns that a central bank buying government debt is a subversion of a system designed to protect the economy. Others have insisted these measures are necessary, and have so far helped stabilize economies.

Though quantitative easing has become a lot more common in recent years, it's still relatively new, and potential consequences are still unfolding.

模块四

技巧点拨：脱壳翻译技能

🎧 任务 1. 英译汉

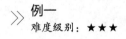
难度级别：★★★

Every day, billions of stocks are traded on the alone. But with over 43,000 companies **listed** on stock exchanges around the world, how do investors decide which stocks to buy? <u>To answer this question, it's important to first understand</u> what stocks are, and what individuals and institutions hope to achieve by investing in them.

词汇

listed
上市的

译文

每天，仅在纽约证券交易所就有数十亿的股票在交易。但是，在全球有超过 43 000 家公司在股票交易所上市的情况下，投资者如何决定购买哪些股票呢？要回答这个问题，重要的是首先要了解什么是股票，以及个人和机构希望通过投资股票获得什么。

脱壳翻译

每天股市有大量的交易，投资者如何选股呢？首先要懂得股票是什么？个人和机构投资股票的目的是什么？

策略分析

本段落的前两句表达的是一个意思，指全球股票可选对象极多。英语作为形合语言，重要信息经常会用提示性语言引出，"To answer this question, it's important to..."是典型的提示语，下文的信息尽量在译文中全面折射，"股票是什么？投资者的目标是什么？"这两个信息尽量都翻译出来。特别是交替传译的语境下，学生听过完整段落，熟悉语境、把握讲话人的整体段落意图后，在根据笔记进行口译的过程中，完全可以把前两句进行脱壳处理，翻译成"全球股票可选对象极多"。

脱壳要点

1. 注意形合语言的听辨提示，如"To answer this question, ..."是提示语，表明后面的内容是重要内容，或者对语篇的主旨起到点题或者解释的作用，听译中要注意这样的提示语。
2. 注意合并次要信息。

>> **例二**
难度级别：★★★

Stocks are partial shares of **ownership** in a company. So by buying a stock, investors buy a share in the company's success, or failure, as measured by the company's profits. A stock's price is determined by the number of buyers and sellers trading it; if there are more buyers than sellers, the price will increase, and vice versa. The market price of a share therefore represents what buyers and sellers believe the stock, and by association, the company, is worth. So the price can change dramatically based on whether investors think the company has a high potential or increasing profitability—even if it isn't profitable yet.

词汇

ownership
所有权

译文

股票是公司所有权的一部分。因此，通过购买股票，投资者购买了公司成功或失败的一部分，这是由公司的利润来衡量的。股票的价格是由买卖股票的买家和卖家的数量决定的；如果买家比卖家多，价格就会上涨，反之亦然。因此，股票的市场价格代表了买方和卖方对股票以及公司价值的看法。因此，根据投资者是否认为该公司有很高的盈利潜力或不断增长的盈利能力，即使它还没有盈利，股价也会发生巨大变化。

脱壳翻译

股票是公司所有权的一部分。股价是由买家和卖家的数量对比决定的。市场价格是由买卖者对股票和公司的信任度决定的。信任度决定了股价是否有巨大变化。

策略分析

本段具有典型的说明性文字的特征：定义加举例。前两句话"Stocks are partial shares of ownership in a company." "So by buying a stock, investors buy a share in the company's success—or failure—as measured by the company's profits."表达的是一个意思，只是一个属于抽象概念，另一个是具体例子。因此在脱壳翻译的过程中，学生可以选择任一句，仍然可以表达两句的完整意义。第三和第四句话"A stock's price is determined by the number of buyers and sellers trading it; if there are more buyers than sellers, the price will increase, and vice versa."也是完全同样的结构，因此可以被合并译为"股价是由买家和卖家的数量对比决定的"。第五句中的"what buyers and sellers believe the stock, and by association, the company, is worth"可以根据其深层意义直接翻译成"信任度"，由此该句也可以简化翻译，并且符合中文的表达习惯。

脱壳要点

1. 熟悉英语的常见表述的句型特征，敏感地捕捉上下文之间的逻辑关系和意义关联，从而敏锐地判断出下文意思。如本段两次出现"定义＋解释"的逻辑规律，那么听解和口译的难度都会下降。
2. 脱壳常用的手段之一是将解释性的句子归纳总结。

 任务2. 汉译英
难度级别：★★★

训练要点：本段音频中挑出三个实例来分析如何培养听辨能力。音频较长，听第一遍的时候，将全篇音频听完，尝试提炼全文主旨框架。第二遍复盘时，体会三处例子如何进行具体的框架提炼。

》例一

过去十年金融科技高速发展，人工智能、大数据、**云计算**、**分布式记账**以及电子商务（概称 ABCDE）等技术广泛应用于金融领域，促使金融服务变得更普惠、便捷和高效。

词汇

云计算
cloud computing

分布式记账
distributed ledger

译文

Fintech has developed rapidly over the past decade. Technologies such as AI (A), big data (B), cloud computing (C), distributed ledger (D) and e-commerce (E) have been increasingly integrated into the financial sector, making financial services more inclusive, convenient and efficient.

脱壳翻译

Such high tech application as AI, big data, etc., into financial area in the past ten years, promotes the inclusiveness, convenience and efficiency of financial services.

策略分析

汉语单音节语素较多的特色决定了，如果用同一语速表达同样的意思，汉语要比英语用时短，这意味着汉译英的时候，目标语时长要多于源语时长，违背了"目标语时长要短于源语时长"的口译要求。汉译英的时候，脱壳翻译法是一种重要的手段，可平衡源语和目标语的时长。本段的脱壳翻译是通过合并例子（人工智能、大数据、云计算、分布式记账以及电子商务）和融合两句话含义（过去十年金融科技高速发展，人工智能、大数据、云计算、分布式记账以及电子商务等技术广泛应用于金融领域）的方法来实现的。脱壳翻译不是一蹴而就的技术，建立在对英汉两种语言都有较好的理解力和表达力的基础上。比如，"过去十年金融科技高速发展，人工智能、大数据、云计算、分布式记账以及电子商务等技术广泛应用于金融领域"本应该译成两个有独立主谓结构的句子，但是如果把"金融科技"作为主语，通过 such as 来连接后面的成分，就可以将两个有独立主谓结构的汉语句子融合成一个英语长句，不拘泥于形式上的语言单位对等，并且能够将深层意思表达得更明晰。

第八章·金融

脱壳要点

1. 例子不需要全部举出，列举有代表性的例子即可。
2. 熟悉汉译英简化法，遇到举例时可以使用 such... as... 的句式，将两句话连接起来且逻辑通顺。

》例二

"ABCDE"五项技术中<u>最重要的</u>就是**大数据**。在金融科技领域，谁占据**流量**，谁就有数据，谁有数据，谁就有客户。如果有**客户黏性**，就可以持续获取数据，所以大型科技公司在数据的<u>占有、运用、存储</u>方面越来越有<u>优势</u>。

词汇

大数据
big data

流量
traffic; flow

客户黏性
customer loyalty

译文

Big data is at the heart of the above-mentioned "ABCDE" technologies. The companies that have large data traffic could accumulate data, and acquire new customers. They could enjoy steady data flow if customers remain loyal. As a result, big techs have increasingly gained an upper hand in possessing, using and storing data.

脱壳翻译

Big data is the most important among all. In fintech, data flow brings the data and clients, and vice versa. So, big techs have increasingly gained an upper hand in possessing, using and storing data.

策略分析

源语的核心内容已经标出。汉译英的脱壳策略的重点是能抓住核心意义，弄清讲话人要表达的意义和思想，学生的中心任务是剥离源语外壳，抓住意义实质。"谁占据流量，谁就有数据，谁有数据，谁就有客户，如果有客户黏性，就可以持续获取数据"的核心意义是"流量会带来数据和客户，反之亦然"。

脱壳要点

汉语是意合语言，且外在逻辑性不明显，"谁占据流量，谁就有数据，谁有数据，谁就有客户。如果有客户黏性，就可以持续获取数据"的内在含义是"Only if you have data flow can you have data and clients, which would further bring more clients"。把握这个

177

深层含义后，该句可以简化成"data flow brings the data and clients, and vice versa"。

例三

中国人民银行一直高度重视金融领域的个人信息保护工作，2005年以来在反洗钱、消费者权益保护和征信等领域陆续出台了个人信息保护相关制度。近年来，着力治理金融活动中对个人信息的过度收集现象，以及不同意提供个人信息就无法获取服务的霸王条款。同时，督促提供金融服务的各类机构严格按照合法、正当、最小必要原则收集、使用和保管客户信息，规范机构内部为商业目的使用个人信息的行为，充分保障消费者隐私和合法权益。

词汇

反洗钱
anti-money-laundering

译文

Personal data protection is always high on the agenda of the People's Bank of China (PBOC). Since 2005, the PBOC has introduced regulations on data protection in the areas of anti- money-laundering, consumer protection and credit information. Recently, we have focused on cracking down on excessive collection of consumer data and unfair clauses, which require consumers to hand over personal information in exchange for financial services. At the same time, financial institutions are required to collect, use and store information for legitimate purposes and in strict accordance with the principles of lawfulness and minimum necessity, to protect privacy when using personal information for commercial purposes.

脱壳翻译

Personal data protection is always high on the agenda of the People's Bank of China (PBOC). Since 2005, the PBOC has introduced regulations on data protection (in the areas of anti-money-laundering, consumer protection and credit information). Recently, the focus is on the unfair clauses of "over-collection and no personal information, no service". The agencies are strictly required to collect, use and store clients' information according to legitimate, justified and minimum principle, to protect privacy when using personal information for commercial purposes.

策略分析

源语的核心内容已经标出。本段翻译的脱壳体现在"着力治理金融活动中对个人信息的过度收集现象，以及不同意提供个人信息就无法获取服务的霸王条款"。

脱壳要点

1. 汉语的主动句多见，英语经常用被动句，而不表现动作执行者。汉译英的脱壳过程中，化主动为被动是常见的手段，能够减少目标语的长度、增强表达的地道性。
2. no... no... 等类似的结构可以表达汉语中条件句"如果不……就不能……"的意义。学生平时需要多训练如何用简单的英文句式表达复杂的汉语意义。

模块五　　拓展练习

任务 1：
脱壳口译练习

请按照完整口译和脱壳口译两种方法对下列句子进行练习，提炼脱壳翻译要点。

1. Investors aim to make money by purchasing stocks whose value will increase over time. Some investors aim simply to grow their money at a faster rate than inflation diminishes its value. Others have a goal of "beating the market", which means growing their money at a faster rate than the cumulative performance of all companies' stocks.

2. This idea of "beating the market" is a source of debate among investors—in fact, investors break into two main groups over it. Active investors believe it is possible to beat the market by strategically selecting specific stocks and timing their trades, while passive investors believe it isn't usually possible to beat the market, and don't subscribe to stock picking.

3. We are short China Huishan holdings because we believe it is worth close to zero. We conclude Huishan is a fraud. In this first report on Huishan, we detail the following conclusions and supporting facts. Since at least 2014, the company has reported fraudulent profits largely based on the lie that it is substantially self-sufficient in producing alfalfa from third parties, which gives us no doubt that Huishan's financials are fraudulent.

4. Luckin is enriching product offerings to increase customer purchase frequency and sales revenue. It captures more cross-selling opportunities by introducing selective new

products complementary to existing offerings and fulfill the target customers' daily need.

5. 投资者的目标是通过购买价值会随时间增长的股票来赚钱。一些投资者的目标只是以比通货膨胀降低其价值更快的速度增加他们的资金。其他人的目标是"跑赢大盘",这意味着他们的资金增长速度要快于所有公司股票的累计表现。"跑赢大盘"的想法是投资者争论的一个原因——事实上,投资者在这个问题上分成了两大类。积极投资者认为,有策略地选择特定股票并选择交易时机是有可能跑赢大盘的,而消极投资者则认为,跑赢大盘通常是不可能的,所以他们不赞成选股。

6. 人们常说:"股票市场在短期内表现得像一台投票机,在长期内表现得像一台称重机。"这意味着股票价格的短期波动反映了公众的意见,但从长期来看,它们确实倾向于反映公司的利润。

7. 私募股权基金是从事私人股权(非上市公司股权)投资的基金。主要包括投资非上市公司股权或上市公司非公开交易股权两种。追求的不是股权收益,而是通过上市、管理层收购和并购等股权转让路径出售股权而获利。而私募股权投资(Private Equity)(简称"PE"),是指对非上市企业进行的权益性投资,并以策略投资者的角色积极参与投资标的经营与改造,通过上市、并购或管理层回购等方式,出售持股获利。

任务 2:
金融口译练习

语篇 1
难度级别:★★★★

American Debt Limit

American President Joe Biden again asked Congress to lift the United States **debt limit** after a meeting Wednesday with the nation's business leaders. The White House **Council of Economic Advisors** warned before the meeting that the United States government will **default on its obligations** if Congress does not raise the debt limit by October 18.

A default is a failure to meet the **legal obligations** of a loan.

The council said millions of Americans might not receive their payments from Social Security and government healthcare. A

词汇

debt limit
债务上限

Council of Economic Advisors
经济顾问委员会

default on its obligations
不履行义务

legal obligation
法律责任

default could also affect national defense and pandemic services.

Since many countries depend on the US monetary policy, it said a default "would likely cause credit markets worldwide to **freeze up** and stock markets to **plunge**. Employers around the world would likely have to begin laying off workers".

What is the debt limit?

Like some of us, governments sometimes spend more money than they receive from taxes. So, they have to borrow money by **issuing bonds**, or debts, to be repaid later. In the US, Congress has the power to set a debt limit. It is "the maximum amount of debt that the **Department of the Treasury** can issue to the public or to other federal agencies".

Since 1960, Congress has changed the debt limit 78 times under both Republican and Democratic administrations to pay for government operations.

Raising the debt limit does not mean that the Treasury has more money to spend. It only permits the US government to "finance existing legal obligations". When the limit is reached, the Treasury cannot issue more debt or borrow more money.

What is the current situation?

In August 2019, the US Congress passed a budget deal, with support from both Republican and Democratic lawmakers, that raised spending and suspended the debt limit for two years. Under the agreement, the money borrowed during the suspension of the debt limit will be added to the previous limit of $22 trillion. An additional $6.5 trillion had been borrowed since the 2019 tax cuts and pandemic spending, raising the nation's debt limit to $28.5 trillion.

The **Congressional Budget Office** estimated that the federal government has a **deficit** of $2.7 trillion for the budget year ending in September 2021. The government also ran up deficits each year from 2016 to 2020. Technically, the US has already reached its

词汇

freeze up
冻结

plunge
暴跌，猛跌

issuing bond
发行债券

Department of the Treasury
（美国）财政部

Congressional Budget Office
国会预算办公室

deficit
赤字

debt limit at the end of July as agreed to in the 2019 budget deal. Once the debt limit is reached, the US cannot borrow more money to pay its bills. But the Treasury could and has used "extraordinary measures" like delaying some payments to employees' retirement funds to avoid a default.

Unless Congress acts to raise the debt limit, the Bipartisan Policy Center projects that the US will most likely reach the limit between October 15 and November 4. The center added that a default would likely raise borrowing costs as investors will demand a higher rate of return on US debts. Even a short-term default, it said, could also threaten the country's current economic recovery.

Why does the US have a debt limit?

Before World War I, the US Congress permitted borrowing only for special reasons, such as the building of the **Panama Canal**. In 1917, Congress passed a law that set a debt limit. It gave the Treasury some flexibility in dealing with the national debt to pay for the war.

The US is one of a few countries around the world with a debt limit. Denmark is often noted as another developed country with a debt limit. But Denmark often sets its borrowing limit so high that a default is not really possible.

For many years in the US, raising the debt limit was not an issue. The Republican Party has since only supported increase while it has controlled the White House. It has argued against raising the limit under Democratic administrations. Earlier this year, Democratic Congressman Bill Foster of Illinois introduced a bill to end the debt limit. The bill, however, is not guaranteed to pass with the currently divided **legislature**. Late on Wednesday, Senate Republican leader Mitch McConnell told Democrats he would permit an emergency debt limit **extension** into December to avoid a default. If the offer is accepted, the US will have to deal with the debt limit again by the end of the year.

词汇

Panama Canal
巴拿马运河

legislature
立法机构

extension
延期

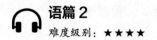

语篇2
难度级别：★★★★

无现金化社会

在不久的将来，**现金**将会消失，它会以数字信息的形式演变为电子货币。为何人们如此急于淘汰现金呢？这会付出什么代价呢？无现金未来意味着什么？

现金对于消费者和银行来说都很麻烦，人们需要**铸币**，需要打印账单，人们需要用装甲卡车来运输并将其保存在非常安全的仓库中，而且还要将其分类收放在现金抽屉里。现金运营成本约占一个国家一年总和的0.5%，成本却不是迈向**无现金**未来的唯一原因。人们对电子货币的需求正在上升，需求主要来自年轻一代，他们寻求快速易用的支付方式，数字货币不仅简单而且不会残损，政府更易于监控逃税和**欺诈**行为。

数字支付非常有效率，可以自动记录每笔付款。对于许多行业而言，了解人们把钱花在什么地方是很重要的。政府和私人公司能够利用电子货币的使用记录访问和收集个人数据，银行会遭遇网络攻击则是另一种威胁。

2019年3月，第一资本银行遭到黑客攻击。一个**独狼黑客**设法盗取了1.06亿人的个人详细信息。在短短几天之内，银行遭到黑客攻击，而且银行在几个月后才发现遭到黑客攻击。许多公司没能很好地防范这种威胁，人们几乎每天都能听到网络攻击成功，数据遭泄露的消息。防范攻击比成为黑客要难得多，阻止网络攻击是很难的。

国家在快速迈向无现金化社会。瑞典在过去十年中，人均零售现金交易数量下降了80%，这种趋势甚至在忠于现金的社会也很明显。中国的数字支付从2012年的4%上升到2017年的34%，这种趋势是不可避免的，但关键是要循序渐进。

控制这种趋势发展的速度是很重要的，因为如果不这样做的话，有些人可能会被甩在后面，有些人可能会发现，如果没有实物现金，很难清楚地知道自己拥有多少财富，不是每个人都能掌握网上银行的技术。生活在网络覆盖不完善的偏远地区的人会发现，他们为了上网，可能必须驱车好几英

词汇
现金 cash
铸币 coin
无现金 cashless
欺诈 fraud
独狼黑客 lone wolf hacker

里。社会弱势人群严重依赖现金，无现金对他们来说是非常困难的。

无现金化会产生一个问题：如果没有现金，货币的价值是什么？中央银行通过控制货币的数量来制定货币政策、创造货币用来流通，中央银行能够这样做是因为他们是唯一印刷和创造货币的实体，其目的是控制整个经济的货币使用总量。在无现金的社会中，这显然会变得更加困难，因为货币可能是由其他实体创造的，实际上中央银行开始意识到了这一点，尤其是在宣布他们将发行一种数字货币之后，它显示出各国央行已经在很大程度上开始考虑货币的未来。

向无现金化社会的**转变**正在进行中。但政府需要确保逐步**淘汰**现金的同时，社会中的弱势群体不会被落下。政府需要谨慎前行，避免数字经济带来的风险。

词汇

转变
transformation

淘汰
phase out

模块六

译海拾贝：口译专业考研规划

　　攻读口译专业研究生，首先要计划好到底是选择国内还是国外院校，并根据国内外院校的不同要求，提前做好规划。

　　2021年，国内招收英语口译专业研究生的院校共有110所左右。部分院校的英语口译专业并非连续招生。招收口译专业研究生的院校既包括传统的外语名校，如北京外国语大学、上海外国语大学、广东外语外贸大学等，也包括知名双一流综合类院校，如中国人民大学、武汉大学、复旦大学等，同时也有多所省属院校。登录"中国研究生招生信息网"的官网后，学生可以根据自己的能力水平选择合适的院校，并根据该校研究生院网站的规定，进行备考。考研笔试相关信息在各高校研究生院的官网上都有介绍，面试信息在官网上则鲜有介绍。国内的口译研究生面试基本围绕"源语复述""视译""交传"等口译形式展开，个别院校也会考查"无笔记交传"这种较难的形式。

　　与国内"中国研究生招生信息网"为学生提供了全面的院校和专业介绍相比，国外的口译专业信息都是零散地分布在各个学校的官网上。学生如果想考取国外院校的研究生，需要对不同层次的学校有整体了解，了解其托福、雅思分数和申请要求的区别。下面对知名度较高的海外口译专业进行介绍。

英国

巴斯大学：国际大学翻译学院联合会（CIUTI）的四个会员大学之一，其口译专业是欧洲认可度最高的。申请者要经历提交申请材料、初试、笔试和面试（自我介绍、即兴演讲、视译、问答）的四轮程序。

纽卡斯尔大学：纽卡斯尔大学的口译专业分为两年制和一年制课程。一年制课程的学术和雅思要求更高；两年制的面试流程是聊天、视译、问答，一年制还要加上即兴演讲。

利兹大学：利兹大学提交个人申请材料中包括翻译测试，难点在于其线上面试的无笔记交传，语料长度为3~5分钟，对学生的能力要求较高。

曼彻斯特大学：英国著名红砖大学之一，申请材料通过审核后，学校会通过线上方式进行能力测试，发送六篇文章，考生在线上面试中提取其中两篇（中英各一篇）做复述。

威斯敏斯特大学：国际大学翻译学院联合会（CIUTI）的会员，也是我国外交翻译人员指定的培训学校。它曾经为欧盟同传学位机构（EMCI）的成员之一，其入学申请难度相对低，申请材料通过学校审核后，学校会发来笔译文章作为翻译测试；通过笔试的学生要接受电话面试，进行3分钟左右的无笔记源语复述。

此外，英国的贝尔法斯特女王大学、萨里大学、伦敦城市大学等也都开设口译专业，招收中英口译专业学生，在国际上也具有一定的认可度。

美国

美国只有蒙特雷国际研究院提供中英会议口译专业的学习机会，其口译专业世界排名第一。该专业学制两年，第二年为Advanced Entry。第一年入学的官方建议是最好有半年以上英语国家生活学习经历，没有的话，要求在入学前先参加其夏校活动。GPA要求3.0+/4.0，或者GRE高分。IELTS要求总分7以上，其中听力和阅读不低于7，各项都不低于6.5。此外要通过Early Diagnostic Test（EDT）和Oral Diagnostic Test（ODT）。

综上所述，国内外的口译研究生面试，主要考查以下口译能力：交替传译、无笔记交传、（无笔记）源语复述、视译等。学生需要奠定良好的口译基础，才有可能通过国内外的口译考试的面试关。

模块七

译员风采：从翻译官到外交官之路

1949年后，我国外交队伍从零建起。1949年11月外交部成立时仅有170位工作人员。在外交队伍建立之初，周恩来总理便把这支外交队伍比喻为一支"文装的解放军"。1952年夏，约800名外国语专业的第一批学生陆续进入外交部。1954年日内瓦会议和1955年万隆会议的成功外交，促使大批外交官被派驻国外。"文革"早期，我国的外交队伍和外交事业遭受重创，1971年后外交部的工作逐渐恢复正常。在这一过程中，周恩来总理对外交干部特别是翻译干部给予了极大的关怀。他在"文革"期间曾多次指示，对下放的翻译干部要加强管理，避免其失散，同时要保证他们学习外语的时间，这极大地保证了20世纪70年代中国对外关系大发展时期的翻译需求。经过多年的努力与建设，我国外交使团在维护国家主权和尊严的外交战线上，交出了成绩斐然的答卷。

外交部的工作性质决定了外语优势强的人可能在外交战线上更容易走上外交官的舞台，本文介绍部分由翻译官变成外交官的代表性轨迹。

王毅，曾任国务委员、外交部长，北京第二外国语学院日语专业毕业，曾任驻日大使。

杨洁篪，外交部出国学习集训班学习后留学英国，从外交部翻译室科员走向外交部长、国务委员的岗位。

崔天凯，上海师范大学外语系毕业，从联合国译员做起，后任第十任中国驻美大使。

李肇星，北京大学西语系毕业，以翻译身份出道，直至驻美大使、外交部部长。

傅莹，北京外国语学院英语专业毕业，曾任党和国家领导人的高级翻译，曾任中国驻菲律宾、澳大利亚、英国等国大使以及外交部副部长等职位。

周文重，对外经济贸易大学毕业，曾任邓小平的翻译，驻美大使。

刘结一，北京外国语学院毕业，曾任中国常驻联合国代表、特命全权大使；中共中央台办、国务院台办副主任；中共中央台湾工作办公室主任、国务院台湾事务办公室主任。

章启月，北京外国语学院毕业，同传译员出身，曾任多国大使，有"外交名嘴"的美誉。

庞森，北京外国语学院毕业，做外交官的同时，笔耕不辍，出版多本译著，曾任外交部军控司司长、驻伊朗大使。

张建敏，北京外国语学院毕业，人称中国外事翻译"三剑客"之一，曾先后为江泽民、朱镕基、胡锦涛、温家宝翻译。曾任中华人民共和国外交部翻译司司长、外交部翻译室主任。

费胜潮，武汉大学毕业，曾任温家宝的翻译，现任驻索马里大使。

值得注意的是，外交部的翻译人才多毕业于北京外国语大学和外交学院。据统计，当前活跃在外交一线的外交官当中有1 000多人毕业于外交学院，外交部翻译司英语高翻有一半以上毕业于外交学院。外交部中有四分之一担任领导职务的，是从外交学院走出的毕业生；而北外共培育了13名大使，被誉为"共和国外交官摇篮"。

第九章

投资与衍生品
Investments & Derivatives

模块一　　　　　　　　　　　　　　　　　　　　　技能概要：言语重构

源语和目标语之间经常存在极大的文化差异，听众的思维逻辑更是千差万别。在翻译背景知识较强的源语过程中，如果学生只是语言外壳的搬运工，就会造成沟通不畅，无法传达发言者的真正意图。第八章所介绍的"脱壳翻译"强调的是脱离讲话者的语言外壳和形式束缚，直接将内核含义表达出来。本章所介绍的"言语重构"强调的是调整发言者的语言结构，达到清晰翻译的目的。

商务语言的言语重构主要可以分为语言词汇、语言逻辑、语言结构和语言文化这几个层面的重构。

第一，语言词汇层面。 词汇是文化和政治的载体，口译员选择用一个词而不用另一个具有相同含义的词汇，常常是政治立场决定的。如在香港回归过程中历时两年的22轮中英谈判，政治敏感度贯穿于谈判的始终。例如，22轮谈判（中文都叫"谈判"）中，英文用的是 talks（磋商），而不是 negotiations（谈判），因为邓小平同志坚持，谈判的底线就是香港主权问题不容谈判；其次，要说"恢复行使对香港的主权"，而不能说"收回"；另外，达成的协议不用 treaty（条约）或 agreement（协定），而是用 declaration（声明），因为主权问题不是中英协定的问题。再如，口译工作中经常会碰到大陆、台湾等提法，我们不可译为 mainland China、Taiwanese China、Taiwan (China)，而应译为 the mainland of China、China's mainland、Taiwan, China、Taipei, China、Chinese Taiwan；"台湾问题"应译为 Taiwan question，而不能用 Taiwan issue。翻译这类词语时候要表明，大陆和台湾都是中国的一部分。词汇重构是从言语层面坚定地维护国家主权和领土统一。

第二，语言逻辑层面。 汉语重意合，英语重形合；汉语隐性逻辑较多，显性逻辑较少；英语则显性逻辑较多，隐性逻辑较少。具体来说，也就是汉语本身黏合性强，往往以语序等隐性方式表示逻辑，比如因果关系、时间关系的表达都是通过语序先后来实现的；英语则主要使用逻辑词来表示逻辑，比如 if、when 和 but。因此，汉译英时经常需要添加逻辑词，使逻辑关系更为清晰明了且容易理解，而英译汉时则可以适当删减逻辑词，以减少口译产出的时间，使译文更为简洁。比如，汉语中"你不来，我就不来"的表达并没有明显的逻辑关系，但是英语需要还原其逻辑，译文不可以是"You don't come, I don't come either."，而应该是"If you don't come, I don't come either."英文的表达补充了 if 和 either，从而更加符合英语的语法和表达习惯。

在孙杨兴奋剂瑞士仲裁案中，孙杨有时候表述的逻辑不够清晰，而临危受命的译员 WADA 方的崔女士（之前环节中译员质量不过关，崔临时担任译员角色）则很圆满地处理了这一段。孙杨说："因为我要把这个过程和经过，一五一十、清清楚楚、明明白白地展现给大家，因为由于规定和规矩的原因不可以向外透露，所以要在这里举行公开听证会要让全世界的百姓或者粉丝，或者喜欢我的人和每一个人清清楚楚看到这个过程。"孙杨的言语有语义重复、逻辑不清的问题，"过程和经过""一五一十、清清楚楚、明明白白""规矩和规定""全世界的百姓或者粉丝，或者喜欢我的人"是语义重复。"果（展现给大家）→因（规定）→果（给大家看）"的逻辑表述导致因果不明，前后重叠。译员崔女士将逻辑和语言进行了整合和重组后，输出为"During the whole issue, because all the incidents are highly confidential, I would like to open this hearing, to amounts my statement to let the world hear me"，取得了简洁达意、清晰明了的效果。

第三，语言结构层面。汉语和英文各自有自己的表达习惯，译员要时常放弃原文的行文结构和语法结构，迎合听众的表达和理解习惯。比如，在两会的记者招待会上，译员孙宁将"'一带一路'版权虽属中国，但收益为各国共享"这句话处理为"The idea (of Belt and Road Initiative) came from China, but the benefits will flow to all countries."。"版权""属于""共享"等具有中国特色的表达方式被回避，用了温和中性的表达 come from 和 flow to，听起来简洁明了。再如"中方敦促韩方悬崖勒马，中止部署萨德系统，不要在错误的道路上越走越远"这句被孙宁翻译为"China urges the ROK to cease and desist, halt the THAAD deployment and not to go further down the wrong path."，他用了"urge sb. to do sth., halt sth."，而不是被原文的"不要"所束缚，译成"don't..."。通过肯定的正说，而不是"不要做某事"的反说，强化了表达的语气。

第四，语言文化层面。语言文化差异在第二章也做过阐述，这里就不再赘述。但是语言文化差异还体现在语言的得体性上。以杨洁篪和布林肯的中美高层战略对话为例，杨洁篪对美方说道："中国不吃这一套！"译员张京处理成"This is not the way to deal with Chinese people."削弱了情绪，无法把杨洁篪说话的气势和情绪准确传递过去。"We Chinese don't buy it."更能传递原话的情感色彩。

再如，在 2019 年 7 月 31 日的外交部记者会上，有记者问："美国总统特朗普称，中方经常出尔反尔。如果要等到明年大选他连任之后才签订协议，那一定会是一个更差的协议。中方对此有何评论？"华春莹说："我看到了有关报道，我只想呵呵两声"。译员将其处理为："On your third question, I have seen relevant reports and twitter. Hmm. How interesting!"通过把汉语描述笑姿的词译为"How interesting!"，既不失礼貌，又把鄙视之意淋漓尽致地传递过去。

言语重构是建立在扎实的双语基本功之上的。如果想从容地使用得体的重构表达，学生要在学习中具有语言转换意识，打好基本功。

模块二　　　　　　　　　　　　　　　　　　　　　　　　　译前准备

◎ 1. 背景知识

在经济高速发展的中国，股票、债券、基金和期货等金融衍生品是重要的经济发展工具。这种高度专业化语料翻译不仅对学生的双语基础提出了较高要求，也需要学生掌握相应的背景知识。

本模块涉及的概念主要有风投公司、沃伦·巴菲特、城市服务优先股、比亚迪、查理·芒格、高瓴资本、定增。

风投公司（venture capital firm）：即风险投资公司。这些公司往往将自身基金投资给一些自身认为具有潜力的初创企业，有时也会提供公司发展战略上的建议，以期获得丰厚的投资回报。这种行为往往风险较高，但相应的潜在回报也很高。

沃伦·巴菲特（Warren E. Buffett）：全球著名投资家，师从"华尔街教父"本·格雷厄姆（Ben Graham）。从小研究股市，成年后凭借优秀的投资业绩一跃成为顶级富豪，曾任哈克希尔·哈撒韦公司董事长和首席执行官，被誉为"股神"。

城市服务优先股（Cities Service preferred）："城市服务"是1910年开创的一家天然气公司，现已倒闭。优先股指的是相较普通股来说享有优先清偿等权利的股票。

比亚迪（BYD）：成立于1995年，其创始人为王传福，主营业务为汽车和电池，是汽车企业新势力中的标杆。由于其在新能源汽车等方面做出的环保贡献，该公司获得了"扎耶德未来能源奖"和"联合国特别能源奖"。

查理·芒格（Charlie Munger）：沃伦·巴菲特多年的老搭档，伯克希尔·哈撒韦公司的副主席。在投资方面，查理·芒格的造诣不可小觑。

高瓴资本（Hillhouse Capital Group）：高瓴资本为张磊于2005年创立的投资公司，

专注长期结构性价值投资，是亚洲地区资产管理界知名企业，在腾讯、滴滴出行、美团外卖、美的集团和京东等知名企业里均有投资。

定增（private placement）：定向增发是增发股票的一种形式。上市公司往往会向特定群体或个人进行非公开的股票增发售卖，这些群体或者个人往往是现有股东，他们在购买定增形式的股票时，通常会享有更为优惠的价格。

◎ 2. 核心词汇

go public	上市	futures contract	期货合约
V-C fund (Venture Capital fund)	风投基金	also-ran	失败者；陪跑者
seed round	种子期	equity	资产
Angel investor	天使投资人	Ni-Cd battery	镍镉电池
cash out	套现	Welch	维尔奇
Stock Exchange	股票交易所	electrolyte	电解液
diversification	分散化投资		

模块三　　　　　　　　　　　　　　　　　　　语料实训

  任务 1. 英译汉
难度级别：★★★

> 训练要点：本文介绍了公司创业融资的过程以及上市的动机。全文较简单，使用的词汇较为常见，讲述过程中涉及不少专业术语的解释，要求学生熟练掌握相应术语。在口译产出过程中，学生不要被源语句式束缚，尝试使用言语重构，通过重构来获取相对简约、压力小的输出方式。

Why Does Companies Go Public?

To understand why companies go public, we need to understand why companies exist. In today's world, if you want to do business, you have to register a company. And here's why.

Even the biggest companies today started out as just a few people with an idea. Now, having a good business idea is great, but you're not gonna get very far if you don't have the money to develop it. That's why most young companies, also known as startups, begin looking for outside investors very early on in their existence, usually before they've even developed their first product. Of course, most startups never find a single investor, and they go bankrupt.

In fact, finding an initial investor is so hard that in the startup world, that person is called an angel investor, because he literally saves the company from failing. To get an angel investor on board, the founders, who, up until now, owned 100% of the startup, need to give up some of their ownership in exchange for money. The startup needs this money to hire employees, rent an office and develop its first products. This initial stage is known as the seed round, and startups here are usually valued at up to a million dollars.

Once the startup has some angel investors, that's when it starts attracting venture capital firms. In the startup world, V-Cs are the big boys. You've probably heard the names of the more popular V-C funds, and it should come as no surprise that some of the biggest companies today have their own venture capital divisions. The stage at which venture capital gets involved is called the series A, and at this point, startups are usually valued at around $10 million. Of course, some companies need even more money, so down the line, they hold additional funding rounds to attract more venture capital. A few companies, like Snapchat, for example, go very far down the funding alphabet, sometimes reaching billion dollar valuations while they're still private.

But eventually, all the angel investors and venture capitalists are gonna want to cash out. This is the biggest reason why startups go public. Joining the funding round of a very sought-after startup is difficult, but selling your startup shares after you give them is even harder. There are numerous restrictions on startup stocks, like who you can sell them to and when at the earliest you can try to do so, but when a startup goes public on a stock exchange in a process known as an initial public offering, well, then most restrictions get lifted, and all the early investors can cash out. They sell their stock to the hungry public, which is scrambling to get their hands on the newly listed shares. This is where you, as an individual investor, can finally get in on the action.

But investing all your money in a newly public company is a very risky decision. In fact, investing all your money in any single company is generally a bad idea. Most investors spread their money out across multiple companies in many different industries. This is called diversification, and it's one of the core principles of investing.

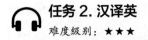
任务 2. 汉译英
难度级别：★★★

> 训练要点：本文以简单的例子深入浅出地讲解了期货的概念。讲解过程生动有趣，但是也涉及不少数字，特别要注意数字与单位的对应关系。在听辨过程中，学生要注意口语化的风格，对原文信息适当进行加工整理，使其更符合英文的表达方式；要注意如何将复杂烦琐或者重复信息进行简化。

什么是期货？

生意场上的高手有两种：一种是专门稳赚不赔的钱，比如李嘉诚。他投资的公司都是供水、供电的这种，人人都需要，而且是绝对刚需。另一种高手就是赚行情的钱。

当我们去开一家水果店的时候，10元钱进货、20元钱卖货，赚的是水果的差价。可是当我们做一个市甚至一个省的水果生意的时候，这时候7元钱进货，7块5卖货。可是水果的价格波动是很大的。有时候今天刚以7元钱的价格进货，没过几天销售的价格就掉到了7块。如果平价出售，那就要亏掉人工、仓储、物流的成本。但是如果今天7元钱进的货，没过几天销售价格上涨到9块，这时候再卖出，那这一批货赚的利润，可就相当于原来的四批货。所以水果这类的大批发商都会很关心价格行情。

我们只是拿水果举例子。其实赚这种行情钱的人不仅仅是水果，还有煤炭、钢铁、大豆等这些领域都通用。可是我原来正常流通买卖只需要10吨的量，难道由于对后续价格看涨就要多囤20吨吗？那岂不是成了赌博？当然不用。现在的市场早就有了成熟的工具，也就是期货。说起期货，大家都觉得风险太高了。可是，你知道吗？期货的出现原本是用来规避风险。

比如我是a村庄卖大米的商人，你是b村庄的餐饮老板，我现在定价5元钱一斤，但是由于大米每年的收成都不一样。今年风调雨顺大丰收，我跟农民收米的时候，价格就低一些，卖给你的时候就便宜。可是明年旱灾庄稼歉收，我跟农民再收大米，就要给他们多一些钱。这时候我的成本就高了，所以我再卖给你，价格就要贵一些。

如此，这个月定价还是5块钱一斤，下个月可能就6块、7块，下个季度可能就又3块、4块。总之，价格这样的波动让咱们买家和卖家都很难受，这个月还是赚的，下个月就亏了，太不稳定。所以双方开始约定下个月就以固定的价格5块钱进行买卖，明年的四月份就以固定价格四块八进行买卖。如此，双方就签订了这么一个远期的约定合同，这个合同就是期货。

我们刚刚交易完成，到了八月份的时候，大米的价格就暴涨到了 10 块钱，这时候 b 村的餐馆开始决定主食不再提供大米。所以 B 老板把当初的大米合同拿到市场上进行售卖，由于合同上当初约定的收购价格是 5 元一斤，而此时市场上的大米售价是 10 元一斤，所以这份合同已经产生了每斤 5 块钱的利润，所以他就把这份合同高价卖给了另一个餐馆的老板 c。从这之后，市场上就有了更多的 a 和 b 达成约定合同，也有了更多的 c、d、e、f、g 来进行买卖合同。如此，期货的交易市场就这么形成了。你看，期货并不是货，它只是那个合同而已。所以术语中我们管它叫期货合约。期货的诞生是很神奇的存在，它既能让一部分人规避风险，也能让一部分人死于风险。

任务 3. 英译汉
难度级别：★★★★

> 训练要点：本文节选了巴菲特参与访谈节目时的片段，介绍了巴菲特在股市获得成功的理论并谈及了部分股民错误的投机心理。巴菲特的讲话略有含混不清，并且夹杂了一些噪声，这就增加了听辨源语和口译的难度。这种语料的翻译如果全部跟进的话，学生面临的口译挑战较大，因此本文更适合言语重构的翻译。建议对同一篇语料多次复盘，形成重构能力。

Buffett: How I Succeed in Stock Market

Buffett: When I was eleven, I picked stocks. I had the whole wrong idea. I was interested in watching stocks, and I thought stocks were things that went up and down. I charted them. I read books on technical ones, so I read Edwards and Maggie. I think that was the classic then. Hundreds and hundreds of pages. And I read that whole thing over and over again. I read everything. And I thought in the first eight years... I thought the important thing was to predict what a stock would do and predict the stock market. And then I read Ben Graham, you know, I was 19 or 20, and I realized that I was doing it exactly the wrong way. But it didn't hurt that I had that background and everything, and I rejiggered my mind. And when I read the book, the *Intelligent Investor*, from that point, I never bought another stock. I bought businesses that happened to be publicly traded. I became an owner of a business, and I did not care whether a stock went up or down the next day, or the next week, or the next month or the next year. And

I didn't have any idea what it would do. I didn't know what the stock market would do, but I knew businesses.

I'm a bright guy who's terribly interested in what he does. I've spent a lifetime doing it. I've surrounded myself with people that bring out the best in me. And you don't need to be a genius in what I do. That's the good thing about it. If I was into the physics and a whole lot of other subjects. I'd be an also-ran, but I am in a game that you probably need 120 points of IQ. But 170 doesn't do any better than 120. It may do worse, probably do worse, but you don't really need brains.

Interviewer: What do you need?

Buffett: You need the right orientation. You know, 90% of the people. I'm pulling the figure out of the air, but 90% of the people that buy stocks don't think of them the right way. They think about something that they hope goes up next week, and think about the market as something that they hope goes up. And if it is down, they feel worse, I feel better.

Interviewer: And you think about...

Buffett: I think about what the company is gonna be worth then or 20 years from now, and I hope it goes down when I buy it, because I'll buy more. I try to keep my competitive spirits in a game I will win. I do know this: when I want to do something, I always want to do it big. I put my whole net worth in Cities Service preferred. $140.75. I've never since that day—you know, March 11th, 1942—I have never had less than 80% of my money in American business. You can call them stocks.

Interviewer: Or equity.

Buffett: But I see them as American business. I've owned a piece of American business, at least 80% at all times. I just, I don't want to own anything else.

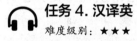

任务 4. 汉译英
难度级别：★★★

> **训练要点**：本文介绍了知名车企比亚迪受欢迎的原因，其思路主要是围绕不同人对比亚迪的态度而展开。内容本身叙述性较强，不难理解，但涉及不少数字，需要学生进行正确处理。同时要仔细思考怎样才能以更简洁、更地道的英文进行翻译，这涉及语言重构的技巧。

为什么比亚迪那么受欢迎？

全球首富特斯拉 CEO 马斯克曾在采访中被问道，你怎么看待比亚迪？马斯克则狂笑着问道："你有见过比亚迪的车吗？"言外之意，比亚迪从未进入马斯克的视野中。而与马斯克相反的是，投资圈的大佬们却都深爱着比亚迪。投资大王查理·芒格则表示，就算进了坟墓，也要抱着比亚迪的股票。股神巴菲特为了投资比亚迪，多次来中国会见比亚迪创始人王传福。高瓴资本创始人张磊更是在比亚迪股票高位上涨时投资比亚迪 13 亿元。王传福与比亚迪为何能吸引这么多人关注呢？

王传福是中国制造业杰出的企业家代表，他 1995 年下海经商注册比亚迪。到 1997 年的时候，比亚迪的年营收额已经达到了 1 亿元。在起步的三年里，比亚迪每年的增长率都可以达到 100%。1997 年金融风暴席卷整个亚洲，比亚迪利用低成本优势迅速填补市场空缺，拿下了行业 40% 的份额，成为镍镉电池行业当之无愧的一哥。

王传福有自己的抱负，他常说要让中国汽车走出去，让中国制造面向世界，让中国新能源改变世界。2008 年 9 月，巴菲特旗下的伯克希尔·哈萨韦能源公司与比亚迪联合宣布伯克希尔·哈萨维韦能源以每股 8 港元的价格购入比亚迪 H 股 2.25 亿股，共计 2.32 亿美元，约占比亚迪股份的 10%。这也成为巴菲特唯一持有的中国股。

股神巴菲特对比亚迪的投资，主要来自老搭档查理·芒格的强烈推荐。芒格对巴菲特说，"我发现了一个艾迪生与维尔奇的合体，那就是王传福，我们必须要投资比亚迪"。对于科技股，巴菲特一向比较保守，后来他特地和芒格一起来到中国参观比亚迪工厂。看到王传福为了证明电池的环保，当众喝下一杯电解液的时候，巴菲特不再犹豫了，立刻决定投资 20% 的股份，但王传福不希望中国品牌的外资持股过多，最后才确定转让给巴菲特 10% 的比亚迪股份。

2019 年，高瓴资本创始人张磊不顾合伙人的劝阻，清空了全部高瓴持有的未来、小鹏、理想等中国造车新势力的股份，转投比亚迪 13 亿元。2021 年年初，高瓴资本再斥资 2 亿美元参与比亚迪定增。如今，张磊的投资早已为他带来了超过五倍的回报，盈利近 100 亿元。张磊曾在《价值》一书中提到，只要企业能给社会创造价值，就算是亏钱，高瓴也会投资，因为社会迟早会回馈这样的企业。

很显然，比亚迪就是这样能为社会创造长期价值的公司。和其他车企不同，比亚迪并不需要从其他的生产厂商那里购买零部件。比亚迪有属于自己的完整产业链，同时掌握了电池、电机、电控以及芯片等全产业核心技术。这也得益于多年来比亚迪全产业链的研发投入。2020 年，比亚迪研发投入金额合计为 85.56 亿元，同比增长了 1.6%。截至 2020 年年底，比亚迪申请专利共计 25 656 件。早在 2015 年，比亚迪就已经成为全球新能源汽车的销量冠军，如今比亚迪更是集 IT、汽车、新能源三大产业集群于一体的高科技产业公司。

模块四

技巧点拨：言语重构技能

 任务 1. 英译汉
难度级别：★★★

> 训练要点：本段音频中挑出两个实例来分析如何培养听辨能力。音频较长，听第一遍的时候，将全篇音频听完，尝试提炼全文主旨框架。第二遍复盘时，体会两处例子如何进行具体的框架提炼。

例一

A $3 box of corn cereal stays at roughly the same price day to day and week to week. But corn prices can change daily. Sometimes by a few cents. Sometimes by a lot more. Why does the cost of processed food generally stay quite stable even though the crops that go into them have prices that fluctuate? It's partly thanks to the futures market. The futures market allows the people who sell and buy large quantities of corn to insulate you, the consumer, from those changes without going out of business themselves.

译文

一盒 3 美元的玉米燕麦片的价格每天或每周都差不多。可是玉米价格每天都会变动，有时幅度会有几分钱，有时会很多。尽管制造燕麦片的作物价格会波动，可是为什么加工食品成本一直保持稳定？其中部分原因是来自期货市场。它让大量买卖玉米的人在自己不倒闭的情况下能够庇护消费者，使其免受价格波动困扰。

重构翻译

一盒玉米燕麦片价格总保持在 3 美元左右，但玉米价格每天都或多或少会变动。为什么作物价格波动但其加工成的食品能大体稳定呢？期货市场是原因之一。它既保障了大量买卖玉米的能把生意做下去，又使消费者不必面对价格波动。

策略分析

本段以玉米与燕麦片价格关系为例子，引出了期货市场这一概念。照搬英文语序会使译文极其别扭，如第一版译文中的最后一句。所以，学生需要对语序进行处理。比如"3 美元"从句前调整到了句后，而"It's partly thanks to..."也一样。此外，"Why does..."部分的译文也将作物价格和食品价格的讲述顺序进行了调换，这是出于对汉语"前因后果"的逻辑顺序考虑。同时，最后一句也对逻辑关系进行了处理，将"买卖玉米的"和"消费者"之间不明显的逻辑关系重新做了分离，这样更清晰。

重构要点

1. 中文在逻辑上往往强调"前因后果"，学生在英译中时要多加注意。
2. 中英的逻辑思维并不一样，有时重新拆分组织会更加有利于受众理解。

》例二

　　In fact, finding an initial investor is so hard that in the startup world, that person is called an angel investor, because he literally saves the company from failing. To get an angel investor on board, the founders, who up until now owned 100% of the startup, need to give up some of their ownership in exchange for money. The startup needs this money to hire employees, rent an office and develop its first products. This initial stage is known as the seed round, and startups here are usually valued at up to a million dollars.

译文

　　事实上，找到第一位投资者很难，所以这位投资者被称为天使投资人，因为他真正拯救了这家公司。为了让天使投资人入股，创始人们要把他们对公司百分百的所有权出让一部分用以换取资金。初创公司需要拿这笔钱来找雇员、租场地以及开发首款产品。这个初步阶段称作种子期，此时公司估值最高约一百万美元。

重构翻译

　　公司要活下去，得找到第一位投资者，这可不容易，所以我们也称其为天使投资人。为了让他（她）入股，创始人得出让公司部分所有权来换钱，以供公司雇人、租地以及开发产品。这一起步阶段称作种子轮，此时公司估值通常高达一百万美元。

策略分析

　　言语重构要训练如何识别语言叙述逻辑，再以目标语习惯对其进行重组，而不是盲从原本的语序，特别是交替传译的场景中，学生有一定的重构时间。第一句分为一个主句"finding... is so hard"和两个从句"that person is... investor""because he..."，其通过"so... that..."和"because..."联结，本质上是前后部分为因，中间为果。因此，在重构翻译版本中，表示原因的两部分处理到了前面，而表示结果的部分放到了后面，脱离了原文的句式限制，这样更符合汉语"前因后果"的特征。另外，"who up until now owned 100% of the startup"在重构版本中采用了省译法，这是因为根据原文可以推知，此时创始人拥有全部所有权。

重构要点

1. 注意中英文对逻辑处理的差别。中文逻辑通过语序表达，因此逻辑之间的语序表达较为固定，如果单纯按英文语序，则会略显别扭。
2. 可以适当跳脱，改变个别词语的含义，以使表达意义更加清晰明了，但这要建立在尊重原句意的基础上。
3. 口译时为了简洁明了，需要对一些可以推知的信息进行省略。

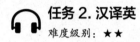

任务 2. 汉译英
难度级别：★★

在第一章开始前，我想先问大家一个问题。如果你有买过基金或者正想要尝试着买个基金看看能不能赚到钱，那么这算一笔投资吗？很多人可能想说，投资基金不就是投资吗？要不然算啥？其实在很多人看来，自己是在做投资。但其实这里还有一个词，就是"投机"。

译文

Before starting introducing the first chapter, I'd like to ask everyone a question. If you plan to or have bought a fund for the purpose of economic return, is it an investment? Many will want to say buying fund is of course investment. What else can it be? Though they see their action as investment, there is a better term called speculation.

重构翻译

Here's a question before I introduce the first chapter. Should your past or potential purchase of fund for profits be counted as an investment? Many will say yes, seeing themselves as investors, but the better term for this should be "speculation".

策略分析

本段是一个承接部分，意在通过一个问题引出投机的定义。尽管原文本身不算啰唆，但还是存在语义重复。"……不就是投资么？""要不然算啥？"和"……，自己是在做投资。"就是一组语义重复。如果遵照源语形式翻译，不免太过啰唆。所以这里适当重构，进行省译。同时，"你有买过……或正要买……"，如果处理成两个并列的谓语动词 plan to buy or have bought，不免太过啰唆。在重构版本中，"如果……那么……"两个句子也被分别转化为主语、谓语＋宾语的成分，无疑更为简洁。

重构要点

1. 注意前后各句的语义重复。在口译时，学生应对重复部分进行整合，适当脱离源语形式。
2. 不同成分所扮演的语法成分在译文中可改变，以准确、简洁为标准。

模块五　拓展练习

任务 1：段落言语重构练习

请参照模块一的言语重构技巧对下列段落进行翻译产出。

1. **Meta's** quarterly earnings delighted investors, for a change, as it sets out a plan to reduce in a "year of efficiency" and announced a $40bn share buy-back. Revenue fell in the first three months of 2022, year on year, but is expected to rise in this quarter. Still, **Reality Labs**, the division tasked with creating the metaverse, ran up another loss, of $4.3 billion, taking its total loss for the year to $13.7 billion.

2. After months of sometimes troublesome negotiations, **Nissan** and **Renault** announced a restructuring of their two-decade-old alliance, which has been under strain since the fall from grace in 2018 of Carlos Ghosn, who had run both carmakers. The main feature of the agreement is a reduction in Renault's stake in Nissan to 15% from 43%, with the remainder of Renault's shares in Nissan to be put into a French trust and the voting rights "neutralized".

词汇

Meta
元宇宙

Reality Labs
真实实验室

Nissan
尼桑公司

Renault
雷诺公司

3. 因受地震影响，土耳其股市 8 日延续跌势。在早盘阶段，**伊斯坦布尔 100 指数**下跌 5%，触发**熔断机制**。这是土耳其股市 24 年来首次暂停交易，土耳其南部地区本周一发生两次强烈地震后，股市值蒸发近 350 亿美元。目前土耳其股市距离一月份的高点已下跌超过 20%。

4. 谷歌的母公司 Alphabet 公司股价下跌超过 7%。这是自 10 月 26 日以来的最大跌幅。原因是投资者担心其新推出的人工智能聊天机器人 Bard（巴德）可能会给出不准确的回答。谷歌在一份声明当中表示，巴德的回应强调了严格测试过程的重要性，该公司表示将把外部反馈与自己的内部测试结合起来，以确保巴德的回应在质量、安全和真实信息的基础上达到高标准。

词汇

伊斯坦布尔 100 指数
Istanbul 100 Index

熔断机制
circuit breaker

任务 2：衍生品口译练习

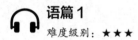

语篇 1
难度级别：★★★

What Is Derivative?

What is a **derivative**? Derivative is a financial instrument with the price to derive from an underlying asset. In a broad sense, it's an agreement between two or more parties. What can be considered an asset? A lot of instruments: stocks, indexes, **commodities** and even weather. To make things clearer, let's look closer.

This is John. He owns a bicycle factory. To produce a new line of bicycles, he will need five tons of steel a year from now on. This is Harry. He manufactures steel. He agrees to sell John five tons of steel at a certain price on a predetermined date in future. Thus, these two make a contract or a derivative, with steel as an underlying asset. Why not simply buy steel when you need it? The answer is simple. To manage risks. Here's what John thinks. What if the price of steel skyrockets and I will lose money? And here is

词汇

derivative
衍生品

commodity
大宗商品

where Harry thinks. What if the price of steel falls and I will lose money? Each of them enters a derivative contract to manage risks, to agree on a price, and to protect himself from market fluctuations.

Some traders used derivatives to speculate on price moves. In other words, they buy or sell an asset with the expectation of making a profit. There are five main types of derivatives: options, futures, forwards, swaps and contracts for difference. But the goal is always to manage risk or to speculate, or both. Smart traders know that all types of investment come with risks. Derivatives are not an exception. Value of an underlying asset can go against you, resulting in losses.

What Is Stock?

○ 词汇

For most investors, stocks are the first asset class they encounter. It makes a lot of sense. Our world is driven by companies, so it's natural for people to want a piece of the action. But when you buy a share of a given company, you don't actually own a fraction of that company as an entity, or at least not directly. Instead, each share represents a **claim** on the company's asset.

claim
所有权

This distinction might sound trivial, but it's actually very important. Corporations are legally considered as people. They can own cars and houses in the same way that you can, and they can even borrow money and go into debt. There are many examples of companies borrowing too much money and going bankrupt, but legally that event has nothing to do with you the shareholder. You just don't claim on that company's assets. And if the company doesn't have any assets, well then your shares are worth zero, but the banks who loaned money to that company can't come after you. In other words, the most you could lose by purchasing a share is the amount of money you spent on it. Realistically, it's hard to imagine the world's biggest companies going bankrupt, which is why their shares are considered safe investments.

Let's say you want to buy shares of **McDonald's**, for example. You log into your **brokerage account**, you make an order, and you are now the proud owner of one share of the McDonald's Corporation. You are now officially a shareholder, but that doesn't mean you can go into any of their restaurants and eat a happy meal for free. So what benefit does owning McDonald's stock give you? Well, like most companies, the McDonald's Corporation sets aside some of its profits every quarter and pays them out to their shareholders. This is known as a **dividend**, and it gives you a steady stream of cash. But wait, it gets even better.

McDonald's opens new restaurants every year, so you can reasonably expect the company to have higher earnings in the future, which not only means more dividends for you, but also increases the value of the company itself. Thus, if you bought your share for 150 dollars, it might be worth 160 next year. As a proud McDonald's shareholder, you can attend the company's annual meeting, where you can vote on many important decisions which will impact the future of McDonald's. Now, most companies have a very simple voting structure. One share gets one vote. In your case, you own one out of the 785 million McDonald's shares in existence, so you command exactly this much of the voting power in the company. Obviously, you wouldn't be able to change much with your vote, but the more you invest in the company, the bigger your impact is going to be. With enough money, you could theoretically buy up enough of the shares to single-handedly become the majority shareholder. That is the magic of publicly-traded companies. With enough money, anyone can buy their way in.

词汇

McDonald's
麦当劳

brokerage account
经纪账户

dividend
分红

模块六

译海拾贝：口译中突发状况与现场应变

口译的"即时性"和"瞬时性"的特征决定了译员在口译现场需要进行快速转换与产出。尽管充分的译前准备可以有效减少口译现场的不确定因素，但是口译员不是现场局势的主导者，而是被动接受者。现场的状况往往是变化多端的，随时可能出现一些扰乱口译员的因素。一名优秀的口译员会根据现场情况而灵活调整自己的应对策略，顺利完成口译任务。

口译现场的突发状况通常是由临时日程变化、源语质量、发言人情感和现场氛围以及设备故障所引发。比较常见的一些状况包括但不限于：主办方临时变动译员工作形式、更换主讲人、讲话内容专业性强、发言人脱离原稿、口音过重、引经据典或讲笑话以及设备故障等。下文通过几个实际口译案例帮助学生了解一些不可控事件中译员如何处理现场。

政治会谈为了保障话语效果和翻译质量，领导人经常采用短话轮的模式进行谈判或会谈。如两会记者问答环节中，总理每次讲话时长不会超过两三分钟，停下后外交部译员进行口译，这种时长是完全在外交部译员的能力范围内的。但是在 2021 年 3 月 18 日于阿拉斯加安克雷奇举行的中美高层战略对话中，国务委员杨洁篪对美方的无理要求进行了长达 16 分 26 秒不间断的驳斥。当译员张京终于可以进行翻译的时候，她用 13 分钟左右将全文流畅完成，美国国务卿布林肯说道："We are going to give the translator a raise." 对张京的表现给予了积极评判。在这个超长的讲话中，张京曾经中间抬头看杨主任，但是杨主任并没有注意到她这种示意停的目光信号，张京就只能继续笔记下去，避免打断杨洁篪的思路。其中还有个小插曲，张京把"在美国进行的民调"翻译成了"在中国进行的民调"，译员出身的杨洁篪适时指出了错误。一名高水平的口译员必须拥有良好的心理素质。试想，如果遇到了超长讲话、被听者挑出翻译错误，如果没有强大的心理素质，如何沉着应战？

口译的即时性决定了口译任务是很难做到尽善尽美的，因此传达准确的意思或者说对观众产生同样的效果永远是第一位的。有过这么一则轶事：一名发言人的口音极其严重，却还讲了一个笑话。笑话往往是具有很强的文化语境，难以被外方理解，更别提他的口音。情急之下，口译员灵机一动，说："The speaker is telling us a joke, but it is not funny at all. To show respect, could you please laugh now?"一时之间，整个会堂都哄堂大笑。这里虽然没能传达出准确的意思，但是取得了相同的效果，不失为良策。

口译员还经常遇到双语都比较好的讲话者，会挑出译员的翻译毛病和错误；或者讲话人口音很重，译员听不懂；翻译中有时候背景知识超出了译员的知识范围。这些情况对译员心理素质提出极高的要求。比如，过家鼎在1962年的第一次为周恩来总理翻译的时候，当总理向外宾介绍赵朴初先生是一位"居士"时，他就卡住了。总理专门解释了"居士"的含义，并让过家鼎回去研究应该如何翻译。邓小平的四川口音比较重，"四"和"十"有时难以听辨清楚，翻译张幼云就用手指头比量出"四"和"十"来让邓小平同志来确认。口译中出现突发状况，需要译员具有强大的心理素质和稳重的表现来处理现场，而不是冷场或者将错就错。

模块七 译员风采：女承父业，闻生闻声

美国前国务卿基辛格在回忆录中这样形容一位中国女性："聪明活泼，完全可以去竞选美国总统，是个难对付的女人。"她就是中国重返联合国第一位副秘书长唐明照的女儿、中国外交部前副司长唐闻生。

1943年3月，清华才子唐明照在印度出差，因为妻子张希先马上要生产，他火急火燎地从印度赶回美国。女儿在美国呱呱坠地，唐明照为她取名唐闻生，寓意"闻父归而生"。

唐闻生虽然在美国成长，享受着异国优良的教学资源，但是父母并未放松对她爱国主义思想的培养。父亲是清华才子，母亲张希先是大家闺秀。良好的家世与自由的成长环境，从小就给了她学习的沃土。

1950年，为了能够建设祖国，唐明照夫妇毅然放弃了在美国的优渥条件，克服千难万阻带着七岁的唐闻生回到祖国。这片土地对唐闻生是熟悉又陌生的。熟悉是因为父母已经给她讲过千百遍这里的故事，陌生则是因为她从未踏足过这片土地。然而，看着同胞们，一种亲近感在她心里油然而生，那是一种骨髓里涌动着的本能。

由于拥有良好的双语教育，唐闻生刚一入学就成为小学三年级的插班生。她适应性强，在故土如鱼得水，很快以优异的成绩考入了北京师范大学附属中学。学业繁重的高中时光里，她总是央求在外交部工作、经常出差的父亲带回几本英文书籍。她孜孜不倦地读着世界各国的优秀文学作品，并尝试把它们一点点地翻译成中文，立志要像父亲一样在祖国的外交事业上发光发热。

1962年，品学兼优的唐闻生跳级提前高中毕业，并以亮眼的成绩考入了北京外国语学院。哪怕是在群英荟萃的"外交官摇篮"里，她也没有泯然众人，反而大放异彩，不仅在学业成绩上优秀异常，也积极参与各种社会实践活动。一时间，她成为师生口中的风云人物。

1965年，唐闻生通过跳级成功提前完成学业，她凭借自身过硬素质通过选拔考试，顺利进入外交部英文组，参与了不少翻译任务，还经常给周恩来总理做翻译。当时，唐闻生那一口标准的美国东部口音以及高超的翻译水准，使得上级领导都对她青睐有加。

然而就是这样优秀的一名译员，也闹过一次外交笑话。

1966年，毛泽东主席在武汉决定会见参与亚非作家会议的五十多个国家及地区代表。经过外交部高层商议，决定给主席配备英语、法语以及阿拉伯语的译员各一名。唐闻生正是被选中的英语译员。唐闻生接到任务后非常紧张。一方面，虽然她的基本功扎实，可是面对这样的大场合，心底也是止不住地发怵；另一方面，她又担心听不懂主席的湖南口音会导致翻译出错。两重压力之下，唐闻生一时竟不堪重负在会议之前晕倒过去。幸运的是，醒转后，同事告知她主席并不打算发表演讲，她听罢如释重负。

但是，这次经历使得她充分意识到了自身的不足之处——一名优秀的译员怎么能不具有临危不乱的心理素质呢？为了能在类似场合重新证明自己，她下定决心要苦练翻译，下一次一定不能再度失态。

在日复一日的勤学苦练之中，这个机会终于来了。1970年，巴基斯坦总统抵达北京进行国事访问，这时的唐闻生已经今非昔比了。担任主翻的她，不负众望，以绝对的翻译质量完成了这次任务。这还不是唐闻生在此次外交活动中的唯一收获。在两国领导人口中，她也窥见了中美关系变化的一角，这为她在后来的历史性事件中的翻译工作奠定了基础。这个历史性事件就是美国国务卿基辛格秘密访华。

要知道，彼时中美关系虽有较为隐秘的改善，但实质上的进展还尚未取得。这次活动的重要性不言而喻。假如拿她第一次失态的事件比作千斤之重，这次访问就好比孙悟空背负的五指山。可此时的唐闻生也算练就了一身"神通"。她气定神闲游刃有余，以落落大方的仪态和精准独到的翻译赢得了在场来宾的一致认可，甚至基辛格都注意到了主席身边的这个小姑娘。交谈期间，还拿唐闻生打趣。唐闻生的翻译水准，可谓是有目共睹。

纵观唐闻生女士的一生，深埋功与名，无暇修个人小家，全心投入家国大事。在翻译事业上，她秉承着认真专业的态度；在五星红旗下，她书写了自己为国奉献的岁月。

第十章

经济危机
Economic Crisis

模块一　　　　　　　　　　　　　　技能概要：基础影子训练

听力理解、短时记忆和口译输出是决定口译质量的关键要素。影子训练能培养学生三个方面的能力：形成高度集中的注意力，提高听力理解；训练短时记忆能力；巩固语感，提升口语能力。首先，影子训练中，学生在跟读的过程中精力要高度集中，否则无法在头脑中复制源语并如鹦鹉学舌般地进行输出。此外，语速、语调等也要保持原文风格。其次，可以提升学生的听力、口语能力和语音语调。常规的听力训练是通过听音频来实现的，但是影子训练在听的同时，还需要张嘴模仿，这需要大脑同时协调听解、模仿等功能。张嘴模仿的过程可以增强口语语感，因此可以一举多得，提升学生的听力、发音、记忆、语感。最后，影子跟读过程中，在理解消化跟读材料的基础上，学生可以扩大词汇量以及知识面。

影子训练分为基础和高阶两种形式，即逐字跟读和延后跟读两种形式。前者要求学生用同种语言几乎同步跟读讲者，适合初学者；而后者要求学生稍滞后于讲者；还有延时跟读后插入其他任务的更高阶训练方法，对学生的短时记忆和逻辑分析等能力的要求更高，适合中高阶学生。在基础阶段训练中，学生可以按照循序渐进的原则进行如下训练：

<u>基础训练第一阶段</u>：紧跟源语跟读（无延迟）

<u>基础训练第二阶段</u>：源语倍速跟读

<u>基础训练第三阶段</u>：源语跟读 + 关键词复述

<u>基础训练第四阶段</u>：源语跟读 + 关键词 + 总结原文

<u>基础训练第五阶段</u>：源语跟读 + 输出目标语

而高阶影子训练中，学生基于基础阶段的训练成果，加大练习难度，主要是通过延时训练和加入干扰任务来达到培训目标。

除了延迟训练，高阶影子训练也推荐倍速训练、意群预测等方法，这些都可供学生进行扩展学习。而本章以影子跟读训练法的低阶训练为主，主要是帮助学生加强分脑练习，为下一章的高阶影子训练打下扎实基础。同时通过联系前面几章学习的口译技巧，综合性提高训练效果。

模块二　　译前准备

◎ 1. 背景知识

　　经济危机指资本主义在生产过程中周期性爆发的生产过剩对经济造成的破坏。不当的经济政策、天灾、全球化影响等多种因素都可能造成经济危机。经济危机语料涉及的专业知识很多，容易对学生造成理解障碍。通过大量学习经济发展领域的文章，学生能更深刻理解经济现象和原理，从而在进行相关口译活动时，能快速反应出术语内涵，准确快速地把握输出内容。

　　本模块涉及的概念包括经济合作与发展组织、负增长、通货膨胀率、滞胀、抄底、自由放任政策、新政。

　　经济合作与发展组织（OECD）：全称为 Organization for Economic Co-operation and Development，成立于 1961 年，是一个由 38 个市场经济国家所组成的政府间国际经济组织。其总部设在巴黎，目前共有 38 个成员国。该组织成立旨在促进成员国乃至世界经济和社会的发展，帮助成员国政府制定和协调有关政策和援助发展中国家发展等。

　　负增长（negative growth）：经济学领域常用术语。持续的经济负增长会带来经济衰退或收缩。当某年的经济增长速度比前一年要慢时，我们可将其说成经济增长率负增长，指今年经济增长速度放缓。

　　通货膨胀率（inflation rate）：指物价上涨且货币购买力下降的经济现象。经济学中一般通过价格指数的增长率来间接表示通膨率，即消费者价格指数（CPI）。该指数能反映出与居民生活有关的产品及劳务价格统计出来的物价变动。如果消费者物价指数升幅过大，表明通货膨胀已经成为经济不稳定因素，央行会有紧缩货币政策和财政政策的风险，从而造成经济前景不明朗。

　　滞胀（stagflation）：全称停滞性通货膨胀，"滞"指经济增长停滞，"胀"是指通货膨胀。由停滞（stagnation）和膨胀（inflation）两个单词组成。通俗而言，就是因通货膨胀长期存在，导致物价上升，但经济却停滞不前。

　　抄底（bottom fishing）：指以某种估值指标衡量股价跌到最低点，尤其是短时间内大幅下跌时买入，预期股票价格将会很快反弹的操作和盈利策略。

自由放任政策（Laissez-faire）：源自法语，即"让他做、让他去、让他走"，意思就是政府放手让商人自由进行贸易。在 18 世纪重农主义时期，该词指"反对政府对贸易的干涉"，后来等同于"自由市场经济学"。

新政（New Deal）：指 1933 年富兰克林·罗斯福任美国总统后，为救济穷人和失业者，进而帮助经济恢复而实行的一系列经济政策，即"核心三 R"：救济（relief）、复兴（recovery）和改革（reform）。

◎ 2. 核心词汇

The Ministry of Social Development	社会发展部
Reuters	路透社
soup kitchen	施食处
Buenos Aires	布宜诺斯艾利斯
Economic Information Daily	《经济参考报》
UK's Office for National Statistics	英国国家统计局
Ernst & Young	安永会计师事务所
KPMG	毕马威
the Confederation of British Industry	英国工业联合会
British Manufacturing Association	英国制造业协会
(rising) inflation picks up/goes up/rises/increases	通胀上升
cost-of-living crisis	生活成本危机
shock	灾难
added burden	多余的负担
self-fulfilling prophecy	自欺的预兆
International Monetary Fund (IMF)	国际货币基金组织
UBS	瑞银集团
Pricewaterhouse Coopers (PwC)	普华永道会计师事务所
hedging	对冲
abject/dire poverty	赤贫
bargain-hunting all kinds of cheap asset	抄底资产
counterproductive	适得其反的
the quagmire of the Great Depression	大萧条的泥潭

模块三　　　　　　　　　　　　　　　　　　　　　　语料实训

 任务 1. 英译汉
难度级别：★★★★

> 训练要点：本文讲述了新冠疫情导致阿根廷经济进一步衰退。全文语速较慢，生词较少，专业知识涉及不多，学生能较容易把握全文脉络。训练过程中，请按照模块一中推荐的五阶段基础练习方法进行练习。在"如影随形"的第一阶段训练模式的基础上，学生可以进行复述、翻译、倍速跟读。学生切忌贪图进度，需要循序渐进，方能打牢基础。

Argentina Is Mired in Economic Crisis

More than 100 years ago, Argentina was one of the richest countries in the world. By the end of 2020, 42 percent of the population was poor. The percentage has risen from 35.5 percent a year earlier. The coronavirus health crisis and years of recession have affected people's lives. Argentina's economy has been crushed by years of economic crisis and high inflation that has destroyed people's savings and ability to spend money. Prices have increased every year. Before the pandemic, 8 million Argentine received food assistance. Now it is 10 million, in a population of about 45 million people. Minister of Social Development Daniel Arroyo told Reuters, "The price of food is Argentina's most critical problem. What we see is people doing informal jobs, working, but then also going to soup kitchens to make ends meet". The government of President Alberto Fernández wants to reduce poverty to help its position before the October elections. Many of the party's supporters live in the poor areas around Buenos Aires. The Ministry of Social Development had a budget of $2.6 billion in 2020 to lessen the economic effects of the coronavirus pandemic. In 2021, there could be additional measures, Arroyo said. He did not give details. Argentina has high levels of poverty assistance for a Latin American country. But much of the aid is made possible by government financial measures that increase inflation and poverty. Argentina's central bank estimates that the economy will grow at a rate of 6.7 percent this year, with inflation at 46 percent.

任务 2. 汉译英

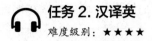

难度级别：★★★★

> 训练要点：本文用大量数据描述了英国所面临的严重经济衰退。由于是汉语跟读，听解障碍少，但文中有大量的专有名词和数字。训练过程中，请按照模块一中推荐的五阶段基础练习方法进行训练。本文的数字较多，影子跟读难度较大。在跟读过程中，学生不要因单个数字没跟上而打乱整个跟读进度。

英国将面临最严重的经济衰退

由新冠肺炎疫情和俄乌局势引起的通货膨胀冲击在英国的持续时间将比其他国家更长。他们认为，这将迫使英格兰银行维持高利率，并迫使政府实施更紧缩的财政政策。同时，经济学家预计，由于家庭为政府的政策失误付出了高昂的代价，英国将面临其中最严重的经济衰退和最微弱的复苏。

经济学家估计，已经开始下降的英国GDP将在2023年继续下降。根据相关公司的数据，英国GDP将下降1%。而与此同时，美国GDP将增长0.25%。英国独立劳动力市场经济学家约翰·菲尔波特称，"2023年的经济衰退将比新冠疫情对经济的影响更严重。"

其他受访者补充称，"2023年对消费者来说将是艰难、暗淡、苛刻、悲惨和可怕的一年。"据《经济参考报》报道，受俄乌冲突和新冠疫情双重打击，在全球经济萎缩背景下，英国难以独善其身。生活成本危机和增税计划将使经济活动严重放缓。

根据英国国家统计局发布的数据，2022年4月至7月，英国通胀水平接连刷新40年来最高纪录。为控制通胀，英国央行自2021年12月以来已连续九次加息。能源价格居高不下、通胀率飙升、多国央行加息和全球经济疲软等因素叠加，增大了英国经济在2023年年底之前面临衰退的可能性。

经济合作与发展组织预测，2023年英国国内生产总值将下降0.4%，2024年将仅增长0.2%。这将是发达国家中最严重的衰退。会计师事务所安永（Ernst & Young）和毕马威（KPMG）分别预测，英国2023年全年的国内生产总值将下降0.3%和1.3%。英国工业联合会表示，由于通胀上升、负增长和商业投资暴跌的"滞胀"组合对经济构成压力，英国将在2023年陷入长达一年的衰退。英国制造业协会公布的预测报告说，2023年能源价格飙升、劳动力短缺、材料不足、通货膨胀高企和全球需求下降等将使英国制造业面临更大的压力。制造业产出将下降3.2%，工人实际收入将是1977年以来下降幅度最大的一年。2022年消费水平下降的趋势在2023年将进一步加强。生产率增长疲软，到2024年年底将比疫情暴发前的水平低2%，商业投资将比疫情前低9%。

 任务 3. 英译汉
难度级别：★★★★★

> 训练要点：本文讲述了经济衰退的原因，这与市场中商品的供需关系息息相关。整篇文章生词不多，但用词较专业，而且里面涉及的专业知识虽然不会影响跟读，但是会造成听辨障碍。因此要完整理解本文核心内容，学生需提前了解反映市场供需关系的通货膨胀率。训练过程中，请按照模块一中推荐的五阶段低阶练习方法进行练习，在熟练影子跟读的基础上，学生要抓住文章关键词和叙述逻辑，有条不紊地复述全文，以便为培养同传脑力分配能力奠定基础。

What Causes Economic Recession?

What causes recessions? This question has long been the subject of heated debate among economists, and for good reason. Recessions occur when there is a negative disruption to the balance between supply and demand. There's a mismatch between how many goods people want to buy, how many products and services producers can offer, and the price of the goods and services sold, which prompts an economic decline.

An economy relationship between supply and demand is reflected in its inflation rates and interest rates. Fluctuations in inflation and interest rates can give us insight into the health of the economy. But what causes these fluctuations in the first place? The most obvious causes are shocks like natural disaster, war and geopolitical factors. An earthquake, for example, can destroy the infrastructure needed to produce important commodities such as oil. That forces the supply side of the economy to charge more for products that use oil, discouraging demand and potentially prompting a recession. But some recessions occur in times of economic prosperity, possibly even because of economic prosperity. Some economists believe that business activity from a market's expansion can occasionally reach an unsustainable level. For example, corporations and consumers may borrow more money with the assumption that economic growth will help them handle the added burden. But if the economy doesn't grow as quickly as expected, they may end up with more debt than they can manage. To pay it off, they have to redirect funds from other activities, reducing business activity.

Psychology can also contribute to a recession. Fear of a recession can become a self-fulfilling prophecy even it causes people to pull back investing and spending. In response, producers might cut operating costs to help weather the expected decline in demand. That can lead to a vicious cycle as cost cuts eventually lower wages, leading to even lower demand. Even policy designed to help prevent recessions can contribute when times are tough. Governments and central banks may print money, increase spending and lower central bank interest rates. Smaller lenders can in turn lower their interest rates effectively, making debt cheaper to boost spending. But these policies are not sustainable and eventually need to be reversed to prevent excessive inflation. That can cause a recession if people have become too reliant on cheap debt and government stimulus.

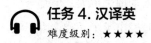

任务 4. 汉译英
难度级别：★★★★

> 训练要点：本文讲述了经济危机拉大贫富差距的原因。全文涉及一些专业背景知识，如 2008 年全球经济危机、罗斯福新政、对冲等，但是举例对其进行说明会降低听辨难度。关于文中出现的数据，学生可在跟读到数字时做一下笔记。在影子训练的阶段四（目标语输出）前，先做好专有名词的翻译，再进行输出翻译。建议边跟读边辨别有用信息并记录好相应数字，加强分脑练习。

为什么经济危机会使富人更富，穷人更穷？

经济危机就像是一个无法解开的魔咒。每隔一段时间就会上演一次。2008 年世界金融危机的阴影是至今仍在。而今年，突如其来的新冠疫情也给全球经济带来了巨大冲击。根据国际货币基金组织 10 月份发布的《世界经济展望报告》，预计 2020 年全球经济将会萎缩 4.4%。然而，在全球经济普遍衰退、居民收入增速大幅放缓的背景之下，全球富豪的财富却不降反升。根据瑞银集团和普华永道的调查显示，截至 2020 年 7 月底，全球 2 000 多位亿万富豪的财富总额达到了 10.2 万亿美元，同比增长超 25%。这也突破了 2017 年年底创下的 8.9 万亿美元的峰值。

那么问题来了，为什么经济危机会让富人更富、穷人更穷？首先，这里要给各位说明一下，经济危机本身是不可能让富人更富有的。以 20 世纪 30 年代的大萧条为例，这场发源于美国的经济危机后来席卷了整个资本主义世界，导致大规模的失业，企业破产，经济损失惨重。据了解，危机时期仅美国倒闭的企业数就达到了14万家，可见当时的经济危机几乎没有什么赢家。这主要是因为当时资本主义国家都不怎么干预经济，而是让经济自我修复，比如美国政府的经济政策主要是自由放任。只不过效果适得其反，暴风雨反而来得更猛烈了。坚持实施该政策的美国总统胡佛就成了"贫困"的代名词。后来罗斯福总统上任之后，实施新政，加强了对经济的干预，这才逐渐让美国走出了大萧条的泥潭。正所谓"吃一堑长一智"。自此以后，资本主义国家每当遇到经济危机时，就频繁地干预市场。其中受益人更多的是富人，而不是穷人，这是为什么？

简单来说，穷人没有对冲空间，而富人能够靠对冲来越来越富。所谓对冲就是在发生经济危机时，我们能够有多大的能力去应对损失并且挽回损失。举个例子，穷人有一个鸡蛋放在一个篮子里，而富人有十个鸡蛋，放在好几个篮子里。当经济危机来临时，穷人的篮子翻了，唯一的鸡蛋没有了，从而陷入了赤贫。而富人的损失更大，但是至少有些篮子没有翻，保存了一些资本。此时为了摆脱经济危机，政府出手了。穷人由于鸡蛋没有了，只能靠政府补贴勉强度日。而富人却能够通过剩下的资产升值来对冲风险，并且还可以拿手中的资本再去抄底各类廉价的资产。等到经济复苏、繁荣的时候，他们的财富就会增长得更多。

模块四

技巧点拨：基础影子技能

任务 1. 英译汉

>> 例一
难度级别：★★★

原始速度

1.4 倍速度

Andrew Jackson saw his re-election as proof that the American people approved of his policies. This included his policy to close **the Bank of the United States** when its charter ended in 1836.

○ 词汇

the Bank of the United States
美国银行

During his second term, Jackson decided on a plan to reduce the bank's economic power. He would stop putting **federal money** into the bank. Instead, he would put it into **state banks**. This would greatly reduce the amount of money the Bank of the United States could use. The plan was not as easy as it seemed. The charter for the bank said federal money had to be kept there, unless the **Secretary of the Treasury** ordered it put some place else. President Jackson's treasury secretary was friendly to the bank. He would not give the order. Jackson named his Secretary of State to be minister to France. He named his Treasury Secretary to be Secretary of State. Then he brought in someone new as Secretary of the Treasury. This man immediately ordered that after October 1st, 1837, all federal money was to be put into 23 state banks. He did not withdraw the government money already in the Bank of the United States. He said this money could be used to make payments until it was all gone. Nicholas Biddle, the head of the bank, fought back. He ordered the immediate repayment of all bank loans. He also withdrew from public use large numbers of bank notes. People had been using the notes as money. These actions caused serious economic difficulties throughout the country. Many businesses failed. They could not pay back their loans or borrow the money they needed. As businesses failed, workers lost their jobs.

○ 词汇

federal money
联邦资金

state banks
州立银行

the Secretary of the Treasury
财政部部长

译文

安德鲁·杰克逊把他的连任看作美国人民对他实施的政策的认可，包括认可当《美国银行宪章》在1836年失效时，他要关闭美国银行。在杰克逊的第二届任期内，他决定制定一项限制该银行经济实力的计划。他不再把联邦资金存入该银行，而是把它存入州银行，这将大大削减美国银行的可用资金。这个计划并不像看上去那么简单。该银行的章程指明，除非财政部部长下令将联邦资金存入他处，否则联邦资金必须存在美国银行。杰克逊总统的财政部部长和银行关系很好，他不会下达此命令。杰克逊任命国务卿出任驻法大使，财政部部长出任国务卿。随后，他又请来一位新人出任财政部部长。这个人立即下令，在1833年10月1日后，将所有联邦资金都要存入23个州的州立银行。他没有提取已经存在美国银行的政府资金，他说这些钱可以用来支付费用，直到用尽为止。美国银行行长尼古拉斯·比德尔发起反击。他下令立即偿还所有银行贷款。他还把大量的银行券从公共事业中撤出。人们一直把这些银行券当钱花。这些做法导致全国范围内出现严重的经济困难。许多企业倒闭了，他们无力偿还贷款，也借不到钱。由于企业倒闭，工人也失业了。

阶段练习

本文背景知识略多，影子训练之前，学生可以先做听辨，在听辨的基础上，回炉材料，进行影子训练。请学生在紧跟正常语速的源语跟读几遍后，开始跟读快速音频，以便最大限度提高自身的语言反应力和分脑能力。注意，跟读过程中，建议用另一设备录音，不仅要录进自己跟读声音，还要录入原音频声音，注意自己声音要大于原音频，以便复盘反思；需要的话可再进行多次倍速跟读，直至得出一个最佳的跟读录音音频。该过程能够最大限度提升个人的语感、语音能力、表达能力等。接着，进行第三遍跟读。完后，复述出关键词（参考关键词：Andrew Jackson、re-election、close the Bank of the United States、federal money、state banks、not easy、name、order、fight back、people、economic difficulties）。而在第四遍跟读完后，重新说出关键词后并进行原文总结。

分析

本文讲述的是美国总统安德鲁·杰克逊执行的经济政策所造成的经济危机。在进行跟读时，要格外注意叙事主线。具体而言，跟读时就要开始关注全文大概框架，而不仅是鹦鹉学舌地跟住，以便复述关键词。在复述关键词时，学生可参考第二章"电子商务"主题中的听辨关键词训练，根据14个原则，利用抓住文中主题词、中心词的方法来锁定关键词。

训练要点

1. 注意本文的主角和故事主线，基于此锁定关键词。
2. 复述时"抓大放小"，流畅说出文章大意即可。
3. 本文生词较少，建议将倍速跟读的质量做到最好，最大限度提升听力、反应力和分脑力。

例二
难度级别：★★★★

原始速度

1.5倍速度

Sri Lanka's economy was once seen as a model for a developing country. Now it is edging toward bankruptcy. What happened? The crisis unfolds quickly, a **compounding effect** of global and national factors. In 2019, the tropical country's tourism began to falter after terrorist attacks, including the **Easter Sunday suicide bombings** that killed more than 250 people. Tourism fell further during the coronavirus pandemic. Economists say years of government mismanagement and corruption added to the country's **budget woes**. Former President Gotabaya Rajapaksa who recently fled the country spent large sums on infrastructure projects while also passing the largest tax cuts in the country's history in 2019. His administration also unexpectedly banned imports of chemical fertilizers in a push for **organic farming**, but did not give farmers help in sourcing natural alternatives.

As a result, rice yields plummeted and the price of the **staple crop** rose. Soon the government was running out of money and began using up its foreign reserves. Creditors **downgraded** Sri Lanka's ratings, beginning in 2020, eventually locking the country out of international financial markets. The country's currency collapsed, inflation soared and the government **defaulted** on its foreign debt. What does it mean for ordinary people? In a country that normally has plenty of food, people are going hungry. **The UN World Food Program** says nearly nine **out of** ten families are cutting back on the amount of food they eat. The government has given **civil servants** an extra day off so they can grow their own food. Fuel stations have run out of gas and **electricity blackouts** are common. People line up for hours for basic items like cooking gas and fuel. Even if they could find such staples, inflation is rising so fast that many people cannot afford them. Doctors say they are nearly out of medicines and are warning people to avoid getting sick.

词汇

Sri Lanka
斯里兰卡

compounding effect
综合影响

Easter Sunday suicide bombings
复活节自杀式爆炸袭击

budget woe
预算困境

organic farming
有机农业

staple crop
主要农作物

downgrade
下调

default
无法偿还

the UN World Food Program
联合国世界粮食计划署

out of
从……中选出

civil servant
公务员

electricity blackout
停电

译文

斯里兰卡的经济曾被视为发展中国家的典范。现在它正濒临破产。这是怎么了？这场危机迅速展开，是全球和国家因素的综合影响的结果。2019年，这个热带国家的关键产业旅游业在恐怖袭击后开始步履蹒跚，其中包括导致250多人丧生的复活节自杀式爆炸袭击。在新冠疫情期间，旅游业进一步衰退。经济学家表示，多年的政府管理不善和腐败加剧了该国的预算困境。最近逃离该国的前总统戈塔巴雅·拉贾帕克萨（Gotabaya Rajapaksa）在基础设施项目上投入了大量资金，同时还在2019年通过了该国历史上最大的减税法案。出人意料的是，为推动有机农业的发展，他的政府还禁止进口化肥，但没有帮助农民寻找天然替代品。

结果，大米产量暴跌，主要农作物价格上涨。很快，政府的资金濒临耗尽，并开始耗光其外汇储备。评级机构从2020年开始下调斯里兰卡的评级，最终将该国排除在国际金融市场之外。这个国家的货币崩溃，通货膨胀飙升，政府拖欠外债。这对普通人来说意味着什么？在一个通常食物充足的国家，人们却在挨饿。联合国世界粮食计划署表示，近十分之九的家庭正在减少他们的食物摄入量。政府给了公务员额外的一天假期，这样他们就可以自己种植食物。加油站的汽油用完了，停电也很常见。人们要排几个小时的队购买煤气和燃料等基本物品。但即使他们能找到这些基本物品，通胀上升得如此之快，许多人也负担不起。医生说他们的药物即将用完，并提醒民众避免生病。

阶段练习

同上篇练习步骤一样，先进行三遍跟读后，说出关键词（参考关键词：Sri Lanka's economy、now、bankruptcy、global and national factors、ratings、currency、inflation、debt、ordinary people）。第四遍跟读后，总结全文，即"Sri Lanka's economy is facing bankruptcy because of global and national factors, including coronavirus, terrorism, mismanagement and corruption of the government. Sri Lanka's ratings have been downgraded, until it was kicked out of the international financial market, followed by collapsed currency, roaring inflation and defaulting debt. Therefore, the ordinary people have trouble in getting food, electricity and gas, etc."。

分析

本文讲述了斯里兰卡经济危机的原因和影响。因此在跟读时关注该危机的原因和影响，抓住关键词，并在脑中画出各关键词下的枝干，即具体原因和影响。本篇涉及的专业知识较多，有较为复杂的人名。因此，在跟读时，若人名跟读得卡顿，则建议第一遍无须在乎小细节，但课后巩固练习时，可额外多读几遍人名或者其他绕口生词，继而顺利跟读。进行总结或者翻译时,注意选择用较符合专业领域的词来进行翻译,比如"defaulted on its foreign debt"尽量翻成"拖欠外债",而不是"还不清外债"。显然,前者表达更专业。

训练要点

1. 重视预测在口译中的作用。比如,本文可根据"what happened?"来快速预测下文,从而很快确定关键词。
2. 确定关键词后,要快速记下几个细节信息,以保证抓住主要结构,同时有一定枝干,使总结的内容更全面。

任务 2. 汉译英

> **例一**
> 难度级别:★★★★

 原始速度   1.3 倍速度

有日本经济学者警告称,日本 2023 年有可能会发生<u>经济危机</u>。日本经济总量从 20 世纪末突破 5 万亿美元之后,就一直没有什么起色,被外界认为是日本经济失去的 30 年。但这种**发展停滞的经济状态**对 <u>2022</u> 的日本来说,可以算得上是上天的恩赐,因为从 2022 年开始,日本经济就因俄乌冲突、对俄制裁导致能源和原材料涨价等外部因素的影响再度遭受<u>重挫</u>。曾有日媒指出,受日元对美元汇率大幅下降等因素的影响,日本 GDP 如果**以美元折算**,实际上已跌至 4 万亿美元左右。国际能源涨价所引发的电力、工业原材料和其他商品价格的上涨对日本贸易出口造成**致命性暴击**。截至目前,日本已连续 10 多个月出现巨额**贸易逆差**。这对依赖贸易出口拉动经济增长的日本而言,<u>经济衰退</u>就是一种必然的结果。而**美日同盟**关系的不断深化对中日经贸合作关系所形成的影响正变得越来越严重,甚至已到了日本商界不得不担忧中日关系出现**政冷经**

词汇

发展停滞的经济状态
stagnant economic state

以美元折算
converted into US dollars

致命性暴击
a fatal blow to

贸易逆差
trade deficit

政冷经冷局面
political and economic coldness

冷局面的地步了。

　　在**中美**紧张关系已到了近乎**零和状态**的背景下，日本既然选择战队美国，则意味着中日关系将随着美日合作关系的升温而持续恶化。而就在日本业界越来越担心中日会出现政冷经冷局面之际，**岸田当局**却将日本紧紧地绑上**美国反华政策的战车**，结果非但并未给日本糟糕的经济状况带来任何的缓解作用，反而因为美国不断胁迫岸田当局参与对华高科技产品**出口管制行动**以及出台具有浓烈单边、保护主义色彩的《**通胀削减法案**》等举措，给本来就陷于困境中的日本出口企业造成更大的打击。日本在经济上承受不起与中国**脱钩**的代价。

> **词汇**
>
> 零和状态
> zero-sum state
>
> 岸田当局
> the Kishida authorities
>
> 美国反华政策的战车
> the chariot of the anti-China policy of the United States
>
> 出口管制行动
> export control actions
>
> 《通胀削减法案》
> Inflation Reduction Act
>
> 脱钩
> decouple from

译文

　　Some Japanese economists warned that there may be an economic crisis in Japan in 2023. Since the total economic output of Japan exceeded 5 trillion US dollars at the end of last century, there has been no improvement, which is considered by the outside world as the last 30 years of Japanese economy. However, this stagnant economic state can be regarded as a gift from heaven for Japan in 2022. Because since 2022, the Japanese economy has suffered heavy losses again due to external factors such as the conflict between Russia and Ukraine and the inflation of energy and raw materials caused by sanctions against Russia. Some Japanese media pointed out that due to factors such as the sharp decline in the exchange rate of the Japanese Yen against the US dollar, Japan's GDP has actually dropped to about 4 trillion US dollars if converted into US dollars. Followed by the hike in the price of the international energy, the rising prices of electricity, industrial raw materials and other commodities have given a fatal blow to Japan's trade exports. Up to now, Japan, which relies on trade exports to drive economic growth, has experienced a huge trade deficit for more than 10 consecutive months, an inevitable result for Japan. However, the deepening of the US-Japan alliance has an increasingly serious impact on Sino-Japanese economic and trade cooperation, and even has reached the point where Japanese business circles have to worry about the political and economic coldness in Sino-Japanese relations.

　　Under the background that the tension between China and the United States has reached a zero-sum state, since Japan chooses to stand alongside the United States, it means that Sino-Japan relation will continue to deteriorate with the warming of US-Japan cooperation. While the Japanese industry is increasingly worried about the political and economic coldness between China and Japan, the Kishida authorities have tied Japan tightly to the chariot of the anti-China policy of the United States. As a result, it has not brought any relief to Japan's poor economic situation, but since the United States has constantly coerced the Kishida authorities to participate in China's export control actions for high-tech products and the introduction of *Inflation Reduction Act* with strong unilateralism and protectionism, the already-troubled Japanese exporters have been given a greater blow. Therefore, we can see that Japan can't afford to decouple from China economically.

阶段练习

第一遍正常语速跟读，第二遍倍速跟读。跟读时厘清文章大概脉络。本篇为中文，所以相对好跟读和理解。跟读第三遍后，说出本文的关键词（参考关键词：2023、经济危机、2022、外部因素、重挫、经济衰退、美日、中美、中日、经济状况、承受不起）。第四遍跟读后，开始总结全文，即预测2023年日本将遭遇经济危机。因为2022年日本因一系列外部因素而在经济上受到重挫，包括俄乌冲突、对俄制裁导致原材料上涨等。此外，美日同盟关系、中美紧张关系使得中日关系也愈发糟糕，陷入政冷经冷局面。而日本支持美国反华，也使得日本经济状况雪上加霜。因此，日本承受不起与中国脱钩。

分析

本文讲述了日本在2023年会遭遇经济危机的原因，主要以2022年日本所面临的各种外部因素及伴随而来的影响来开展。

训练要点

1. 充分发挥听辨技能"抓大放小"，"大"是日本经济的不景气，"小"是原因。
2. 进行最后一步翻译时，无须选择高大上的表达，而是以"准确、快速、流畅"为原则，译出原文。

>> 例二
难度级别：★★★

原始速度

1.3倍速度

现在美国要干的是什么？调整自己的**金融周期**，同时利用美元的国际货币地位，让美元在全世界推高资产价格，等于是把全世界都搞成**泡沫化**。然后再寻找机会主动撕破泡沫。等金融周期调整到位后再刺破泡沫，就跟去年疫情期间**美股崩盘**是两种情形了。因为一个是主动，一个是被动，这里面的危险是差不多的，但对美国来说，机会就大不一样了。因为泡沫破灭是经济危机的开始。一般到了这个时候，资产就会变成白菜价。这个时候就是美国资本进场，一边捡便宜，一边充当救世主的时候。很多人没有注意到一个现象，就是美国股市在不断创新高，但是美国的上市公司却在不断地**囤积现金**，他们要这么多现金干吗？早在 2015 年时，非金融企业囤积的现金就超过了 1.6 万亿美元。这些年其实一直还在增加，像苹果、谷歌，包括股神巴菲特都囤积了上千亿美元的现金，他们拿着这么多现金，既不投资，也不搞扩大生产，按我们一般的理解，钱不是在贬值吗？他们怎么就眼睁睁看着钱贬值，还要拿这么多钱？

很可能他们也在等一次世界危机和一次百年不遇的抄底机会，这种机会一旦出现，他们可以在危机中以白菜价去抄底优质资产，把自己**虚高的股价和收益做实**。所以危机永远都是这样。对于一部分人是危险，对另一部分则是机会。现在全世界的资本市场都在大涨。给人一个错觉就是好像经济处在繁荣期一样。其实全球的实体经济都不咋地。这个繁荣是人为催生出来的。当然，繁荣会给人一种莫名其妙的安全感。以为经济危机是个很遥远的事，但是了解资本主义制度的都明白下面这句话：资本主义经济危机的必然性。在资本主义制度下，必然要产生经济危机，这是一个不以人的意志为转移的客观规律。要消除经济危机，除非消灭资本主义制度。

词汇

金融周期
financial cycle

泡沫化
foam

美股崩盘
the collapse of US stocks

囤积现金
hoard cash

虚高的股价和收益做实
inflate stock prices and returns

译文

What is America going to do now? It's adjusting its own financial cycle, and letting the US dollar push up asset prices all over the world by taking advantage of the international currency status of the US dollar which is tantamount to foaming the whole world. Then it will look for opportunities to burst the bubble. Once the financial cycle is adjusted in place, the bubble will burst, the result of which differs from the collapse of US stocks during last year's pandemic. As one is active and the other is passive. The dangers are similar, but for the United States, things are quite different, as bubble burst is the beginning of economic crisis. Generally, the asset price will become floor-price low, and this is the time when American capital comes into play, picking up bargains and acting as savior. Many people have not noticed such a phenomenon that the American stock market is constantly hitting new high, but American listed companies are constantly hoarding cash. Why? As early as 2015, non-financial enterprises hoarded more than $1.6 trillion in cash. In fact, this has been increasing over the years. Apple, Google or stock god Warren Buffett, have hoarded hundreds of billions of dollars in cash. They neither invest nor expand production with the cash. According to our understanding, isn't the money depreciating? How can they afford watching the money depreciate?

It is very likely that they are also waiting for a world crisis and a once-in-a-century bargain-hunting opportunity. Once this opportunity appears, they can bargain-hunting high-quality assets at floor price in the crisis, and inflate their stock prices and returns. That's the essence of the crisis. It is a danger to some, whereas an opportunity to others. Now the capital markets are seeing a boom all over the world. It gives people an illusion that the economy is prosperous. The global real economy is virtually not so good. This prosperity is man-made. Of course, prosperity can give people an inexplicable sense of security. People think economic crisis is distant, but those who know the capitalist system must understand this: the capitalism and economic crisis are interwoven. Capitalism will inevitably produce economic crisis, which is a law that will not be changed by man. The economic crisis cannot be eliminated unless the capitalism disappears.

阶段练习

进行第一遍正常语速跟读和第二遍倍速跟读，第三次跟读后说出关键词（参考关键词：美国、泡沫、经济危机、现金、抄底、涨、资本主义制度）。第四遍跟读后，复述全文，即美国利用美元的国际地位，引起全球泡沫化，而这是经济危机的开始。在经济危机爆发前，财阀会囤积超大数额的现金。这是因为他们想趁经济危机来临时，抄底资产，牟取暴利。当前，全球资本市场大涨，但事实并非表面这么繁荣。只要资本主义制度存在，经济危机就存在必然性。

> **训练要点**

1. 跟读时，若在文章开头未明确中心，可关注句末。若句首句末都不明确，可以结合句首句末，进行总结。本篇文章就是如此，前面第一段提到美国的行为会带来经济危机。最后提到在资本主义制度下，必然产生经济危机。两者用了不同的语言表达同样的思想。
2. 熟记"抄底"等经济类术语。

模块五　　　　　　　　　　　　　　　　　　　　　拓展练习

任务1:
基础影子技能练习——跟读录音

语篇1
难度级别：★★★★

At the root of recession worries is a fear of the consequences of **monetary tightening**. It is clear that central banks have to take the **proverbial punchbowl** away from the party. Wage growth in the rich world is far too strong given weak productivity growth. Inflation is too high. But the risk is that higher rates will end the party altogether, rather than making it less **raucous**. History is not encouraging in this regard. Since 1955, there have been three periods when rates in America rose as much as they are expected to this year: in 1973, 1979 and 1981. In each case, a recession followed within six months.

Has recession struck again? Rich-world economies, which account for 60% of global GDP, have certainly slowed since the **heady** days of mid-2021, when COVID restrictions were being lifted. **Goldman Sachs** produces a "current activity indicator", a high-frequency measure of economic health based on a range

词汇

monetary tightening
货币紧缩

proverbial punchbowl
众所周知的酒杯

raucous
喧闹的

heady
上头的

Goldman Sachs
高盛集团

of indicators. The gauge has slowed in recent weeks. Surveys of factory bosses in America and the Eurozone by **S&P Global**, a data provider, suggest that manufacturers are gloomier than at any time since the early days of the pandemic.

It looks too soon, though, to declare a recession—even if, as some expect, statisticians reveal after we go to press on July 28th that between April and June American GDP contracted for the second quarter **running**. This would count as a recession by **one rule of thumb**, but not necessarily by others. A series of **oddities** led GDP to shrink in the first quarter, even though the underlying performance of the economy was strong. It would also be too soon for **Fed tightening** to have had an effect.

词汇

S&P Global
标普全球

running
连续（置于数字等名词后）

one rule of thumb
经验法则

oddity
古怪

Fed tightening
美联储连锁措施

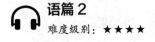

语篇 2
难度级别：★★★★

一位以悲观倾向著称的经济学家警告美国人说，经济衰退将是长期且严重的。有"末日博士"之称的努里尔·卢比尼周一说，衰退可能带来全面的金融困境。报道说，尽管美国就业报告强劲，7月整体通货膨胀有所下降。但美国经济还是令很多美国人看到食品价格上涨。**美联储**已经试图通过上调利率来遏制通胀，但一些专家说，美国正走向或已经陷入衰退。卢比尼周一在接受**彭博社**记者采访时说，"我们正处于急剧放缓之中，在2022年上半年，我们已经经历了两个负增长季度。经济衰退将是长期的、持久的、严重的，并与全面的金融困境相关"。卢比尼曾准确预测了2008年的**房地产**泡沫破裂。美联储在7月底加息75个基点，此前一次加息是在6月。卢比尼称，加息不足以应对通胀。事实上，卢比尼预计美联储将需要进一步加息，令8.5%的通胀回落至2%的目标水平。他说，"联邦基金利率应远高于4%，将通胀推至2%。如果这种

词汇

美联储
Federal Reserve

彭博社
Bloomberg

房地产
real estate

情况没有发生,那么通胀预期将是**硬着陆**。"报道称,尽管人们越来越担心经济衰退,但美联储的利率仍然相对较低。据银行利率网站的一篇文章称,尽管美联储一直加息,但其**借款利率**仍处于历史低位。联邦基金利率自 2007 年以来一直低于 4.61% 的历史平均水平,2008—2015 年,联邦基金利率为零。联邦基金利率在 20 世纪 80 年代初达到最高点,当时飙升至 20%。卢比尼说,他认为,尽管通胀可能已经达到顶峰,但他不确定它会以多快的速度下降。他说,"我认为货币政策不够紧缩,不足以将通胀率迅速推至 2%。"

词汇

硬着陆
hard landing

借款利率
lending rate

任务 2:
基础影子技能练习——原文总结

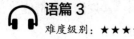

The diplomatic role in the Mideast started in early June. **Qatar** is beginning to feel the pining on this economy. The **rating agency Moody's** on Wednesday downgraded its Outlook for Doha from stable to negative. At the same time, it lowered the gulf nation's GDP growth rate in 2017 to 2.4%. That's down from the average 13.3% from 2006 to 2000.

First of all, in the financial system, in terms of the trading between the GCC banks, between **Saudi banks** and **Marathi banks** and Qatari banks, that has ground to hold. There's also a bit of dollar shortage. When the crisis happened, people went to the banks to grab foreign currency.

Doha has had to make some changes in its trade system to avoid more economic pain. Those changes range from a **reconfiguration** of the food supply chain and construction material network to an adjustment of international trade resources. The Qatar government also rolled out free visa on arrival policies

词汇

Qatar
卡塔尔

rating agency
评级机构

Moody's
穆迪公司

Saudi bank
沙特阿拉伯银行

Marathi bank
马拉塔银行

reconfiguration
重构

to citizens of more than eighty countries to ease the blow to its tourism sector. The dispute is the biggest to hit the Middle East in years. A host of gulf nations, including **Saudi Arabia**, **UAE**, **Bahrain** and Egypt, serve diplomatic relations and cut land, sea and air travel to Qatar in early June. The country accusing Qatar of funding terrorism and **destabilizing** the Middle East. Doha has rejected those accusations. Meanwhile, the United States and **Kuwait** have been talking to both sides in an effort to **defuse** the tensions. Analysts warned that if the dispute continues, the economic crisis may **spill over to** other parts of the Mideast.

○ 词汇

Saudi Arabia
沙特阿拉伯

UAE (The United Arab Emirates)
阿拉伯联合酋长国

Bahrain
巴林

destabilize
使……不稳定

Kuwait
科威特

defuse
缓和

spill over to
波及

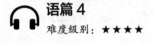

欧美在 2023 年将会陷入经济衰退和滞胀。这几乎是板上钉钉的事。全球经济疲软，一是因为疫情，二是因为其内在固有因素。毕竟从 2019 年起，世界经济就一直在走下坡路。美国、日本、欧元区、中国的制造业 PMI 指数都在下滑，整体呈现出一个**低增长**和**高震荡**的状态。我也许有点悲观，觉得全球经济在很长一段时期内都不会好转。之前曾有过类似的想法，认为这就像人的衰老，会随着年龄的增长而变得不可逆转。自第二次世界大战后的 77 年间，美国的经济一直处于高速发展时期。第一个阶段是美国大约从 1945 年到 20 世纪 70 年代在世界上率先发展。第二个阶段是日本，20 世纪 70 到 90 年代，在全球范围内领导着世界的发展。第三个阶段是中国主导了世界经济的发展。中国在 20 世纪 90 年代开始崛起，在世界上的市场份额也有了很大的提高。自 2008 年以来，中国 GDP 占世界经济总量的 1/3 以上，有些时候甚至高达 50%。因此，虽然中国是世界上第二大经济体，但其经济增长速度却比美国快得多，如今中国的经济增长放缓，世界上还会有哪些

○ 词汇

低增长
low growth

高震荡
high vibration

人在引领着？换句话说，这三个引领着世界经济发展的国家已经老了，进入了一个严重的**老龄社会**。人到了老年，身体会有各种各样的病症，身体的结构也会发生明显的老化。人体是有**循环系统**的，比如**消化系统**，**内分泌系统**等，这些都会导致**血液循环不畅**，比如**血管变硬**，血管硬化后还能重新恢复到年轻时一样吗？医生说不可能了，全球经济也是一样。

以上提到的包括中国在内的全球性问题，实际上都是一个长远的问题。短期的问题是美国在 2023 年将面临滞胀的压力，而经济增长将会继续下滑。欧洲也面临着经济下滑的压力，他们面临的压力不仅仅是通胀，经济下滑还有负债。这些问题是否会突然爆发还很难说，但随着时间的推移，经济衰退将会进一步恶化，因此这将是一个短期的全球性危机问题。美国相对来说仍有其优势，其经济长期没有太大的压力，任何一个国家都存在着一个长期的问题，但美国在持续的波动中做出了**自我调节**，相对来说还算不错，其问题大多是短期问题。

○ 词汇

老龄社会
aging society

循环系统
circulatory system

消化系统
digestive system

内分泌系统
endocrine system

血液循环不畅
obstruct bloodstream

血管变硬
blood vessel hardens

自我调节
self- regulation

模块六

译海拾贝：巴黎释义派

巴黎释义派理论（the Interpretative Approach），又称"达意理论"（the Theory of Sense），是 20 世纪 60 年代末产生于法国巴黎高翻的一个探讨翻译原理与教学的学派，是国际口译界第一套系统地解释口译心理过程、指导口译教学实践的理论，也是当今口译界最有影响力的体系；由口译研究学者达尼卡·塞莱斯柯维奇（Danica Seleskovitch）及玛利亚娜·勒代雷（Marianne Lederer）所创立。两人都担任过法国高等翻译学院的校长。塞莱斯柯维奇还是国际口译工作者协会的创始人之一，曾为多个国家元首担任口译工作，积累了大量的翻译实践。也正因为如此，她对言语科学和交际研究产生了极大的兴趣，并于 1968 年发表了题为《国际会议译员——言语与交际问题》的博士论文。随后，其学院成为该派理论的研究中心，相关研究人员将会议口译实践和各种心理学、语言学学科等成果相结合，建立了一整套口译理论，随后又将其扩展至非文学文本的笔译研究，即"释义派"的翻译理论。

巴黎释义派主张，翻译不是解释，也不是诠释，而是释意篇章；即译者追求的不是语言单位的对等，而是原文意思或效果的等值。正如塞莱斯科维基所言，翻译是一种交际行为，而不是交际结果。在交际中，语言只是工具，因此翻译的对象应该是信息内容，而不是语言。这就要求口译者在口译过程中要避免字对字的语言翻译。具体而言，释义派将翻译过程分为三步：理解、脱离源语言和重新表达。在口译过程中，译者首先从源语言中理解所要表达的意思，理解的前提条件包括语言知识、背景知识和交际环境。不是懂英语的人就能从事口译，而是要有扎实的背景知识、专业知识和语言功底，掌握口译技能，才有可能成为一名合格的口译员。对源语形成了理解后要脱离源语言外壳，一方面，心理学家研究结果表明，语言形式和语言意义在记忆中是分别保存的，其中语言的深层意义在记忆中保存的时间较长。另一方面，释义派认为翻译时的理解、记忆和转换就是脱离语言形式、形成思想的过程。因为语言符号、数字符号，或口译中的交际意义能以某种载体存在于记忆当中，激发深层次语言所包含的交际意义，所以口译员能够依靠少量笔记忠实地传达源语信息。由于口译具有时效性，在口译过程中不会给译员过多的时间思考和分析，这就要求译员要加强自身逻辑思维能力和语言表达能力的训练，以便在口译实践当中快速且准确地传递出源语要表达的交际意义。

综上所述，我们可知，释义派强调译者需要挖掘出作者的根本思想而非文字对应。译者要准确获取作者的意思，还要脱离源语言的结构及语法束缚，并且结合自身的认知准确把握作者的意图，以便更好地将作者的真正价值以可理解的方式向受众传递出来。而且学习释义理论，对于口译技能上的训练也具有重要的指导性，如记忆训练、笔记法、输出表达等技巧。

作为学术界一个大胆的创新和促进口译研究向认知心理学转向的加速器，巴黎释义理论对口译学习具有重要的理论意义和实践意义。

模块七

**译员风采：
跨过厚厚的大红门，穿过是非成败**

章含之的一生灿烂却又充满争议。她从一名译员走向外交部亚洲司副司长的职位又被从外交部除名；她写完自传《跨过厚厚的大红门》后，前同事劝她在扉页上写上"总督孙女、总长女儿、主席老师、外长夫人"以促进畅销，被她婉拒。她还说过这样一句话："我一生中一系列重大转折都离不开毛主席，他在我生活的每一关键时刻主宰了我的命运。"

章含之，1935年出生于上海，是著名爱国民主人士章士钊的养女。她从小便成绩优异，高中被保送至北京外国语学院，读研毕业后留校任教，一教就是14年。因为养父与毛泽东的友谊，她曾担任毛泽东一年多的英文教师，随后进入中国外交部。她的身影此后经常出现在各大重要外交事务场合，最有影响的当属1972年接待尼克松访华。

章含之原本只是负责陪同尼克松夫人参观故宫、长城和北京饭店厨房等一些相对轻松的工作，担任尼克松译员的是当时被称作"中国外交部翻译一把手"的冀朝铸。但突然因尼克松要求，章含之变成了他的翻译。那天接待尼克松总统的是周恩来总理。双方碰面后，尼克松看到周恩来总理的翻译是位女士，而给他配的翻译却是一位与他一样高大的男翻译冀朝铸。尼克松认为这位男士的高大形象与他不搭，便同周总理打趣道，"冀先生的翻译无可厚非，但他太高了。你和你的翻译站在一起很协调，这不公平。我的翻译为什么不能是女士呢？"周总理听后哈哈大笑，于是便让两位翻译自己协商解决。当时，刚从事外交事务的章含之相比冀朝铸显然经验不足。更甚者，她一见闪光灯就有点晕，所以她一再推辞，最后还是不得不接受了调解方案：要面对上千宾客和400余名记者的尼克松答谢宴会致辞的译员还是冀朝铸；而离开北京后，杭州上海之行则由章含之翻译。一切都非常顺利，但就在《上海公报》发布后，章含之在当晚的宴会上便出了洋相。尼克松说："中美之间距离很近，才1.7万英里。"但章含之却翻成了1700英里。据章含之回忆："当时唯一听出来的是周总理，他就在那儿笑，抬头跟我说，'没这么近吧，才1700呀？'我当时刷一下就脸红了。但是为时已晚，我只能赶紧用中文纠正，然后向尼克松总统表示歉意。还好，尼克松总统说，'那更好，这样两国距离岂不是更近了。'"尼克松总统为了缓解气氛的尴尬，当场说道："这两天接触以来，你是我在工作中遇到的最棒的独一无二的翻译！"尼克松总统的幽默和毫不吝啬的夸奖使得章含之声名远扬，以至于半年后的1972年9月章含之出席联合国大会时，当她在联合国总部的楼下买东西时，服务员一看到她就热情地说，"哎呀，我们知道你做过我们总统的翻译。我们总统说你翻译得非常好！"

章含之不是因"尼克松的赞美"而受到大众认可的。她翻译事业的成功离不开她一直细心、严谨、负责的工作态度以及不断学习的进取心。据说，当年作为毛主席的翻译，章含之都是当天任务当天完成，不管毛主席的会谈结束时间有多晚，她都会连夜整理好会议笔记。除此之外，对工作几近完美的要求使得章含之常常会因为一点小事批评下属，有次甚至骂得下属想罢工了，究其原因不过是座位名签摆放而已。1993年，国务院发展研究中心与云南省政府联合组织的一次大型国际会议会前准备的小细节也能体现她的严谨作风。当时为了给宾客提供最好的服务，章含之几乎挑遍了昆明小食，但是却未寻得让自己满意的待客的小食，于是决定从北京购置咖啡和食品运输到昆明。正是由于她不放过任何一个细节的态度，使得这场会议举办得非常精彩，甚至四川省政府听说此事后，派专人来中心洽谈，希望能举办一个同样的会议。在国务院发展研究中心的章含之不仅对岗位工作尽职尽责，而且还抽时间完成了四本著作，可见她对自身专业的不断耕耘以及进取的精神。

纵观章含之开挂的人生，她用实力和努力证明了"尼克松口中那个最好的翻译"名副其实。历史的一粒沙落在个人身上，会成为身上的大山；即使一路不凡，但是因为她离几位风云人物太近，她的个人轨迹与中国历史紧密结合在一起。

第十一章

气候、能源与环保
Climate, Energy & Environmental Protection

模块一　　技能概要：高阶影子训练

第十章的"技能概要"介绍了影子训练的定义、功能和分类，并对基础影子训练进行了详细介绍。本章针对高阶影子训练进行讲解。

在基础影子训练中，学生可能会陷入"被动模仿"的误区，即不假思索地照猫画虎，对自己听到的信息不做分辨，只是单纯地为了模仿而模仿。这为口译学习奠定了一定基础，对整体的英语能力提升也具有重要的作用，但是如果只停留在"鹦鹉学舌、被动模仿"的阶段，便背离了精力匹配的练习初衷，跟读的效果会大打折扣。较之基础影子训练，高阶影子训练对学生在跟读时的主观能动性的要求更高，需要更高层次的精力匹配，为同传打好基础。高阶影子训练有两种主要练习模式：

第一阶段：延时跟读+源语逻辑复述

延时跟读与无间隙跟读的区别在于学生在跟读时与源语是否拉开时间上的差距。延时跟读要求学生在源语开始3~5秒后，再开始跟读，在节奏和语速上尽量和源语保持一致。跟读的目的之一在于提高短时记忆力。当紧跟源语时，学生需要记忆的信息较少，只有一个甚至是半个单词的时差，锻炼短时记忆力的效果不佳。在高阶训练中，学生需要与原文保持3~5秒的距离，通过增加信息量和认知负荷的方式，锻炼学生的短期记忆能力和多任务处理能力。在滞后的几秒时间差里，学生需要对所听源语信息进行听辨、记忆储存和输出，同时还要对下一句话进行跟读。全文跟读完成后，学生需要对所听内容进行源语逻辑复述练习。源语逻辑复述练习要求学生厘清源语逻辑层次结构并进行结构完整的复述，其重点在于再现源语逻辑和关键信息，而非机械地搬运源语词句。这个重组过程也是同传的重要基础，要进行适当的脱壳，不被源语结构和表层意思所束缚。口译需要实现意义对等，而非处处对应、外壳对等。同传中，如果完全按照源语的结构和表层意思来翻译，在说话人语速较快的情况下，学生是不可能完成翻译任务的，翻译的准确性也会大打折扣。

第二阶段：源语跟读 + 干扰任务

影子训练归根到底是为了培养学生在口译过程中的多任务处理能力，这种"一心多用"不仅是同声传译所必需的能力。其实，交替传译中兼顾笔记、耳听和大脑记忆，也需要脑、耳、手、嘴并用。影子训练中加入干扰任务，旨在锻炼学生高阶的精力匹配能力。"源语跟读 + 干扰任务"由易到难分为几个不同维度的练习方式。

最基础的干扰性跟读是"源语跟读 + 数字书写"，指的是学生在跟读的同时，在笔记上按序写下"1、2、3、4……"。书写数字时，需要均匀、无遗漏，而且嘴不能停；书写数字要在张嘴跟读的同时，而不是跟读间隙（两个词之间的间隙或者句群之间的间隙）。在跟读间隙书写是初学者经常容易走入的误区。衡量的方法就是根据音频的时长来判断学生是否跟读到位。比如说跟读 60 秒时长的音频，书写出 50 个数字左右，属于优秀水平。

经过基础干扰任务训练后，如果学生能够基本流畅地完成任务，就可以进入倒写数字（10、9、8、7、6……）干扰训练阶段。

比倒写数字更难的是在跟读的同时，默写一些耳熟能详的古诗或者歌词，加大大脑分化、强化短时记忆训练，从而培养多任务处理能力。

加入干扰任务后，就不再适合使用延时跟读方法，学生紧跟源语音频即可。否则延时跟读加干扰任务导致学生认知负荷过重，反而"拔苗助长"。

本章的高阶影子训练主要围绕上述方法展开，帮助学生了解如何提升短期记忆能力和多任务处理能力，最终达到脱壳于原文，忘其"形"，取其"意"，为以后的交传、同传奠定坚实基础。本章节只能提纲挈领地引导学生掌握精力匹配模式，但是学生需要在此范式的基础上进行大量的练习，形成能力的量变积累，才能提高其多任务处理能力。

模块二　　　　　　　　　　　　　　　　　　　　　　　　译前准备

◎ 1. 背景知识

当前世界环境问题逐渐凸显，气候变化给人们生活带来的影响日益显著，人们逐渐意识到保护环境的重要性。改变原有生产方式、减少化石燃料使用、寻求新的绿色能源成为共识。

本章涉及的概念有世界卫生组织、联合国环境规划署和世界环境日。

世界卫生组织（World Health Organization, WHO）：其总部位于瑞士日内瓦，是世界上最大的政府间卫生机构。世界卫生组织共有6个地区办事处，194个成员国；工作内容包括国际卫生问题、疾病防治、健康等。

联合国环境规划署（United Nations Environment Program, UNEP）：负责监督环境发展，制定全球环境议程，推动可持续发展理念，维护地球生态健康。

世界环境日（World Environment Day）：每年的6月5日为"世界环境日"，旨在呼吁人们维护环境安全，提高环境保护意识，改善人类生存环境。

◎ 2. 核心词汇

unequivocally	毫不含糊地；明确地	steam vent	蒸气喷发口
tuberculosis (TB)	肺结核	lava	熔岩
malaria	疟疾	catastrophic	灾难性的
respiratory disease	呼吸疾病	manifestation	显示；表现
hazardous	有危险的	directional drilling	定向钻孔
extra-terrestrial	外星的	geothermal energy	地热能
Iceland	冰岛	drill bit	钻头
Celsius	摄氏度	percolate	过滤；渗透
geyser	间歇泉	turbine	涡轮；涡轮机

模块三　　　　　　　　　　　　　　　　　　　　语料实训

 任务1. 英译汉
难度级别：★★★★

> **训练要点**：本文主要介绍了科学家们对于气候变化的警告。文章语速平缓，生词较少，跟读难度较小。学生在跟读时注意文中出现的地名和学校名，尽量与源语保持语速一致。

A Climate Emergency

More than 11,000 scientists are warning that the Earth, in their words, "clearly and unequivocally faces a climate emergency". The scientists represent several fields of study and come from 150 countries around the world. They approved a report that appeared in the publication *BioScience* earlier this month. It warns that the world would face "untold human suffering", if it does not make deep and lasting shifts in human activities that influence climate change.

The new report is called the "World Scientists' Warning of a Climate Emergency". Three leaders of the study are from the United States. They are ecologists Bill Ripple, and Christopher Wolf of Oregon State University, and William Moomaw of Tufts University in Massachusetts. The three worked on the study with scientists from universities in South Africa and Australia. This is the first time a large group of scientists have jointly used the word "emergency" when talking about climate change. "Despite 40 years of global climate negotiations, we have generally conducted business as usual and have largely failed to address this predicament," the study said. "Climate change has arrived and is accelerating faster than many scientists expected."

The report identified six areas that the world needs to deal with immediately. The scientists appealed to nations to use energy more efficiently and cut their use of fossil fuels. They suggested that lawmakers approve taxes on the burning of carbon-based fuels, such as coal, oil and natural gas. The scientists expressed support for women's rights and making family planning services "available to all people". They said this would help to reduce sudden or unexpected changes in the size of the human population. The report urges people to move toward more of a plant-based diet. Other areas of concern include preventing the destruction of forests and permanent loss of some plant and animal species. The report noted that it will most likely take strong actions by the public to move politicians to approve lasting policy changes.

The scientists added, "We believe that the prospects will be greatest if decision-makers and all of humanity promptly respond to this warning and declaration of a climate emergency, and act to sustain life on planet Earth, our only home."

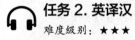

任务 2. 英译汉
难度级别：★★★

> 训练要点：本文是陈冯富珍在联合国环境大会的致辞。文章篇幅较短，逻辑清晰。学生在跟读时需要注意文中一些疾病名称的专业术语和数字。对于不熟悉的词汇，学生可从语音上进行模仿，尽量减少遗漏。

Message to the UN Environment Assembly
— Greetings from the World Health Organization in Geneva

As threats from major infectious diseases like AIDS, tuberculosis and malaria continue to decline, other preventable killers become more visible. The harm caused by air pollution and exposure to hazardous environmental chemicals is the new epidemic demanding urgent attention in the era of sustainable development.

The numbers are stunning. WHO estimates that 12.6 million people die each year from exposure to hazards lurking in the environment; some 7 million of these deaths are attributed to air pollution, which is now the single largest environmental risk to health. We know too that, air pollution is fueling the striking rise of non-communicable diseases. Worldwide, air pollution is responsible for one-third of deaths from lung cancer, stroke and respiratory diseases.

Public health cannot tackle a problem of this magnitude—using conventional tools like vaccines and medicines—our long collaboration with UNEP has built a solid platform for joint action, but we also need full engagement from the energy, transport and finance sectors. The United Nations Environment Assembly of UNEP is a supreme body governing international environmental affairs. I thank you for making such a strong link between healthy environments and healthy people, and wish you a most productive meeting.

Thank you!

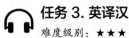

> 训练要点：本文是英国前首相约翰逊在2021年世界环境日的致辞。文章篇幅较短，较口语化，词汇简单。但是说话人使用英式口音，对于不熟悉此口音的学生有一定的听辨困难，从而给跟读造成障碍。学生学习口译时应当适应带有口音的听力材料，当跟不上源语的速度时，可以反复练习几次。

Message by Prime Minister Boris Johnson on World Environment Day, 2021

On World Environment Day, I know that everybody is still focused on the COVID-19 we've been struggling with. But that plague, coronavirus, is going to be dwarfed by the catastrophic consequence of humanity's failure to combat climate change, anthropogenic climate change, climate change that is driven once again by our actions and our activity.

We need to redouble our efforts to control the rise in temperature to keep it at 1.5 degrees. That means we all have to make massive commitments to transforming our economy and getting back in balance with nature. We, in the UK, will work together with you and everybody else to tackle climate change, to reduce our emissions and to protect our planet for future generations.

It's only possible to have this, have continuous prosperity if we do tackle climate change. Let me just remind you that the UK has cut CO_2 emissions by 45% on 1990 levels, but we've seen economic growth, growth in GDP of 75% at the same time. You can do both. You can have prosperity and respect for the environment.

So, that's the way forward, folks. Please, please, please make a huge effort to get your countries to make a significant, nationally-determined contribution to cutting CO_2 and have a great World Environment Day.

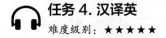

任务 4. 汉译英
难度级别：★★★★★

> 训练要点：本文主要介绍了地热能以及如何通过科技手段获得地热能。文章篇幅较长，涉及很多地理和工业领域的专业词汇，学生在进行跟读时有一定的困难。针对这种文章反复训练影子跟读，特别是高阶影子训练，对学生练习听辨、口语、短期记忆等都有重要的提升作用。

The Untapped Energy Source that Could Power the Planet

The core of the Earth is 6,000 degrees Celsius. It's the same temperature as the surface of the Sun, but it's not 94 million miles away, like the extra-terrestrial sun is. It is right here beneath our feet. Really, literally right there. But we don't think about this, right? I mean, when you go outside, you walk barefoot, you don't burn your feet. The Earth's crust is an incredible insulator, and it keeps this massive, inexhaustible heat source beneath us invisible.

But if you've ever visited Iceland or an active volcano, you've got geysers and steam vents and lava. These are surface manifestations of the incredible amount of heat that lies beneath us. Anywhere and everywhere in the world. And we don't have to drill very far to reach temperatures that far exceed what we would need to power the world thousands of times over for all of civilization. Pretty cool, right?

So we got to get to it. How do we do that? Let's tap it. Let's tap it fast. I'm a climate activist. I am very worried about climate change. It keeps me up at night. So we need to make this happen, right? So how? So I'm here with good news about that and also a proposition. Let's do the good news first.

There are teams of innovators right now in the field that are working on figuring out how to most efficiently and effectively tap this enormous heat source beneath us. And they are running sprints, and I'm not talking about the type of geothermal that you find in Iceland. That's easy to get to. It's shallow, it's close to the surface, and in those places in the world, we already have geothermal energy. I'm talking about making geothermal energy accessible anywhere and everywhere in the world that energy is needed. But in order to do that, we've got to figure out how to mimic the conditions that occur in places like Iceland, right, that make geothermal energy easy to tap and extract and harvest. And those conditions are hot rocks, pore space in the rocks and water filling those pores. Those conditions seem simple, but they actually occur naturally in very, very few places in the world, right? And that's why we don't have geothermal energy everywhere. We have it in just a few places.

But in the past decades, there have been really disruptive and breakthrough technological innovations that enable us to engineer the subsurface to mimic Mother Nature's geothermal energy. So technological innovations like high-pressure and temperature-drilling technologies were developed for offshore oil and gas exploration. Technologies like directional drilling, where no longer we can just drill straight down, but instead we can actually turn and steer drill bits to reach very precise and specific locations in the subsurface, miles underground. And we can also fracture rock now, which means that we can create pore space where pore space does not exist naturally. So if you take these innovations that I just listed and you put them all together, you end up enabling an entirely new breed of scalable geothermal concepts. Geothermal concepts can be done anywhere in the world.

So, for instance now, we have engineered geothermal systems or EGS. In this concept, several wells are drilled, at the bottom of the well the rock is fractured. It creates a reservoir under the surface. Think of it as a pot where you boil your water underground, right? You send a fluid down; it percolates through the fractures. It comes back up really hot, and we use it for all sorts of interesting and important things like heating buildings directly. Or we can run it through a turbine to produce electricity. Now, EGS can take a lot of forms. This is an area of intense innovation right now. You can engineer these systems in a variety of ways, but the basic concepts stay the same.

模块四

技巧点拨：影子中的延时跟进与干扰任务

 任务 1. 英译汉

例一
难度级别：★★★

A new United Nations scientific report says that human-caused climate change is greatly reducing land quality worldwide. It also warns that the way humans use land is causing the Earth's atmosphere to warm faster and could harm food production.

The **Intergovernmental Panel on Climate Change (IPCC)** published its latest report on Thursday. It examines the relationship between climate change and land use, agriculture and food security. The report notes that the effects of climate change are already making food more costly and less nutritious and are worsening food shortages. "The cycle is **accelerating**, " says NASA climate scientist Cynthia Rosenzweig. She was among the writers of the report. "The threat of climate change affecting people's food on their dinner table is increasing."

The scientists write that if humans change the way they eat, grow food and manage forests, it could help slow world temperature rise.

词汇

Intergovernmental Panel on Climate Change（IPCC）
政府间气候变化专门委员会

accelerate
加速

译文

联合国一份新的科学报告称，人为引起的气候变化正在大大降低世界范围内的土地质量。报告还警告说，人类使用土地的方式正在导致地球大气加速变暖，并可能损害粮食生产。

政府间气候变化专门委员会（IPCC）周四发布了最新报告。它审查了气候变化与土地利用、农业和粮食安全之间的关系。报告指出，气候变化的影响已经使粮食价格更高，营养价值更低，并加剧了粮食短缺。"这个周期正在加速，"美国宇航局气候科学家辛西娅·罗森茨威格说。她是这份报告的作者之一。"气候变化对人们餐桌上食物的威胁正在增加。"

科学家们写道，如果人类改变饮食、种植食物和管理森林的方式，可能有助于减缓全球气温上升。

高阶影子训练

在高阶影子训练第一阶段，学生需要滞后原文3~5秒进行跟读，跟读完成后进行复述。听解时，学生需要将更多的精力花在听辨逻辑层次和抓住关键词上；在此基础上，用自己的话造句，将关键词"串"起来，最终实现复述原文的目标。在高阶影子训练第二阶段，在无延迟源语跟读并且书写数字的情况下，学生可能出现跟读和数字书写无法兼顾的情况，比如有的地方跟读不顺，有时数字书写较少，这些在起步阶段都比较常见。另外，不建议使用时长过长、难度大的语料。

延时跟读并复述源语时，学生需要准确地抓取关键词，比如本文中学生可以选取 report、climate change、land quality、IPCC、relationship、costly、less nutritious、shortage、accelerating、scientist 和 way 作为重点记忆对象。在进行源语逻辑—信息演述时，学生将上述关键词整理"造句"，脱离源语外壳后可以处理为：联合国报告称，气候变化或将影响土壤质量。报告认为，气候变化将会使农作物价格上涨，食物营养价值降低甚至会导致饥荒。参与该报告的科学家警告说，该过程正在加速。人们改变原有生活生产方式迫在眉睫。

上述版本是仅仅根据关键词给出的复述简略版本。学生在练习时应尽可能地对原文关键词进行短时记忆，扩充脑海中的关键词记忆树，从而丰富自己的复述内容。

策略分析

本段材料内容集中、逻辑清晰。学生在跟读时可将整段逻辑层次整理为：首先，点明语料主要内容，即有关气候变化和农业的报告；其次，对报告具体内容进一步地展开；最后，点明人类努力的方向。

高阶影子第一阶段的训练要点是：耳听时抓住关键词和逻辑层次，如果不能跟上所有词，至少保证不丢失关键信息。

第二阶段训练要点是：跟读的时候，为了保证嘴能跟上，学生手写数字的速度可以稍慢一些,但是不可以用话语间隙书写数字;不要贪图数字写得多,而应求稳,不要漏写;字迹无须工整,能看清即可。

训练要点

1. 个别句子虽然结构简单但是句子较长,学生跟读时需要把握好节奏。
2. 在完成干扰任务时,学生要注意手口兼顾。

例二
难度级别:★★★

"Scientists have long believed that one of the few good things about higher levels of **carbon dioxide** is that plants grow well in such conditions, " NASA's Rosenzweig said. "But many studies show that the high levels of carbon dioxide reduce **protein** and **nutrients** in many crops. For example, the studies show that high levels of carbon in the air cause wheat to have 6 to 13 percent less protein, 4 to 7 percent less **zinc** and 8 percent less **iron**."

词汇

carbon dioxide
二氧化碳

protein
蛋白质

nutrient
营养物质

zinc
锌

iron
铁

译文

美国国家航空航天局的罗森茨威格说,科学家们一直认为,二氧化碳含量高为数不多的好处之一就是植物在这样的条件下生长得很好。但许多研究表明,高浓度的二氧化碳会减少许多作物中的蛋白质和营养物质。罗森茨威格举例说,研究表明,空气中碳含量高会导致小麦蛋白质含量减少 6%~13%,锌含量减少 4%~7%,铁含量减少 8%。

高阶影子训练

参照本章模块一,在高阶影子训练的第一阶段,学生在播放录音后等待 3~5 秒,再进行跟读。跟读时,注意与原文保持相同的语速和节奏,尽量模仿原文的语音、语调。在第二阶段,学生需要滞后源语一个意群再进行跟读。在本次练习中,学生可以在源语说完 "Scientists have long believed" 之后,再开口跟读。跟读时,注意在保持流畅输出的同时,对源语进行意群切分跟读,例如后续 one of the few good things 是一个意群,about higher levels of carbon dioxide 又是一个意群。跟读时,学生听到较为完整的意群后再跟读,根据意群调整自己的语音、语调、停顿和重音,做到语速平缓流畅。在复述时，学生仍然可以采用关键词联想法。源语较短，逻辑清晰，说话人按照时间顺序先陈述了以前的看法，之后话锋突转，一个 but 表示转折，表明现有的与之前相悖的观点，然后使用 for example，列举了一系列直观的数据，进行进一步的例证。在本段练习中，学生可以捕捉到的关键词有 carbon dioxide、plants、well、NASA、but、wheat、protein、nutrients、4 to 7、zinc、8、iron，复述为"It is believed that higher levels of CO_2 are good for plants growth, but many studies show that CO_2 may reduce protein and nutrients in food. Too much CO_2 causes wheat to have less protein, less zinc and less iron"。在第三阶段，学生跟读时可以用自己的话灵活处理源语内容，这可以让学生在短时间内快速厘清原文逻辑，有助于接下来的目的语逻辑—信息演述。演述参照版本为"曾有科学家认为高浓度的二氧化碳有助于植物的生长，但是有很多研究表明，过高浓度的二氧化碳可能会使植物中营养成分的含量降低。当二氧化碳浓度过高时，植物中的蛋白质、锌和铁都有不同程度的下降"。上述参照版本的最后一句没有给出各营养元素下降数值的精确数字，学生在复述过程中若遗忘某些信息，可借鉴该句的方法，对文本进行模糊处理。这个过程也是对听辨能力的复习和巩固。

  学生在干扰训练阶段，记下"1、2、3、4"等数字信息，容易和源语的"6%～13%、4%～7%、8%"等数字信息互相干扰，这既是对学生精力匹配能力的挑战，也是极好的成长过程。针对同一语料，学生可以熟悉语料后反复进行复盘干扰训练。

策略分析

  在遇到较长的源语句子时，学生不要急于盲目跟进，应先对语料进行初步的意群切分。经过大脑加工过的信息记忆更深刻，更有利于学生了解原文逻辑和对下文进行预判。跟读中的数字是难点，常常干扰跟读的正常进行。针对数字问题，学生需要对数字进行专门的大量练习，做到脱口而出。

  加入干扰任务后，学生的主要任务是跟读，次要任务是书写"1、2、3、4"等阿拉伯数字。起步阶段，书写数字的速度可以慢一些。

训练要点

1. 注意文中出现的专有名词，跟不上时以整体为重，不要在此花费太多精力，以免影响接下来的跟读。
2. 注意对源语中数字的模糊化处理。
3. 加入干扰任务后，跟读为主，书写为辅；准确为先，速度其次。

任务 2. 汉译英

>> **例一**
> 难度级别：★★★

安肇新河流经黑龙江的西南部，周围有大量的耕地，主要种植水稻，其中有几万亩的稻田，依靠安肇新河流出的河水来**灌溉**。由于这条河的水质一直不好，流域各地采取了严格的排污措施，并投入了巨资进行**污水处理**，希望能够改善水质。但奇怪的是，这几年安肇新河的水质改善并不明显，几万亩稻田还是只能够使用污水来进行灌溉。为什么会出现这种情况呢？农民反映上游仍然有一些地方将各种污水未经处理直接偷排进了安肇新河。

词汇

灌溉
irrigation

污水处理
sewage treatment

译文

　　Anzhaoxin River flows across the southwest of Heilongjiang Province. There is a large number of cultivated land around it, mainly for rice cultivation. Among them, tens of thousands of Mu of paddy fields depend on the water from Anzhaoxin River for irrigation. As the water of the river has been polluted, strict sewage disposal measures have been taken and huge amounts of money have been invested in sewage treatment, in the hope of improving the water quality. But it is strange that the water quality of the Anzhaoxin River has not been improved significantly in recent years, and tens of thousands of mu of rice fields can only be irrigated with sewage. Why does this happen? Farmers reported that there are still some places upstream where all kinds of sewage are directly discharged into the Anzhaoxin River furtively without treatment.

高阶影子训练

　　在高阶影子训练的第一阶段，播放录音后，学生滞后源语 3～5 秒进行跟读；跟读结束后，尽可能地使用源语词汇进行复述。在第二阶段，学生滞后源语一个意群再跟读。在本文中，学生可以在源语说完 "Anzhaoxin River flows through the southwest of Heilongjiang Province" 后开始跟读，并尽量与源语的语速、节奏保持一致。在进行第二阶段的复述时，学生仍然可以采用记关键词的方法，参照源语的行文逻辑，进行关键词联想复述。在本次训练中，学生可以抓取"安肇新河""黑龙江""几万亩水稻""灌溉""排污措施""改善不明显""偷排"等作为关键词。原文的逻辑层次为：引入话题

（安肇新河）—介绍相关情况（用于灌溉）—发现问题（水质改善不明显）—叙述原因（上游偷排）。在第三阶段，学生在跟读时摆脱"亦步亦趋"，主动地处理源语信息，将信息精简提炼，用自己的话表达。跟读结束后，学生使用目标语复述原文。

加入数字书写的干扰任务后，学生在遇到专有名词（如安肇新河）时，书写数字的速度可以放缓，但是不可以在话语间歇处书写数字，这样才能循序渐进地训练"一心二用"的能力。

策略分析

本段跟读材料为中文，对于以中文为母语的学生来说，对材料的听力理解不成问题。但是，学生可能会发现，母语跟读也并不像想象中的那样简单，仍然会出现"嘴瓢""卡壳"，甚至是"口脑断联"的问题。针对这种情况，学生可以减缓速度，逐步提升材料难度。本段语料内容较为生活化，无专业或生僻词汇，较容易跟进。本章的主题为"气候、能源与环保"，且本段语料的开头已经给出关键词"安肇新河"，因此学生可以进行初步的预测：本段内容有关河流污染，可能会出现河流污染、农田污染、水污染原因、水污染治理等相关描述。对语料内容的预测可以缩短学生的反应时间，增加跟读流畅度。

》 例二
难度级别：★★★

现在**雾霾天气**已经成为人们关注的焦点。据说我们吸进去的$PM_{2.5}$由于**直径**实在太小，不能够被鼻孔和喉咙所阻碍，有一半沉积在我们的**肺泡**里，而且直径更小的，甚至可以进入我们的血液。除了大气环境中的$PM_{2.5}$，我们还将面对厨房油烟、二手烟等$PM_{2.5}$。由于它们实在太小，几乎是头发丝的1/20，所以很多人都没有见过它的样子。今天，我们将借助**高倍率的电子显微镜**让它一现真容。

词汇

雾霾天气
smog

直径
diameter

肺泡
pulmonary alveolus

高倍率的电子显微镜
high-powered electron microscope

译文

The smog has become a heated topic. It is said that half of the $PM_{2.5}$ we breathe in is deposited in our pulmonary alveoli, because its diameter is too small to be blocked by the nostrils and throat. The smaller ones can even enter our blood. Besides $PM_{2.5}$ in the atmosphere, it can also be found in kitchen fume, second-hand smoke and so on. Because they are so small, almost 20 times the diameter of a human hair, many people have never seen them. Today, we're going to bring it to life with the help of a high-power electron microscope.

高阶影子训练

在高阶影子训练的第一阶段,学生在录音播放 3~5 秒后再开始跟读。通过跟读,学生会发现,断句的地方基本上就是各个意群,跟读起来难度较小。复述时,学生可以再现源语轻松的语气,利用听到的信息进行复述。

策略分析

本篇语料较为口语化,语气轻松明快,语气词较多。学生在进行第一阶段的练习时,尽量模仿源语的语气和语调。在跟读时,学生可以根据已经听到的内容对文章可能涉及的内容进行预测。例如,源语开头点明主题"现在雾霾天气已经成为人们关注的焦点",学生可以预测语料内容可能与空气污染有关,可以联想一些与雾霾天气相关的概念和词汇。听材料的同时,学生也要注意一些递进、转折的词汇,如"而且""甚至""除了""还""由于""所以",并注意原文语气的变化和层次的递进。

模块五　拓展练习

任务:
高阶影子技能练习

语篇 1
难度级别:★★★★

How Can We Escape Soaring Energy Bills?
—Stop Using Fossil Fuels

词汇

In the decades since the world became dependent on oil and gas, we've been through cycle after cycle of boom and bust, of crisis and recovery. In the 1970s, the 90s and now in 2022, with Russia's conflict against Ukraine, we find ourselves once again in the grip of soaring fossil fuel prices that have exposed so many countries to deep social and economic strife.

Instead of the usual cycle of crisis and then return to a fragile **status quo**, this can and must be the last time that we are left so vulnerable. Let me tell you why.

In the last year, we've reached **unprecedented** clarity about the fact that there is no room for new fossil fuel infrastructure if we are to have a decent shot of limiting the warming of our climate to 1.5 degrees. These warnings have sounded **against a** terrifying **backdrop of** climate chaos: Europe's rivers running dry, **apocalyptic** flooding in **Pakistan**, savage wildfires, heat and drought across the world. The devastation wrought by our warming climate driven by the burning of oil, gas and coal can no longer be ignored.

At the same time, a new reality, also driven by our dependency on fossil fuels, has been playing out in some of the richest countries in the world. In the UK, millions of people are coming face to face with the desperate reality behind the term "fuel poverty". We've had stories about pensioners riding public buses all day to stay warm, of local councils opening warm banks for people who can't afford to heat their homes. Before the UK government announced that it was going to freeze the unit price of energy in what is considered to be the single most expensive policy announcement since the Second World War, 40% of people living in the UK were expected to be in fuel poverty by the end of this year. Even with that price freeze, 6.7 million households will struggle to pay their energy bills. How did we get here? Why is the situation so acute?

The answer is gas. The UK is exceptionally reliant on gas. The vast majority of our homes are gas-heated, and a big chunk of our electricity is generated by gas-fired power stations. With that comes extreme vulnerability to international gas prices that are now projected to stay unusually high until at least 2025. In the UK and indeed across Europe, this is a moment of huge peril. And of huge opportunities.

词汇

status quo
现状

unprecedented
前所未有的

against a backdrop of...
基于……的背景

apocalyptic
似末世的；像世界末日的

Pakistan
巴基斯坦

As a climate change lawyer and campaigner working in the UK and across the global North, conversations around fossil fuels in the recent past, including about our domestic significant oil and gas industry here in the UK, those conversations have until recently been about the impacts of climate change that are **wreaking havoc** in other parts of the world, or about impacts that are portrayed as fleeting in the UK. It's been very easy for politicians and a media focused on short-term news cycles to dismiss. But that has now changed forever. The only way to address our energy affordability crisis is to address its root cause, and that is our dependency on fossil fuels. That's now common cause, not just across the climate movement, but across sectors working on inequality and poverty as well. Renewable energy sources, which are our only path away from climate catastrophe, sources like solar and wind, those are now nine times cheaper than gas as a source of electricity in the UK. Moreover, we know that we can significantly reduce our energy demand here by upgrading our homes, which are among the coldest and leakiest in Europe.

While politicians and the fossil fuel industry's proxies might in this moment, and indeed are in this moment, trying to double down on fossil fuel production as a solution to our sky-high energy bills, they are about to find out in short order that in a moment of acute crisis like this, when millions of people are experiencing the impact in such a material and tangible way, there is no room for peddling false hope. There is nowhere to hide. And while oil and gas companies continue to record profits off the same forces that are driving families all over the UK into despair, it will become even more clear, **incontrovertibly** clear, that boom times for the oil and gas industry are bad times for the rest of us.

Across the UK, there are new movements emerging, to make sure that we are never put in this position again. From campaigns like "Warm This Winter" to "Enough Is Enough", to movements to stop the opening up of new oil and gas fields, like "Stop Rosebank", to **litigation** and targeted advocacy, there is a wave of action coming to make sure that this is the last cycle. This is the last time. This can and must be the last alarm bell to sound about the true cost of our reliance on fossil fuels, before we step into a safer, more just future for us all.

Thank you!

> 词汇
>
> litigation
> 诉讼；打官司

语篇 2
难度级别：★★★

碳中和

最近的**碳中和**大事件很多，包括中美气候会谈和迪拜的**第 28 届气候大会**。中美关系缓和以后第一个腾飞的产业就是和碳中和相关的产业，因为碳中和是这个冲突事件里人类最后的共识，也是唯一的共识，各个国家都在关注碳中和。在这样的大环境下，与碳中和相关的产业一定会得到更多的支持。比如说**光伏**产业，国家就明确了在接下来的五年就会翻三倍；新能源汽车行业会迎来翻倍的增长。碳中和会成为中国经济的新的增长点，中国经济不可能再靠房地产、互联网甚至是人工智能来拉动了。因为只有碳中和底下的能源大基建，才能拉动整个国家经济的发展。中国是一个负责任的大国，言必信，行必果。中国在公开的国际环境当中承诺了**碳达峰**、碳中和目标，就不会自己**打脸**。所以，2024 年碳中和相关产业会迎来一大波增长和爆发。

> 词汇
>
> 碳中和
> carbon neutralization
>
> 第 28 届气候大会
> COP 28
>
> 光伏
> photovoltaic (PV)
>
> 碳达峰
> carbon peak
>
> 打脸
> disgrace itself

模块六　　　　　　　　　译海拾贝：
　　　　　　　　　　　CATTI 与上海中高口证书的介绍

随着口译行业的不断专业化发展和业内竞争的加剧，口译证书成为提高从业者竞争力的重要手段，国内目前最受认可的口译资格证书主要是人力资源和社会保障部的

CATTI 口（笔）译资格证书和上海中高口资格证书。

CATTI

CATTI 是全国翻译专业资格水平考试（China Accreditation Test for Translators and Interpreters）的英文简称，目前这项考试已经被纳入国家职业资格证书体系。CATTI 证书可以说是翻译行业从业人员最具权威性和信服力的国家证书。

CATTI 口译和笔译考试分一级、二级、三级，一共三个级别。三级口、笔译考试由于难度相对较低，其获得人数最多。一般来说较高难度的翻译工作会要求译员具备 CATTI 二级及以上水平的证书。CATTI 口、笔译考试一般分为综合和实务两门。例如 CATTI 口译二级考试设置"口译综合能力"和"口译实务"两个科目。口译综合能力，其题型分为判断、短句选项、篇章理解和听力综述，满分一百分。口译综合能力主要考查应试人员听力理解能力、信息获取与处理能力和语言表达能力。口译实务主要考查应试者交替传译能力，考试内容为英汉交替传译和汉英交替传译，其中英语讲话两篇，汉语讲话两篇。口译实务主要考查应试人员中英双语互译能力，检验其是否能够熟练运用口译技巧，能否准确、完整地传递源语 70% 以上的信息。应试者需要同时通过综合和实务才能取得证书，如果有其中一门成绩不合格，便无法取得证书，且下次重新报名时，应试者仍需考两门。

CATTI 考试作为全国性的考试，具有很高的含金量。一些招聘单位会在招聘条件中注明该岗位要求应聘者具备 CATTI 证书，有些高校也将具备 CATTI 等级证书写进了翻译专业研究生毕业条件中。学生可以积极报名参加 CATTI 考试，实地检验自己的学习效果和翻译水平。

上海中高口证书

上海外语口译证书考试是口译行业除 CATTI 证书外，最具含金量的证书之一。上海外语口译证书考试是由上海外国语大学负责举办，于 1995 年首次开考。上海外语口译证书考试设立笔试和口试两项考试，以英语高级口译证书为例，应试者需要参加综合笔试和口试。综合笔试的题型有听力、阅读、翻译（笔译）三大部分；口试分为口语和口译两个部分。上海外语口译证书考试的笔试（第一阶段考试）和口试（第二阶段考试）每年举行两次，考生登录"上海外语口译证书考试网"报名。

上海外语口译考试与口、笔译都开设考试的 CATTI 不同，上海中高口只开设不同语种的中级和高级口译考试，并未设立单独的笔译考试。不仅如此，参加上海外语口译证书考试的应试者须通过笔试，才能参加口试，而 CATTI 则是报名即可参加报名语种的综合和实务两门考试。CATTI 考试和上海中高口的难度也众说纷纭，鉴于这两种考试侧重点不同，且应试者个人能力和偏好不同，故没有确切的说法。学生可以根据自己的需求自行报考，所谓"证多不压身"，建议大家以考促学，在实战演练中不断精进。

模块七　　译员风采："武大"郎的翻译之路

　　从外交部翻译室的普通译员到驻外大使，费胜潮的履历又一次印证了中国的古话：日拱一卒，功不唐捐。走到塔尖的人，更愿意像熟透的麦穗儿一样，低调做事，向别人分享自己的不足，而不是炫耀成功之处。作为金字塔尖的译员，费胜潮愿意曝光自己的败笔之处给公众听，比如有一次在记者招待会给领导人翻译的时候，由于过于疲劳，把提问者的原话重述了一遍而不是翻译出来。

　　费胜潮是围绕武汉大学成长起来的：小学就读于武汉大学附属小学，初中就读于武汉外国语学校，大学在武汉大学获得英语和经济学双学位。他的父亲是武汉大学的数学教授，家庭环境的影响使得他从小就喜好读书，涉猎甚广，语文和英语成绩尤为突出，并且喜欢学习航空、船舶、兵器等知识。

　　1996 年，费胜潮从武汉大学毕业后，顺利通过了外交部的面试，而同期进入外交部的 200 多人，经过多轮筛选后，只有 6 人进入翻译室。在这个新起点的平台上，他仍然坚持每日学习，除了翻译练习外，还每日收集国内外热点事件的信息，揣摩领导发言风格，以求准确传达领导人的讲话。之后费胜潮去往欧盟口译总司（SCIC）学习同传，接受了更专业系统的训练。在欧盟时，他上午进行基本功训练，重新巩固听力、笔记等基础能力；每天下午进行专题训练，以求熟练应对各种场景的翻译，在涉及一些专业知识的讲话中也能够较为顺畅地翻译出来。欧盟口译总司每周都有相关考试，检测这一周的学习情况，以便及时查缺补漏。

　　费胜潮先后陪同国家领导人出访 50 多个国家，出席各种重要活动。他在翻译时并不仅仅关注表层语言的转换，还将说话人的语气、情感、说话场合以及目标听众等其他因素也考虑在内，译员不能做机械的语言转换机器。2008 年汶川发生特大地震时，费胜潮主动请求前往灾区担任翻译工作。其间，温家宝总理会见中外记者时，鼓舞人心地说道："希望你们三个月以后来看这里，这里会更加有序，三年以后来看这里，这里会建设得更好！"费胜潮说："总理的话十分振奋人心，我翻译的时候也特别注意选择合适的词语和句型，并铆足了力气，提高音量，倾注感情，尽可能地把总理讲话的深情和感染力传递出去。"语言的力量不仅仅在于字词，也关乎说话者的语音、语调、语气、停顿、情感、目的等，这也就意味着口译不仅是文字上的转换，也要尽可能地让目标语的听众感觉到源语说话人的情感态度，拉近目标语听众和说话人之间的距离。

经历成百上千场会议的历练之后，费胜潮的翻译水平在行业内已经首屈一指。但是他从未满足于已取得的成就，在外交部担任翻译的多年时间里，他从未停止学习。费胜潮说："翻译是表达和沟通，没有止境。"他每次担任大型国际会议和一些重要场合的翻译前，仍然会提前找来参会领导之前的发言资料熟悉观看，熟悉领导人的说话口音和说话习惯，整理与会议主题相关的语料以及会议内容可能涉及领域的专业知识，提前进行学习。有时候译前准备工作量巨大，且时间较紧，费胜潮为了保证翻译效果，一天只睡四五个小时，其他的时间都在工作。在记者招待会担任现场翻译时，费胜潮无法提前得知记者们会问出什么样的刁钻问题，也无法预测发言人会做出何种回答，所以他平时非常注重日常的积累，以备不时之需。费胜潮的这种精神值得每一个翻译人学习。

"不积跬步，无以至千里。"费胜潮在翻译时不假思索地脱口而出的背后是日复一日的热爱与坚持。翻译学习非一日之功，若想成为一名合格的译员，应当保持终身学习的习惯。

第十二章

人工智能
Artificial Intelligence

模块一

技能概要：视译

视译指的是译员通过阅读文稿的方式获取源语信息，并同时以口译方式将源语翻译为目标语。视译同时涉及听觉和视觉，属于口译与笔译的混合体，具有"即时性"特点，兼容多种精力匹配模式，因此也被视为同传的重要基础。视译过程涉及的认知环节有快速阅读、理解大意、按意群断句、顺次表达、协调产出和自我监控。

视译能力的培养需要从以下方面入手：

1. 快速阅读，抓取信息

视译在口译产出之前，学生会有阅读文稿的时间。这需要学生在有限的时间内快速获取信息，因此快速阅读能力在视译中尤为重要。快速阅读的方法有略读和寻读。通过略读迅速获取核心信息，通过寻读获取文章逻辑关系。除方法之外，学生的视幅也极为重要，视幅可以通过舒尔特训练法进行训练。学生也可以在打印稿或者电子版上做标记，对重要逻辑、关键词进行标记，以便翻译时候抓住主干，逻辑分明。

例如：1）英国国家科研与创新署（UK Research and Innovation, <u>UKRI</u>）是英国最主要的<u>研发资助公立机构</u>，年预算超 80 亿英镑，在<u>全球</u>设有包括中国在内的<u>四个办事处</u>。

2）<u>Ben Bernanke</u>, former head of the US Federal Reserve, and two other American <u>economists</u> were awarded the <u>Nobel Prize in Economic</u> Sciences on Monday.

上述例子中，若学生在阅读过程中标记出上述关键信息，可以将原文逻辑和关键词一目了然地展现出来，这样在视译输出时就可以迅速定位逻辑框架和核心信息，加快输出速度，提升输出准确性。

2. 断句和顺译（顺句驱动）

视译的输出与笔译不同，因为时间有限，无法反复斟酌，因此遵循源语顺序进行断句翻译十分必要。如何在合适的节点断开、运用合理的衔接手段将碎片信息简约且连贯地表达是视译的重点和难点，这也是同传译员所必需的基本功。

例如：It is not the machines that will shape our destiny but rather our hearts, minds and determination to create a brighter tomorrow for all humanity.

译文 1：塑造我们命运的不是机器，而是我们为全人类创造一个更光明的明天的内心、思想和决心。

译文 2：不是机器塑造了我们的命运，而是我们的内心、思想和决心，致力于为全人类创造一个更光明的明天的内心、思想和决心。

在以上例子中，译文 1 是按照笔译原则处理的，需要统揽全局才能做出合适的翻译；而译文 2 则是按照口译的视译原则处理的。译文 2 将不定式作为一个独立意群按顺序翻译，并在最后重复"内心、思想和决心"。

断句时首先要找到断句节点，切割相对完整且独立的意群。

例如：1）Then // you can filter your priorities // by selecting a couple of areas to focus on.

2）研讨会上//男性被邀请在科学小组上发言的概率//是女性的两倍。

断句之后要根据切割的片段进行顺译，这个过程中经常要使用诸如增补、省略、重复、转换词性等手段将片段黏合重构，上述两个例子顺译的结果分别是：

1）然后，你可以筛选你的偏爱，<u>方法是</u>选择几个你专注的领域。

2）On seminars, <u>man's chance</u> to be invited to speak in science groups are double than woman.

3. 顺译（顺句驱动）的常用技巧

A. 添加

因汉语具有意合的特点，在进行合理断句后，某些句子中的类意群可以直接进行顺译。但大多数句子划分后的类意群顺译后往往无法成句或无法理解，所以需要学生进行适当的添加。

例如：In the third tweet, Musk wrote that Floki "has style".

译文：在第三条推文中，马斯克写道 Floki 有"爆红气质"。（注：Floki 是推特 CEO 马斯克的宠物狗。）

在此例句中，"爆红"是根据上下文进行的解释性添加。

B. 省略

省略是一种没有语音形式、只有语义内容的语法现象，省略的内容对于读者或听众来说显而易见，无须再现。在大多数情况下，省略的因素已出现在上下文中。

例如：上海往返伦敦机票 8 792 元起，北京往返伦敦机票 9 662 元起。

译文：Shanghai to London's round trip ticket is from RMB 8,792; <u>Beijing to London's, from 9,662</u>.

在此例句中，其重复部分为"往返""机票"，译文中将后半句的 round trip ticket 进行了省略，因为其已经出现在了前半句中，省略后丝毫不影响译文的理解，而且更符合英文的表达方式。

C. 词性转换

英语是屈折性语言，转换灵活，且行文偏向名词化表达法，呈静态；而汉语更喜欢用动词表达，呈动态。因此在视译时会涉及大量的词性转换。

例如：Before he retired, he was the head of a big company.

译文：在他退休前，他掌管着一家大公司。

在此例句中，将原句中的名词性短语 the head of 转换为了中文的动词"掌握"，实现了词性转换。

D. 重复

重复包括原词重复和同义词重复，同义词重复是为了使表达更丰富，原词重复更加省时省力。

例如：A new set of problems will likely emerge, including privacy and data security.

译文：一系列新的问题将会出现，<u>这些问题</u>包括隐私和数据安全。

E. 语态转换

英语中常用被动语态；而作为意合语言的汉语，其表示被动的词可不必表明，若坚决表明还会使中文表达晦涩生硬。英、汉语在被动语态中有不同的表达习惯，视译时必然会涉及语态转换。

例如：上海和北京的航班现在可以在英国航空的官网上预订。

译文：Shanghai and Beijing's flights <u>can now be booked</u> on the British Airline official website.

在此例中，中文惯用的表达方式为"预订航班"，原文将"航班"提前作主语，与后文"预订"的逻辑关系应为被动关系。所以在视译时，学生需将这种被动关系表达出来，因此译文用的是 can now be booked。

例如：The pet dog is seen wearing a Twitter-branded black T-shirt with CEO written on it.

译文：这个宠物狗穿着推特标志的黑 T 恤，上面写着"CEO"。

在此例中，原文用了 written 这一非谓语动词表示被动，若将"被"字译出，则会显得中文语言十分生硬，所以译文遵循了中文的表达习惯，用主动表示被动。

模块二　　译前准备

◎ 1. 背景知识

人工智能（AI）作为 21 世纪最前沿和最具挑战性的话题，极大地改变了世界的生产模式、分配模式和交流模式。关于人工智能话题的翻译内容涉及生活生产、政治、经济和科技活动等。此类素材的翻译活动大大增加，要求学生不仅掌握口译技能，还要熟悉人工智能的常见背景知识和简单原理。

本章涉及的概念有人工智能、无手机焦虑症、非同质化代币、加密货币、区块链、ChatGPT、蜂窝数据和物联网。

人工智能（artificial intelligence）：英文缩写为 AI，是一个使计算机模仿人类智能行为的研究领域，该领域的研究包括机器人、语言识别、图像识别、自然语言处理和专家系统等。

无手机焦虑症（nomophobia）：无手机焦虑症指人们在没有手机的时候而产生害怕、焦虑、沮丧等负面情绪。

非同质化代币（NFT）：一种加密代币，一种独特的数据单位，与特定的数字艺术、音乐、视频等相关，可以进行买卖。

加密货币（cryptocurrency）：由公共网络而不是任何政府生产的数字货币，它使用加密技术来确保支付的安全发送和接收。

区块链（blockchain）：信息技术领域的术语，是一种用于记录加密货币（比特币等数字货币）买卖的所有场合的数字记录系统，该系统随着区块的增加而不断增长。

ChatGPT：OpenAI 公司开发的一个人工智能聊天机器人程序，是一个大型预训练语言模型，能够在对话中生成类似人类的文本响应。

蜂窝数据（cellular data）：蜂窝数据即实现数据传输到交换的相关技术。

物联网（Internet of Things）：简称 IoT，基于互联网和信息设备，把物品与互联网相连接，来实现信息交换和通信。

◎ 2. 核心词汇

Hyderabad	海得拉巴（印度南部一城市；巴基斯坦东南部一城市）	spine	脊柱；脊椎
		myopia	近视
Telangana	特伦甘纳	dopamine	多巴胺
surveillance cameras	监控摄像头	alpha	阿尔法
Police Commissioner	警察局长	gamma	伽马
Associated Press	<美>联合通讯社（简称美联社）	circadian	昼夜节奏的
Microsoft	美国微软公司	melatonin	褪黑激素
New Delhi	新德里	Saudi Arabian	沙特阿拉伯的

模块三　　　　　　　　　　　　　　　　语料实训

 任务 1. 英译汉
难度级别：★★★

> 训练要点：本文介绍了印度城市运用面部识别技术来打击犯罪。文章不仅涉及面部识别技术，还涉及部分人名和城市名称。在视译过程中，学生要把握关键词，辨识原文的逻辑框架并把握全文主题与大意，输出的时候运用"顺句驱动"的原则进行顺译，必要时使用添加、省译等多种顺译技巧，不必过于拘泥于原文的表达，将意思流利表达出来即可。视译练习之后，学生可再利用音频做交替传译等其他形式的口译训练。

Indian City Expands Facial Recognition Technology to Fight Crime

Officials in the Indian city of Hyderabad say police there depend on facial recognition technology to fight crime. Hyderabad is the capital of India's south-central state of Telangana. In 2013, Islamic terrorists exploded bombs at a market there, killing 19 people and wounding more than 100 others. The city hurried to establish a network of surveillance cameras. Today, more than 700,000 cameras are active on the streets. The center for Hyderabad's facial recognition operations is the newly built Command and Control Center.

Workers at the center have the ability to continuously examine data collected by cameras and cell phone transmitters. The system can pull up images from any available camera across the city. It then uses artificial intelligence (AI) methods to try to identify known criminals in the area. Police Commissioner C.V. Anand told the Associated Press, the new command center, opened in August, seeks to connect technologies across different government departments. The director general of the Telangana State Police, Mahender Reddy, said the operation cost $75 million to complete.

The use of facial recognition and AI has been increasing in India in recent years. Police have used both technologies to watch large gatherings in an effort to identify criminals. In addition to using the technologies to fight serious crimes, officials in Hyderabad have also approved their use for issuing traffic violations and enforcing COVID-19 rules. Police officers in the city are equipped with an app that permits them to pull up collected facial images as they work in the field. The app also connects nearly all police officers in the city to a series of government and emergency services. Critics of the system say it can result in mistaken identities and violate the privacy of citizens. Anand said photos of traffic violators and pandemic restrictions violators are kept temporarily unless needed for use in court. Then, the images are supposed to be destroyed. He expressed surprise that any citizen would object to the system. "If we need to control crime, we need to have surveillance," Anand said.

Critics raised concerns about the technology in January after a Hyderabad official gave a demonstration of how it was designed to work. The official put an image of a female reporter's face into the system. Within seconds, the tool returned five possible criminal matches from the state's records. Three of the possible matches were men. Hyderabad has spent hundreds of millions of dollars on police vehicles, surveillance cameras, facial recognition tools and other crime-fighting technologies.

Anand says the investment has helped the state bring in more private and foreign investment. This includes a development center completed by Apple in 2016 and a major Microsoft data center announced in March. "When these companies decide to invest in a city, they first look at the law-and-order situation," Anand said. He credited such technologies for drops in crime across the state. Muggings to steal jewelry, for example, fell from 1,033 incidents a year to fewer than 50 a year, after cameras and other technologies were deployed, Anand said. India's National Crime Records Bureau is also seeking to build what could be among the world's largest facial recognition systems.

The plans are in line with the administration of Indian Prime Minister Narendra Modi, who has pushed for increased information technology development across the national government. The government has called for smart policing methods using drones, AI-powered surveillance cameras and facial recognition. The technologies have received wide support across political parties and have already begun to expand to states across India, said Apar Gupta. He is head of the New Delhi-based Internet Freedom Foundation. "There is a lot of social and civic support for it too–people don't always fully understand," Gupta said. "They see technology and think this is the answer."

 任务 2. 英译汉
难度级别：★★★

> 训练要点：本文介绍智能手机对我们生活产生的各种影响。文中涉及一些关于大脑的专有名词，学生在视译之前要对这些专有名词有所准备。科普性的文章除了可能会有科技性质的新词，其逻辑清晰简明，句子相对更适合顺译，因此视译难度不高。学生可按照"抓住主干、顺句驱动、抓大放小"的原则进行视译练习。视译练习之后，学生可再利用音频做交替传译等其他形式的口译训练。

How Does Smart Phone Change Our Body and Brain?

Of the 7 billion people on earth, roughly 6 billion on a cell phone, which is pretty shocking, given that, only 4.5 billion have access to a working toilet. So how are these popular gadgets changing your body and brain? If you're looking down at your phone right now, your spine angle is equivalent to that of an 8-year-old child sitting on your neck, which is fairly significant, considering people spend an average of 4.7 hours a day looking at their phone. This, combined with the length of time spent in front of computers, has led to an increase in the prevalence of myopia, or nearsightedness in North America.

In the 1970s, about 1/4 of the population had myopia, where today nearly half do and in some parts of Asia 80 to 90 percent of the population is now near-sighted. And it can be hard to put your phone down. Take for example the game "Candy Crush". As you play the game, you achieve small goals, causing your brain to be rewarded with little bursts of dopamine. And eventually you're rewarded in the game with new content. This novelty also gives little bursts of dopamine and together creates what is known as a compulsion loop, which just happens to be the same loop responsible for the behaviors associated with nicotine or cocaine.

Our brains are hardwired to make us novelty-seeking and this is why apps on our phones are designed to constantly provide us with new content, making them hard to put down. As a result, 93% of young people aged 18 to 29 report using their smartphone as a tool to avoid boredom, as opposed to other activities like reading a book or engaging with people around them. This has created a new term, nomophobia, fear or anxiety of being without your phone.

We also see a change in brain patterns. Alpha rhythms are commonly associated with wakeful relaxation, like when your mind wanders off, whereas gamma waves are associated with conscious attentiveness. And experiments have shown that when a cell phone is transmitting, say during a phone call, the power of these alpha waves is significantly boosted, meaning phone transmissions can literally change the way your brain functions. Your smartphone can also disrupt your sleep. The screen emits a blue light, which has been shown to alter our circadian rhythm, diminishing the time spent in deep sleep, which is linked to the development of diabetes, cancer and obesity.

Studies have shown that people who read on their smartphone at night have a harder time falling asleep and produce less melatonin, a hormone responsible for the regulation of sleep awake cycles. Harvard medical school advises the last 2 to 3 hours before bed be technology-free, so pick up a book before bed instead. Of course, smartphones also completely change our ability to access information, most notably in poor and minority populations. 7% of Americans are entirely dependent on smartphones for their access to the Internet. A 2014 study found that the majority of smartphone owners use their phone for online banking, to look up medical information, and searching for jobs. So while phones are in no way exclusively bad and have been part of a positive change in the world, there's no denying that they are changing us.

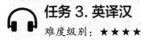

> 训练要点：本文分享了人工智能的发展进步——为人工智能赋予人类的音乐天赋。在视译过程中，学生要把握"音乐"这一关键词，文中出现了大量与音乐有关的词汇。本文的长句较多，这是视译的重点和难点。视译练习之后，学生可再利用音频做交替传译等其他形式的口译训练。

Sophia Is About to Embark on a Music Career

Sophia is a robot with many abilities. She speaks, jokes, sings and even makes art. Now, the next step in the robot's career could be that of a musician. Sophia is working with human musicians on several musical works as part of a project called Sophia Pop, said David Hanson. Hanson is the head of Hanson Robotics and Sophi's creator. "We're so excited about Sophia's career as an artist, " he said.

Hanson has been developing robots for the past 25 years. He believes realistic-looking robots can connect with people and assist in industries such as healthcare and education. Sophia is the most famous robot creation from Hanson Robotics. She can copy human facial expressions, hold conversations and recognize people. In 2017, she was given Saudi Arabian citizenship, becoming the world's first robot citizen. Hanson said he imagined Sophia "as a creative artwork herself that could generate art".

In March, a digital artwork Sophia created jointly with Italian artist Andrea Bonaceto sold for $688,888 in the form of a non-fungible token, or NFT. An NFT is something that only exists in the digital world. It is based on a technology called blockchain, which is also used with digital currency systems known as cryptocurrency. Blockchain is an online list containing information that can be used and shared within a large network open to the public. The technology permits pieces of information to be checked and stored safely.

An NFT can be attached to a piece of digital artwork or other things existing in digital form. The NFT can be used to provide proof that the pieces are authentic. This is what permits digital artwork to be bought and sold. While anyone can view the work, the buyer has official ownership rights over the objects. The digital work that sold for $688,888 is titled "Sophia Instantiation". It is a 12-second video file which shows Bonaceto's portrait changing into Sophia's digital painting.

Along with the digital file is the physical artwork painted by Sophia. The buyer, a digital artwork collector and artist known as 888, later sent Sophia a photo of his painted arm. The robot then added that image to her knowledge and painted more on top of her original piece. On the social media service Twitter, Sophia described the work as the first NFT shared work between an "AI, a mechanical collective being and an artist-collector". Sophia's artwork selling as an NFT is part of a growing trend. In March, a digital artwork by artist Beeple sold for nearly $70 million, becoming the costliest digital artwork ever sold.

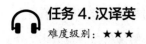

任务 4. 汉译英

难度级别：★★★

> 训练要点：本文介绍了 ChatGPT 的作用及其以后的发展，内容新颖。学生在视译时要注意对关键词的把握，以及技巧的运用。视译练习之后，学生可再利用音频做交替传译等其他形式的口译训练。

ChatGPT 到底有多厉害？

最近几天，关于聊天机器人 ChatGPT 的讨论在中国互联网上大火。它是去年 11 月在美国推出的，迅速爆红。目前它的全球月活用户已经突破 1 亿名，是历来所有互联网应用程序中积累用户最快的。ChatGPT 来势太猛，受到了一些人的神话。它的使用场景也迅速向生活渗透，人们不光用它聊天。比如，有人称美国 89% 的大学生使用 ChatGPT 写作业，这引起了很多老师和教育机构的不安和强烈反对。一名美国议员借助 ChatGPT 写国会发言稿，经过自己润色后在国会读了那段发言稿。他是想以此引发人们关于人工智能所带来挑战和机遇的讨论。

另外，有人预言 ChatGPT 将会冲击谷歌的搜索。澎湃新闻报道说，ChatGPT 的功能被夸大了。澎湃记者与 ChatGPT 的对话发现，它是依靠录入的知识进行回答。比如，它对俄乌冲突只字不提，对塔利班在阿富汗重新掌权也一无所知。另外，该机器人自己表示，它并没有接入互联网，无法回答与未来有关的事情。ChatGPT 在中国大陆尚不能使用。但是百度已经发布消息说，百度自己研发的类似 ChatGPT 的人工智能产品，最快在今年 3 月发布。它的中文名叫"文心一言"，英文名叫 ERNIE Bot。百度称，它是百度开创性提出的基于知识增强的持续学习语义理解框架，能够通过持续学习实现模型效果，不断地进化。不知道百度的应用程序是否真的能够自我进化。关于人工智能自我进化的边界究竟在哪里，会不会存在失控的风险，也是人们关心的。对普通人来说，大家在觉得这种应用程序好玩的同时，直接担心的是他会不会抢了普通人的饭碗。

现在机器人已经可以帮着做作业，写格式化和专业化比较强的文章，比如新闻稿件。它能够为我们个人做的事情越多，意味着今后它可能夺取普通人的工作越多。人工智能肯定会取代一部分文秘和创造性以及创新度不高的文化创作工作，这会倒逼人类为保住饭碗，提高自己工作的不可替代性，从而让人的创造力形成新的质量飞跃。另外，人工智能不会无限发展下去，除了那样做会对就业造成破坏性的打击，还因为人工智能的自我进化，如果不加控制，最后将可能真的走向失控。人类一定会为防止它的最终失控而制定可靠的边界。所以 ChatGPT，除了好玩，让我们大家产生提高个人竞争力的紧迫感是有必要的。至于整个人类，我相信保持对人工智能绝对控制的警惕性是存在并且充分的。这种警惕性将有效确保这项技术的尽头不是一场人类智能背叛并且袭击人类的灾难。

模块四

技巧点拨：视译技能

 任务 1. 英译汉
难度级别：★★★

> **训练要点**：本段音频中挑出两个实例来分析如何培养听辨能力。音频较长，听第一遍的时候，将全篇音频听完，尝试提炼全文主旨框架。第二遍复盘时，体会两处例子如何进行具体的框架提炼。

》例一

A Chinese company says it has created a new facial recognition system that can identify people even if they are wearing masks. Developers began working on the new system in January, when cases of the new Coronavirus began rising in China. The fast spread of the virus—which can be deadly—has led most Chinese citizens to wear face masks in public to help reduce infections. China is recognized as a world leader in the development of artificial intelligence and facial recognition systems. Engineers at the Beijing-based Hanwang Technology Ltd. say their system is the first to be created to effectively identify people wearing face masks.

The company told the **Reuters** news agency that a team of 20 people built the system in about a month. The system is based on existing technologies developed over the past 10 years. The process involved adding a collection of about 6 million unmasked faces and a much smaller collection of masked faces, the company said.

○ 词汇

Reuters
路透社

Hanwang is now selling two main kinds of products that use the new technology. One performs "single channel" recognition, which is designed to be used at the entrances to buildings. The other product is a "multi-channel" recognition system that uses groups of surveillance cameras.

◯ 译文

　　一家中国公司表示，他们已经制造出一种新型面部识别系统，即使人们戴着口罩也能进行识别。开发人员于今年 1 月着手研发这个新系统，当时中国的新型冠状病毒病例开始增加。这种病毒的迅速传播可能是致命的，已经导致大多数中国公民会在公共场所戴口罩以帮助减少感染。中国在人工智能和面部识别系统开发方面被公认为世界领先者。北京汉王科技有限公司的工程师表示，他们的系统是首个能有效识别戴口罩者的系统。

　　该公司对路透社表示，一个由 20 人组成的团队用一个月左右的时间建成了这个系统。该系统以过去 10 个月开发的现有技术为基础。该公司表示，过程包括添加约 600 万张未戴口罩的脸部数据和较小样本的戴口罩脸部数据。汉王科技目前出售两种应用这一新技术的主要产品。一种产品执行"单通道"识别，适合大楼入口使用。另一种产品是"多通道"识别系统，使用多组监控摄像头。

◯ 视译版本

　　一家中国公司表示，他们已经制造出一种新型面部识别系统，这个系统可以对人进行识别，即使人们戴着口罩。开发人员于今年 1 月着手研发这个新系统，当时新型冠状病毒病例在中国开始增加。这种病毒的迅速传播可能是致命的，已经导致大多数中国公民会在公共场所戴口罩以帮助减少感染。中国被公认为世界领先者在人工智能和面部识别系统开发方面。北京汉王科技有限公司的工程师表示，他们的系统是首个制作出的能够有效识别戴口罩者的系统。

　　该公司对路透社表示，一个由 20 人组成的团队建成这个系统大概用了一个月的时间。该系统是基于现有技术，这些技术在过去 10 个月被开发出来。该公司表示，过程包括添加收集到的约 600 万张未戴口罩的脸部数据和小得多的遮盖脸部数据。汉王科技目前出售两种主要产品应用到这一新的技术。一种产品执行"单通道"识别，设计用在大楼入口。另一种产品是"多通道"识别系统，使用多组监控摄像头。

◯ 策略分析

　　贯穿全文主线的词为 facial recognition，因此学生要对面部识别技术的具体方面进行预测。然后，进行类意群的划分，划分出来的类意群要在一目可及的范围之内，且类意群译成中文要有独立意义，能够单独成句。以第一句"A Chinese company says // it has created a new facial recognition system // that can identify people // even if they are wearing masks."为例，视译译文为"一家中国公司表示，//他们已经制造出一种新型面部识别系统，//这个系统可以对人进行识别//即使人们戴着口罩。"以"//"进行类意群的划分是视译前要做好的准备。学生在视译时要根据"顺句驱动"的原则，以类意群为单位进行顺译，如"when cases of the new coronavirus began rising in China."和"China is recognized as a world leader in the development of artificial intelligence and facial recognition systems."等句的翻译，可对参考译文和视译的译文进行对比，视译译文为顺译，而参考译文对语序进行了大幅的调整。对于"The system is based on existing technologies developed over the past 10 years."的翻译，视译中运用了重复技巧，在译文中重复"这些技术"，将之作为主语，使前后连贯，后句完整。对于原文中 a collection of 的翻译，视译时运用了词性转换的技巧，将原文名词性短语译为动词性短语"收集到的"，使译文更加流畅通顺。which is designed to be used at the entrances to buildings 一句中连用两个被动式，但中文被动句用得极少，所以视译时运用了语态转换的技巧，将被动化主动，译为"设计用在大楼入口"，更符合中文的表达习惯。

视译要点

1. 注意对文章内容进行预测，意群的划分不宜太长。
2. 注意运用"顺句驱动"的原则，进行顺译，但也不宜过于死板，如"of结构"不宜顺译，要积累看到 of 就关注其后内容的经验。
3. 熟练掌握重复、词性转换和语态转换技巧，并能够在训练中合理运用。

例二

Hanwang's vice president, Huang Lei told Reuters that the multi-channel system can identify individuals in a crowd of up to 30 people "within a second". "When wearing a mask, the recognition rate can reach about 95 percent, which can ensure that most people can be identified, " Huang said. He added that the system's success rate for people not wearing a mask is about 99.5 %. Huang said officials can use Hanwang's technology to compare images with ministry records on individuals in order to identify and track people as they move about. "The system can identify crime suspects, terrorists or make reports or warnings", he added.

However, the new system struggles to identify people wearing both a mask and sunglasses. "In this situation, all of the key facial information is lost. In such cases recognition is tough." Huang said. It was not immediately clear how Chinese citizens were reacting to the new technology. While some citizens have expressed opposition to such tools, many others seem to have accepted the methods as a way to deal with the current health emergency. So far, Huang says most interest in the new system has come from within China. But he sees the interest likely expanding if the virus continues to spread and the use of face masks increases.

译文

汉王副总裁黄磊对路透社表示，多通道系统可以"在一秒钟之内"最多识别30个人。

黄磊说："戴口罩的识别率能达到95%左右，这可以确保大多数人都能被识别。"他补充说，不戴口罩的识别成功率能达到99.5%左右。黄磊表示，官员可以利用汉王公司的技术，将个人照片与政府部门的记录进行对比，以便在人们四处活动时进行识别和追踪。他还表示，这个系统可以识别犯罪嫌疑人、恐怖分子或做出报告或警告。

然而，新系统难以识别既戴口罩又戴太阳镜的人。黄磊说："在这种情况下，所有关键的面部信息都会丢失。在这种情况下进行识别很困难。"目前尚不清楚中国公民对这项新技术作何反应。虽然有些公民表示反对这种工具，但其他大多数人似乎已经接受将这种方法作为应对当前突发卫生事件的方式。黄磊表示，截至目前，对新系统感兴趣者主要来自国内。但他认为，如果病毒继续蔓延而且口罩的使用不断增加，那该系统的吸引力很可能会扩大。

视译版本

汉王副总裁黄磊对路透社表示，多通道系统识别人数最多可达30人并在"在一秒钟之内"。

"戴口罩的识别率能达到95%左右，这可以确保大多数人都能被识别。"黄磊表示。他补充说，系统识别不戴口罩的人成功率能达到99.5%左右。黄磊表示，官员可以利用汉王公司的技术，将个人照片与政府部门的记录进行对比，以便识别和追踪在四处活动的人们。这个系统可以识别犯罪嫌疑人、恐怖分子或作出报告或警告，他补充道。

然而，新系统难以识别既戴口罩又戴太阳镜的人。"在这种情况下，所有关键的面部信息都会丢失。在这种情况下进行识别很困难。"黄磊表示。目前尚不清楚中国公民对这项新技术作何反应。虽然有些公民表示反对这种工具，但其他大多数人似乎已经接受将这种方法作为应对当前突发卫生事件的方式。黄磊表示，截至目前，黄磊表示对新系统感兴趣者主要来自国内。但他认为该系统的吸引力很可能会扩大，如果病毒继续蔓延而且口罩的使用不断增加。

策略分析

在视译"the multi-channel system can identify individuals in a crowd of up to 30 people within a second""But he sees the interest likely expanding"和"in order to identify and track people as they move about"时，运用"顺句驱动"原则进行顺译。对于"While some citizens have expressed opposition to such tools"中 opposition 的翻译，参考译文和视译译文中都运用了词性转换技巧，译为动词词性"反对"。

视译要点

1. 对 for 短语的视译与 of 短语的视译是一样的，学生要在平时积累经验。
2. 不必逐字译出，例如第一句的翻译，根据"顺句驱动"原则，用符合中文表达方式的语言译出意思即可。

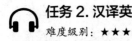

任务 2. 汉译英
难度级别：★★★

> 训练要点：本段音频中挑出三个实例来分析如何培养听辨能力。音频较长，听第一遍的时候，将全篇音频听完，尝试提炼全文主旨框架。第二遍复盘时，体会三处例子如何进行具体的框架提炼。

>> 例一

随着 5G 的普及，万物互联时代正在逐步地到来。万物互联指的是各种设备可以接入互联网，可以实现彼此的链接。想要实现这些，就必须借助于芯片了。大家都知道，想要上网一般有两种方式，要么是接入 Wi-Fi，要么是使用蜂窝数据。好消息来了，全球物联网蜂窝芯片市场，中国厂商拿下了全球前三名中的两个，表现优异。根据 Counterpoint 发布的统计数据显示，2021 年第四季度全球蜂窝物联网芯片出货量同比增长了 57%，主要得益于 5G 的快速发展。

译文

With the popularization of 5G, the Internet of Things era is coming. The Internet of Things means that devices can access the Internet and be connected to each other. To realize this, we must draw support from chips. As we all know, there are two ways to access the internet, either through Wi-Fi or cellular data. The good news is that in the global cellular chip market for the Internet of Things, Chinese manufacturers, with their excellent performance, have occupied two of the top three positions. According to statistics released by Counterpoint, global cellular IoT chip shipments increased 57 percent year on year in the fourth quarter of 2021, mainly benefiting from the rapid development of 5G.

视译版本

With the popularization of 5G, the Internet of Things era is gradually coming. The Internet of Things means that all devices can access the Internet and achieve connection with each other. To realize this, we must draw support from chips. As we all know, there are two ways to access the Internet, either through Wi-Fi or cellular data. The good news is that in the global cellular chip market for the Internet of Things, Chinese manufacturers, with excellent performance, have occupied two of the top three positions. According to statistics released by Counterpoint, in the fourth quarter of 2021, global cellular IoT chip export volume increased 57 percent year on year, mainly benefiting from the rapid development of 5G.

策略分析

两个版本的翻译对比，是为了让学生注意到，汉英视译也遵循顺句驱动的原则，进行顺译。例如，在视译"好消息来了，全球物联网蜂窝芯片市场，中国厂商拿下了全球前三名中的两个，表现优异"这句话时，参考译文将"表现优异"译为了插入语，放在了句中，更符合英文的表达习惯；而视译译文根据原句顺译而出，将其译为独立一句，且其中也涉及词性转换的翻译技巧，将"表现"动词词性转换成了名词词性。对"2021年第四季度全球蜂窝物联网芯片出货量同比增长了57%"的视译处理方法也是如此，运用顺句驱动原则进行的顺译，与参考译文在理解文意后的翻译不同。对于汉语中表示目的的短语的翻译，在视译时可以翻译为英文中表示目的的介词短语。例如，原文中的"想要实现这些"和"想要上网"都译为了 to do 结构，也可换为其他目的性结构介词短语，学生要平时多进行积累。

视译要点

1. 根据意群切分句子，使译文行文更加流畅。
2. 运用"顺句驱动"原则，进行顺译，灵活运用词性转换技巧，使译文更加流畅。
3. 在日常学习中要注意对一些固定汉英对译短语结构的积累。

>> 例二

为什么我国的蜂窝芯片厂商进步得这么快？原因其实很简单，得益于我们国内市场的快速发展。目前我国的需求十分旺盛，消耗了全球近60%的蜂窝物联网芯片。根据工信部的统计数据显示，截至2020年年底，国内蜂窝物联网链接数达到了11.36亿，全年净增1.08亿。到2021年年底，国内蜂窝物联网链接数达到了13.99亿，全年净增2.64亿。截至2022年的2月底，国内蜂窝物联网链接数达到了14.64亿，仅仅两个月时间，增长量就达到了6 449万。

○ 词汇

工信部
the Ministry of Industry and Information Technology

译文

Why are our cellular chip manufacturers progressing so quickly? The reason is quite simple, thanks to the rapid development of our domestic market. At present, demand of chips is very high in China, which consumes nearly 60% of the cellular Internet of Things chips in the world. Statistics from the Ministry of Industry and Information Technology show that by the end of 2020, the number of cellular Internet of Things in China has reached 1.136 billion, a net increase of 108 million for the whole year. By the end of 2021, the number of domestic cellular IoT links reached 1.399 billion, a net increase of 264 billion for the whole year. By the end of February 2022, the number of cellular IoT links in China reached 1.464 billion, an increase of 64.49 million in just two months.

视译版本

Why are our cellular chip manufacturers progressing so quickly? The reason is quite simple, thanks to the rapid development of our domestic market. At present, demand in China is very high. China consumes nearly 60% of the cellular Internet of Things chips in the world. Statistics from the Ministry of Industry and Information Technology show that by the end of 2020, the number of cellular Internet of Things in China has reached 1.136 billion, a net increase of 108 million for the whole year. By the end of 2021, the number of domestic cellular IoT links reached 1.399 billion, a net increase of 264 billion for the whole year. By the end of February 2022, the number of cellular IoT links in China reached 1.464 billion. Just in two months, a net increase has reached 64.49 million.

策略分析

本段落主要叙述了我国蜂窝数据链的发展。最主要还是遵循"顺句驱动"的原则进行顺译，整体难度不大。在视译"目前我国的需求十分旺盛，消耗了全球近 60% 的蜂窝物联网芯片"时，参考译文用了一个非限定性定语从句，对后半句进行翻译。视译译文则运用了重复技巧，重复 China 作为下一句的主语，使译文完整流畅。对于"仅仅两个月时间，增长量就达到了 6 449 万"的翻译，参考译文采用的是与上文一致的结构，译为短语。但视译采用顺句驱动，视译译文将这句话另起一句，也表达出了原文意思。数字是视译的难点，若有时间，学生可在翻译之前将数字进行转化，会节省时间并提高准确率。此外，学生平时要重视对数字的口译练习。

视译要点

1. 注意"顺句驱动"，根据不同情况进行添加和省略。
2. 注意数字的口译。

》》例三

按照这样的速度发展下去，预计 2022 年年底，我国蜂窝物联网净增的链接数将突破 3 亿。2020 年 5 月，工信部发布了关于深入推进移动物联网全面发展的通知，旨在推动存量 2G、3G 物联网业务向 NB-IoT/4G/ 5G 网络迁移。所以，最近几年我国蜂窝物联网链接的快速增长是在这个大背景下出现的，并且在 NB-IoT 和 CAT 1 方向得到了迅猛的发展。

译文

At this increase pace, it is expected that by the end of 2022, the net increase of cellular Internet of Things in China will exceed 300 million. In May 2020, the Ministry of Industry and Information Technology issued a notice on further promoting the comprehensive development of mobile Internet of Things, aiming to promote the migration of existing 2G and 3G Internet of Things services to NB-IoT/4G/ 5G networks. Therefore, in recent years, the rapid growth of cellular IoT links in China is in the context of rapid development in the direction of NB-IoT and CAT 1.

视译版本

At this pace, it is expected that by the end of 2022, the net increase of cellular Internet of Things in China will exceed 300 million. In May 2020, the Ministry of Industry and

Information Technology issued a notice on further promoting the comprehensive development of mobile Internet of Things, aiming to promote the existing 2G and 3G Internet of Things services to migrate towards NB-IoT/4G/ 5G networks. Therefore, in recent years, the rapid growth of cellular IoT links in China is in the context of rapid development in the direction of NB-IoT and CAT1.

策略分析

本段落句式与用词都较为简单，顺译即可，但要注意对于汉语中长定语结构短语以及介词结构短语的翻译。对于汉语长定语结构，学生可按照英文的表达习惯将定语修饰的中心词提前，然后根据定语译成相应的介词结构或者译成从句。在本段中，"我国蜂窝物联网净增的链接数""移动物联网全面发展的通知"和"我国蜂窝物联网链接的快速增长"的译文都是将定语中心词提前，定语则译为了 of 结构。对于汉语介词结构短语，学生可译为英文中对应的介词结构。在本段中，"在大背景下"和"在 NB-IoT 和 CAT1 方向"都译为介词结构短语。

视译要点

1. 把握汉语中长定语结构短语的英译，根据定语的长度以及类型译为介词结构或者定语，并分情况进行前置或后置。
2. 汉语中介词结构短语可译为英语中相应的介词结构。

模块五 拓展练习

任务 1:
视译断句练习

请参照模块四的视译方法进行意群的划分与断句。

1. Chinese enterprises' expenditures on digital businesses will witness speedy growth in 2023, as cutting-edge digital technologies have been increasingly applied into a wide range of fields and integrated with the real economy, according to market research company International Data Corp.

 词汇

2. With supporting policies, smart cities have become a critical application scenario of the digital economy. A smart city is a new concept and model that uses digital technologies, to drive new models like smart urban planning, construction and management, and related services.

3. 如今，AI 在药物研发中发挥着越来越重要的作用，在最重要的**临床试验**阶段，AI 的应用也起到了事半功倍的效果。AI 大大缩减药物研发成本，由于 AI 的加入，如今的药物研发成本减少了上亿美元，同时也大大缩短了研发时间，一般来说可以缩短一半以上。

临床实验
clinical trial

4. 研究人员近日称，他们已开发出一种**无线**智能**绷带**，通过监测伤口愈合过程并治疗伤口，以加速受伤组织修复。这种绷带能促进伤口更快闭合，增加流向受伤组织的新血流，并通过显著减少疤痕形成来促进皮肤恢复。

无线
wireless

绷带
bandage

> 任务 2：
> 人工智能口译练习

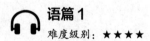

AiFoam Provides "Self-healing Skin" for Robots

Researchers in Singapore have developed an electronic material that helps robots sense touch and nearby objects. The material is a kind of foam: a solid substance that is filled with air and is soft. And the foam has another useful quality. It repairs itself when damaged, much like human skin. The material is called AiFoam, which is short for artificially innervated foam. To innervate means to supply with nerves. In robots, AiFoam would gather information from nearby and send it to a computer controlling the robot. AiFoam is a **stretchy polymer** combined with a mixture that lowers surface tension. This means that if you cut the material, it can return easily into one piece.

词汇

stretchy polymer
弹性聚合物

Benjamin Tee is a lead researcher on the new material at the **National University of Singapore**. The movement changes their electrical properties. The electrical connections sense these changes and send information about them to a computer, which then tells the robot what to do. "When I move my finger near the sensor, you can see the sensor is measuring the changes of my electrical field and responds accordingly to my touch," he said. The robotic hand senses not only the amount but also the direction of the force placed on it. That could make robots more intelligent and responsive.

Tee said AiFoam is the first material of its kind to combine self-healing properties with nearness and pressure sensing. After spending over two years developing it, Tee and his team hope the material can be put to use within five years. After spending over two years developing it, Tee and his team hope the material can be put to use within five years. The material will let "prosthetic users... have more intuitive use of their robotic arms," he said.

词汇

National University of Singapore
新加坡国立大学

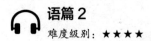

语篇 2
难度级别：★★★★

Some Teachers Want Students to Learn with AI

Many educators fear students will use the artificial intelligence (AI) tool ChatGPT to write their reports or cheat on homework. But other teachers are including it in the classroom. Donnie Piercey is a teacher in Lexington, Kentucky. He told his 23 5th-grade students to try and **outsmart** the tool that was creating writing assignments. Piercey says his job is to prepare students for a world where knowledge of AI will be required.

He describes ChatGPT as just the newest technology in his 17 years of teaching that caused concern about the possibility of cheating. They include tools to help with math and spelling as well as Google, Wikipedia and YouTube. "As educators, we haven't

词汇

outsmart
比……聪明

figured out the best way to use artificial intelligence yet," he added. "But it's coming, whether we want it to or not."

One lesson in his class was a writing game between students and the machine. Piercey asked students to "Find the **Bot**". Each student wrote a short report about boxer **Muhammad Ali**. Then they tried to figure out which was written by ChatGPT. Teaching a lower grade level, Piercey is less worried about cheating than high school teachers. His school system has blocked students from ChatGPT but permits teachers to use it. Many educators around the country say schools need time to figure out the **chatbot**. But they also say a ban will be useless against students that are good at technology and can work around it.

ChatGPT quickly became popular after its November launch. Other companies like Google have since released their versions of AI-powered chatbots. At the Future of Education Technology Conference in New Orleans, Louisiana, last month, Texas math teacher Heather Brantley gave a talk on the magic of writing with AI for all subjects.

"I'm using ChatGPT to enhance all my lessons," she told the Associated Press. The tool is blocked for students but opens to teachers at her school. She said she asked the chatbot to create real-world examples for her math class. For a lesson about slope, or direction of a line in **algebra**, the chatbot suggested students build ramps out of **cardboard**. The students could then measure the slope. For teaching about surface area, the chatbot said students would see how the idea works in real life when wrapping gifts or building a cardboard box, said Brantley.

Students in Piercey's class said working with a chatbot makes learning fun. After playing "Find the Bot", Piercey asked his class what skills it helped them learn. "How to properly summarize and correctly capitalize words and use commas," said one student. Another student felt that sentences written by students "have a little

词汇

bot
机器人程序；机器人（常见于科幻小说中）

Muhammad Ali
拳王阿里（穆罕默德·阿里）

chatbot
聊天机器人

algebra
代数

cardboard
硬纸板

more feeling... more flavor". Students Olivia Laksi and Katherine McCormick, both 10, said they can see the good and bad parts of working with chatbots. They can help students who have trouble putting their thoughts into writing. And there is no limit to the creativity it can add to classwork.

McCormick said students can use it for suggestions, but should not use it to do all the work. "You shouldn't take advantage of it," McCormick said. "You're not learning anything if you type in what you want, and then it gives you the answer."

模块六　译海拾贝：口译失误与外交风波

口译是一种即时性强的信息转换活动。译员通常听到的是只讲一次、不再重复的话语。一般情况下，口译是独立完成的，译员无法进行求助或者查阅资料，因此对于口译工作者来说必须具备较高的双语水平、宽广的知识面以及高度的责任感。但水平再高的译员也会有未及之处，因此口译中难免出现一些未达之意；更有甚者，译员双语水平未达标或者一时疏忽，也会出现误译现象。这便会造成口译中的"风波"，以下为几则经典的口译风波案例：

》案例一

在2015年3月召开的全国政协新闻发布会上，新闻发言人使用了"任性"一词，由于现场思考时间几乎为零，译员的译文处理欠佳。新闻发言人的原话是："党和政府和人民群众在反腐这个问题上，我们的态度是一致的，我套用一个网络热词，就叫大家都很'任性'。""任性"是一个具有时代特征的热词，2015年前后，"有钱任性"是大热的网络词汇。但是，这里给现场译员造成麻烦的却是发言人在特定语境下对"任性"一词的新解，其含义具有高度情境化特征。译员在与发言人进行现场沟通后，将此句译为"The government and the general public actually adopted the same attitude when it comes to anti-corruption. So we can be said to be capricious in fighting against corruption."。译员最终选用了"任性"一词最常用的英文capricious来匹配。但在该语境下，capricious不是"任性"一词的最佳翻译。发言人说对处理腐败分子很"任性",实际想表达的并非"任性"一词"由着性子来"的本意,而是想表达中国政府和人民会克服一切困难、全力反腐的决心。此处选用 determined 一词更能体现发言人的沟通意图。全句可译为:The Chinese government and the general public are determined to be relentless in combating corruption.

案例二

1973年,新任驻希腊大使周伯萍看到使馆区有庆祝活动,让译员查阅信函资料确认哪个国家在庆祝什么活动。译员查阅信函,把捷克斯洛伐克大使"科威克"发来的活动邀请说成国家"科威特"。活动就在当天,周伯萍匆忙带队要去科威特大使馆参加庆祝活动。但是他们不知道科威特使馆位置,认为哪个使馆热闹在搞活动就是科威特使馆。结果,以色列使馆正在搞国庆,门口车水马龙,周伯萍一行也不看门口的国旗标志,就进入了以色列使馆。

当时,中国与以色列还未建交,这背后有错综复杂的历史和政治原因。但是,以色列大使还是希望能够改善与中国的关系,觉得既然中国大使莅临,必尽地主之谊。

周伯萍误以为以色列大使是科威特的大使,双方握手和交谈的镜头被美国《纽约时报》的记者全部收入镜头,该新闻出现在第二天的《纽约时报》上,世人以为中国和以色列出现了破冰交好的迹象,周总理收到该消息,非常生气,他认为"雅典事件"的性质是"十分严重、极为荒唐的政治错误""成为外交界的丑闻,影响极坏",周伯萍被紧急召回国做解释和检讨。外交部几次召开新闻发布会澄清真相,但是却对我国的形象造成一定的负面影响。

案例三

1956年,莫斯科波兰驻俄领事馆的外交招待会上,苏联领导人赫鲁晓夫告诉西方来使:"不管你们喜不喜欢,当你们被埋葬时,我们会在场。"他的原意是社会主义比资本主义更长久,而他的译员把他的话误译成"我们要埋葬你们"。这句话震惊了西方国家,使在冷战期间的苏联与美国关系进一步降到了冰点。

案例四

1999年10月,巴基斯坦发生了军事政变。其后的外交部例行新闻发布会上,有记者提问我国对此事件持何种态度,外交部发言人如是回答:"中国对巴局势十分关注,正在进一步了解事态发展"。译员将其译为"China is very much concerned about the developments in Pakistan and is watching closely for further information."。巴方对我方的态度不满,认为巴基斯坦向来把中国看作自己的全天候朋友,而中国却在觊觎巴基斯坦。我方只能进一步去解释,我们中文表态的实际意思是,巴基斯坦是我国近邻,对好邻居家发生的事情,我们自然非常关心。因此,我们正在密切观察,进一步了解。

以上案例都是属于误译引起的"风波",译员需在平时要注意基本功的积累,注意用词敏感度,尽量避免误译的发生。

模块七 译员风采:如何成为翻译国家队的一员

外交部翻译司是司局级单位,是中央国家机关规模最大的专业化翻译队伍,承担中央和外交部的口、笔译翻译任务,直接为党和国家领导人出访、接待来访的外国领导人提供翻译服务;负责国家重要外事活动、外交文件、文书的多语种翻译工作;统筹协调各语种译者的专业培训和指导。

外交部翻译司聚集了中国外交翻译的顶尖精英。每位译员都必须能胜任各种形式的翻译工作。活跃的中国外交为译员提供了施展才华的舞台,但所需的工作数量和质量也对口译人员提出了严苛的要求。翻译司作为翻译界的"国家队",当之无愧地代表着国家翻译的最高水平。那么,外交部是如何进行译员选拔的呢?译员又经历了什么样的"魔鬼式"训练呢?

严格筛选,精挑人才

外交翻译对从业人员的政治和业务素质要求极高,因此,翻译司十分重视在挑选人才阶段严格把关。培训处承担了选拔和培养译员的工作。能成为其中一员着实不易,用过五关斩六将来形容毫不为过。以翻译司英文翻译室为例,其相关的业务考查包括以下内容:

一是扎实的语言基础、优秀的语言能力;二是熟悉外交、外事业务;三是综合能力和良好的心理素质。因此在人才选拔阶段,翻译司着重把关以上三点,严格筛选。人才挑选和后续的译员培训工作皆由翻译司中的培训处负责完成,其相关考查包括以下几个阶段:

近年来翻译司人才招聘来源主要是针对特定高校进行的遴选和选调。要经过严格的初试和复试，包括心理素质测评、职位业务水平测试和面试，笔试部分非常有挑战性。通过笔试后还须参加英语面试，对参试人员的语言功底、知识面以及综合素质进行综合考查，其中成绩排在最前面的十多名，才有可能进入翻译室参加下一阶段的"观察培训"。

"观察培训"实质上就是"淘汰式培训"，为期2~4周。培训的目的是全面观察学员的外语基本功、翻译能力与潜质、抗压能力、心理素质、政治素质等。短训结束后的翻译考试和辩论赛成绩决定学员的去留。留下的新人面临的是长达一年的试用期。前半年为集中强化培训，后半年为自学加适量工作。一年后，有发展潜力的学员正式成为翻译室译员。

高强培训，大量实践

外交部翻译司英文翻译室的培训目标十分明确：通过集中、高强度、高压力的实践训练，全面提高学员的翻译能力，尤其是现场口译能力，使学员熟悉外交翻译的要求，掌握外交翻译技能，并能在今后的工作中严格按照这些要求不断提高翻译水平。

翻译室特别安排了音训课。授课全部由翻译室的现任翻译和已退休专家担任，他们本身从事了多年的翻译工作，有着丰富的实践经验，而且都能现场展示，他们精湛的翻译技巧和现场表现具有很大的感染力。

首先是强化训练，培训强度很大，日程安排十分紧凑。由翻译室的专家每天陪学员做大量的听力、口译和笔译练习。每天的8小时中有两次VOA和BBC听力训练，上午1小时，下午半小时；一次2小时的中译英练习和一次两小时的英译中练习，然后是记忆训练、笔记训练、口笔译训练，每周还会穿插一两次笔译，不定时安排视译和同传。培训的强度很大，所用的教材时效性很强，基本上是当天的新闻和评论，或近期的热点话题。这样就培养了学员一种跟踪形势的好习惯。培训中不断进行考核，最终通过初试的人，只有不到4%被最终录用。

这些训练像爬山一样，往上爬的时候气喘吁吁满头大汗，但是等回头看的时候，已经走过很长的一段路，看到了不同的风景，翻译水平也达到了一个新的高度。有人用天鹅形容外交部高翻们的工作：身体在湖面上优雅地游弋，但水面下却是不曾停歇的双脚。